CENSORSHIP IN VIETNAM

ALSO BY THOMAS A. BASS

The Eudaemonic Pie
Camping with the Prince and Other Tales of Science in Africa
Reinventing the Future
Vietnamerica
The Predictors
The Spy Who Loved Us

CENSORSHIP IN VIETNAM

Brave New World

THOMAS A. BASS

University of Massachusetts Press
AMHERST AND BOSTON

Copyright © 2017 by Thomas A. Bass
All rights reserved
Printed in the United States of America

ISBN 978-1-62534-295-9 (paper); 294-2 (hardcover)

Designed by Sally Nichols
Set in Monotype Apollo
Printed and bound by Sheridan Books, Inc.

Library of Congress Cataloging-in-Publication Data
A catalog record for this book is available from the Library of Congress

British Library Cataloguing-in-Publication Data
A catalog record for this book is available from the British Library.

∞ The acid free paper used for this publication meets
the requirements of ANSI/NISO z39-1992.

For Bonnie

Fish teach you to keep your mouth shut.
Unfortunately, all my fish have died.
—*Pham Xuan An*

CONTENTS

Preface
ix

CHAPTER I
Culture Ground Zero
1

CHAPTER II
Chaos
4

CHAPTER III
Swamp of the Assassins
7

CHAPTER IV
Wandering Souls
50

CHAPTER V
Stabbing People in the Back with My Pen
88

CHAPTER VI
Vietnam: Brave New World
104

CHAPTER VII
Shiva the Destroyer
141

CHAPTER VIII
Boiled—Steamed—Raw
169

CHAPTER IX
Information
198

Credits
205

Acknowledgments
207

Index
211

PREFACE

Everywhere in the world, free speech is under attack. One of the worst offenders is Vietnam, a sunny police state in Southeast Asia. When a Vietnamese publisher bid to translate my book *The Spy Who Loved Us* into Vietnamese, I decided to conduct an experiment. I would wire the book like a literary seismometer. I would mine the publishing contract with trip switches guaranteeing that I was notified at every move of the censor's pen. Vietnam has not one censor but hundreds, scattered throughout every level of government, and I eventually got to know several of them.

What follows is the picaresque tale of my being censored in Vietnam. It includes my flying to Hanoi to meet my censors—at least the half dozen who would talk to me. These were honorable people, doing their job, but what devastating work it is. After watching my book being sliced and diced, I commissioned an uncensored translation and published it outside Vietnam, on computers hardened against electronic attacks from cyber trolls and government agents. This is when my real education in Vietnamese censorship began. Equal parts alarming and amusing, my story is a cautionary tale for us all.

CENSORSHIP IN VIETNAM

CHAPTER I
Culture Ground Zero

Reporting out of Vietnam focuses on (a) the country's lovely beaches, food, and allure as a tourist destination or (b) Vietnam's abysmal human rights record. Vietnam is a moiré pattern. Squint one way and you get a dynamic, aspirational society zooming into the future. Squint another way and you get an old-fashioned jailer of anyone who refuses to toe the party line. The sunshine lobby focuses on Vietnam's economic development. Human rights reporters focus on patterns of abuse. How does economic advancement relate to censorship? Can the two ride in tandem, as they seem to be doing in China and Vietnam, or does the lack of honest reporting eventually pull the rug out from under your booming economy?

    I have been traveling to Vietnam for a quarter of a century. I have accompanied refugees fleeing the country. I have accompanied refugees returning to the country. I wrote a book on the Amerasian children of the war. I wrote another book about the famed reporter and spy Pham Xuan An. My latest writing on Vietnam is the product of another half dozen years spent looking at censorship in Southeast Asia. I fell into this subject by accident, beginning to examine the issue only because my book about Pham

Xuan An was censored in the process of being translated and published in Vietnam. My most recent trip to Vietnam, in the summer of 2015, was devoted to exploring the country's cultural crisis and meeting with authors, journalists, poets, and other people newly out of jail or headed in that direction.

What I found during this visit was a culture in ruins. Vietnam's best fiction writers no longer write fiction. Its poets no longer write poetry, except for those who circulate their work in underground samizdats. Journalism is a corrupt enterprise controlled by the government. Ditto for publishing. History is a subject too dangerous to study. Freedom of religion, thought, speech—none exists. The country has silenced or driven into exile its intellectual talent. In this wasteland has sprouted a relentlessly commercial culture. The Communist Party of Vietnam, through its state-owned enterprises and its hammerlock on corporate financing, controls the economy at the top. Only because famine forced its hand did it allow pushcart vendors and *petits-commerçants* to compete at the bottom. Can a country this lopsided carry on forever without falling on its face?

The sunshine lobby scorns such talk as alarmist, and it does seem old-fashioned, like something out of a time warp from the 1950s. But the news out of Vietnam *is* alarming. It is alarming for Vietnam, which has to cope with this cultural wreckage, and it is also alarming for the rest of us, who are confronting in our own societies the pressures of censorship and mass surveillance and the rise of commercial interests to the exclusion of all other values. From this perspective, Vietnam is not a time warp from the past but a window into the future. Could this freakish outlier become the new normal?

Walled off from history, living in a society ruled not by law but decrees, and deprived of news because journalism is produced by state-owned entities corrupted by bribery and censorship, the people of Vietnam whirl through space like particles in Brownian motion, rolling endlessly around on their motorbikes, suspended between buying and selling, consumerism and commerce, flirting and fucking. The individual is free to consume and be consumed but not to reflect on the process of consumption. The Vietnamese live in a world of signs and sins, with party slogans posted next to toothpaste ads and all saying the same thing: buy party dogma, buy toothpaste. George Orwell, here is your modern utopia. Aldous Huxley, welcome to your brave new world.

CHAPTER II
Chaos

For those who think that opposition to censorship is a universal value, I offer the following story. I am meeting Nguyen Huy Thiep, Vietnam's most famous contemporary author, at his favorite café in Hanoi, when he pulls from his pocket a well-thumbed volume and begins leafing through the text. "This is a copy of a speech I gave before the Writers Association," he says. "No one understood the slightest thing I was saying."

He begins reading from the speech. "Every person in Vietnam has to cope with three words, which have become products of the propaganda machine: politics, love, and death. Every six-year-old is taught to love Ho Chi Minh. Our teaching is geared toward communist ideology. Vietnamese heads are stuffed with communist ideology. We are brainwashed. It takes twenty years to clear your mind after the first twenty years of brainwashing. The educational system gives birth to a stupid generation. The professors teaching my works are ignorant people who understand nothing about them.

"Love is forbidden in communist society. People have to hide their sexuality. We have created generations of people with fake moral standards. We are a society of hypocrites.

"We make the dead look beautiful. We idealize death. Because we are forced to live for the group, we discourage individuality and diversity. Our literature is full of one-dimensional figures, only good characters and bad characters." Thiep pauses to say that he himself has failed to introduce complex characters into Vietnamese literature. Since 1991, all he has been able to do is watch helplessly as the country retreats into ideology, hypocrisy, and the dead space of its current cultural Year Zero.

After Thiep's speech, I return to the subject of censorship and ask if Vietnam would be better off without it. His answer surprises me and reveals the depth of his pessimism about Vietnamese culture. "Vietnamese society is like an animal that has been caged for too long," he says. "It knows nothing about the outside world. It is arrogant and ignorant at the same time. If released it would run wild and be a danger to itself and others."

He tells a story about Vietnam's isolation. "I went to the United States for the first time in 1986. I was scared. I didn't know how to turn on the water in the sink. I spent half an hour trying to take a bath. It was very embarrassing. I realized after this trip that Vietnam needed to open to the outside world. But if you open too fast, you get dizzy. Censorship slows down the opening process."

"Censorship is reasonable and necessary for the Vietnamese people," he says. "It keeps us from getting dizzy from too fast an exposure to the outside world.

"I know little about other countries. Vietnam is a backward place, ill-educated. It is easy for this society to get chaotic. We have spent much of our history at war. We lack a civilized mind, attuned to art and music.

"Our culture is stolen from other cultures, from the Chinese or the French. We have nothing original to us. Even our Marxist-Leninism is borrowed. We borrow, but we don't dig deep or fully comprehend what we borrow. We lack core values. In Thailand, one sees political protests that can overthrow a president. It would be much worse if these protests were allowed in Vietnam.

The Dream of the Artist (portrait of the writer Nguyen Huy Thiep) by Nguyen Dinh Dang, 1990.

"We are secular. We have no spiritual values. Vietnam could fall into chaos and disorder. This is why we need censorship. It is a brake on our chaotic nature."

CHAPTER III

Swamp of the Assassins

Taking a taxi to the Cau Giay district on the west side of town, I pass several of the lakes that dot downtown Hanoi to arrive at a tree-lined boulevard where Nha Nam, my publisher, occupies an old building with louvered windows that open onto iron-fronted balconies. Already by ten in the morning a dusty blanket of heat and humidity has draped itself over the city. Nha Nam's ground-floor bookshop is filled with translations of Proust, Kundera, and Nabokov, and I am pleased to find a stack of my own books displayed next to *Lolita*. I introduce myself to the receptionist and am led upstairs to meet Nguyen Nhat Anh, the chairman of the company, and Vu Hoang Giang, his vice-director and partner. I had actually met Giang the night before. Without my knowing in advance, he had attended a lecture I gave at the Hanoi Cinémathèque. He had introduced himself afterward, and we exchanged a few words, but today, as he and the chairman of Nha Nam present me with a bouquet of purple lotus blossoms, I fear that my remarks the previous evening may have been too candid.

Nguyen Nhat Anh, a slender man in a black tee shirt, jeans, and sandals, looks more like a coffee shop habitué than the editor of a major publishing company. Known for his literary nose, he works at a desk covered with books and manuscripts piled ten deep. His partner, Giang, wearing an open-necked polo shirt, is a tall, handsome fellow with a ready smile and a small tattoo decorating his right wrist. I imagine they have divided the corporate turf between them, with Anh responsible for scholarship and Giang for sales. Later I learn that many of the manuscripts piled on Anh's desk are actually publishing contracts, while Giang has his own literary interests. In fact, he was the person who finally arranged to get my book published.

Ms. Thu Yen, the editor with whom I have been sparring for the last few years, has not been invited to this meeting. She remains at her desk in the contracts department, while another translator has been hired for the occasion—a young Vietnamese woman, a former office manager at an American law firm. As the scholarly Anh and smiling Giang discuss the nuances of Vietnamese publishing, the young woman's translations get shorter and shorter, until finally she seems on the verge of giving up altogether. Fortunately, I have brought my own translator with me, and we will spend several hours later that afternoon reconstructing the conversation.

I take a seat on the couch in Anh's office. Outside the louvered windows, the cicadas in the trees are making a fearsome racket. Mr. Giang has already warned me an in email about the "tight and rather heavy-handed censorship system of state-owned publishers in Vietnam. This you may not fully imagine." Giang offers me a cup of green tea, and then we launch into a discussion of censorship: how it is handled generally in Vietnam and particularly in my case.

Anh takes the lead, giving lengthy, formal answers to my questions. Giang takes over when the boss heads to the espresso machine next to his desk and brews himself a cup of coffee. I am tempted to ask for a cup myself but decide to be polite and stick with tea. Anh describes how the censors dictate even the smallest details. He gives as an example the fact that political figures must have honorifics. One is not allowed to refer to the founder of the Democratic Republic of Vietnam as Ho Chi Minh. He has to be Bac Ho—Uncle Ho—which inscribes him simultaneously into Vietnamese family structure and history.

"Censorship is a very tough question," says Anh. "We don't really have a system or set of rules for how it is handled. All we know is that lots of publishers didn't dare to publish your book."

The jalousie doors and windows in Anh's office open onto a porch overlooking the street, but they remain closed against the heat. Other than his desk, groaning under its layer of books, and a coffee table, piled with yet more books, the room holds nothing more than the couch on which I am sitting and bare green walls.

"Because another book had been published on the same subject, we thought this improved our chances," he says. "We were sure we could get your book in print."

I ask Anh why he chose a northerner to translate my book, someone who missed the nuances of the language and even the jokes told by its southern hero.

"The differences are like music," he says. "Singers sing the same songs but give them different interpretations. When we translated Tim O'Brien's *The Things They Carried*, we tried to keep it honest to the southern dialect. But in your case, we thought we were dealing with a political book, a work of nonfiction. The people who read these books are northerners, and you have to make the text understandable for them."

I ask Anh and Giang to talk in more detail about censoring my book. They describe the process, which begins with the translation, commissioned from someone who knows how the game is played. Then the book goes to the editor, who removes all the "sensitive" material.

"How does he know what to remove?"

"That's his job," says Anh, referring to Nguyen Viet Long, the original editor of my book, who has since left the company. "Mr. Long was a specialist in nuclear control mechanisms, what they call cybernetics, and similar principles apply in literature. Censorship in book publishing has some known, but also lots of unknown, control mechanisms. We rely on the editor's experience in making cuts to the manuscript. He knows what has a high probability of failing to pass the censors."

"The process is dangerous, dangerous to the author, but also dangerous to the publisher," says Anh. By this point in the conversation, he has kicked off his sandals and is cooling his bare feet on the tile floor. Overhead, a fan swirls tepid air around the room. Temperatures in Hanoi this spring are spiking over a hundred degrees Fahrenheit.

Anh tells me the story of a book of poems the company published in 2006 by an author named Tran Dan. Dan's work has been banned in Vietnam since the 1950s, when he was involved in the *nhan van giai pham* affair. This was Vietnam's version of Mao's cultural revolution, a purging of writers, artists, and musicians who were blacklisted, imprisoned, and banned for fifty years. One of these artists was Van Cao, who, in 1945, composed Vietnam's national anthem. From 1957 until 1986, people were in the peculiar position of being allowed to play but not sing Van Cao's anthem. Only when the words were changed was the song once again performed. Van Cao himself stopped composing long ago, thereby joining the ranks of Vietnamese artists—hundreds of them, from the 1950s to the present—who have been driven into silence or exile.

With Mao long dead and his cultural revolution discredited, Nha Nam thought it was safe to bring blacklisted poet Tran Dan back into print. They obtained a publishing license from a state-owned company in Danang and produced a volume of poems, when all hell broke loose. "The police came to the book fair and seized all our books," says Anh. "Then they raided our offices and destroyed more books. This was terrifying for us. We thought we were going to be closed down and put out of business."

"What went wrong?" I ask.

Anh lowers his voice and mentions the name of an agency named A25.

"Now it's A87," Giang says, correcting him.

Governmental departments that begin with the letter A—which stands for *an ninh*, meaning "security"—are legion, and A25, now known as A87, is the one that deals with publishers.

"In any case, it's Cultural Security, *cuc an ninh van hoa*," says Anh.

"What's their address?" I ask.

"They don't have an address," he says, implying they are everywhere. The two men discuss among themselves in terse sentences what can be said about the A agencies. None of their conversation is translated.

"There is no single organization in charge of censorship," says Anh. "A lot of people are involved." Again, he mentions the Ministry of Public Security.

Giang mentions the Ministry of Information and Communication. "This is the office in charge of publishing," he says.

Anh adds to the list the national police and other organizations. "It's like a cloud," he says. "They are everywhere."

"Usually they don't arrest editors," he says. "This can happen to writers, but editors generally know in advance when they're going to run into trouble."

I ask them to speak in more detail about the censorship involved in publishing my book. This is when I hear for the first time about Nguyen The Vinh. Mr. Vinh is the man who produced the final list of cuts to my book and secured its publishing license. From their description of him, I get the idea that Mr. Vinh is a heavyweight in the publishing world. The former director of various companies, he now works as editor of Hong Duc, the state-owned publisher attached to the Ministry of Information and Communication. This company not only gave my book its publishing license but also put its logo on the title page. Actually, the book has two logos on the title page: Nha Nam's trudging water buffalo, mounted by a boy (or girl) reading a book, and Hong Duc's white H inscribed inside a black D.

I learn another interesting fact about Mr. Vinh. He was the editor who secured the publishing license for Larry Berman's *Perfect Spy*. The Vietnamese translation of this book was supposed to grease the skids for my own book (on the same subject, although reaching opposite conclusions), and who better to perform this feat than the man who had already done it before?

As Anh busies himself making another cup of espresso, Giang takes over the narrative. "Your book was rejected by five or six publishers," he says. "Other publishers who looked at it wanted to interfere a lot, changing the content. They kept asking to cut more and more. We resisted these changes, until finally Nguyen The Vinh agreed to publish it."

"And what changes did *he* demand?" I ask.

Anh is pacing behind his desk. A frown darkens Giang's face. "When you talk to him, you shouldn't be too hard in your questions," he says. "It could affect Mr. Vinh and the chances for your book to remain on sale."

"Who asked Mr. Vinh to get involved?" I ask.

"Mr. Giang approached him," says Anh. I can see that these men are nervous about talking to me in such detail. By now, both of them are sitting with their arms crossed over their chests.

"The publishers at Hong Duc wanted to write a foreword to your book," says Anh. "We rejected this idea."

I can imagine how Hong Duc's introduction would have reworked the standard tropes about Pham Xuan An as a "perfect" spy, an impeccable communist cadre, who nonetheless garnered fulsome praise from his Western admirers. I am grateful to my editors for saving me from this embarrassment.

"Mr. Vinh was the man who took personal responsibility for publishing your book," says Anh.

"If I understand what you're saying, the book could still be censored?"

"Your book could be seized tomorrow," he says. "No one knows where the trouble could come from. We have yet to see any negative signs, but someone can always find 'sensitive' items in a book."

"What subjects would you like me to avoid talking about while I am in Vietnam?" I ask.

"Please remember that Mr. Vinh has his reputation and career on the line," says Anh.

By now everyone knows my opinion of censorship—the cowardly business by which the powerful lie to the weak in order to protect their self-interest. I have no need to repeat myself.

"You shouldn't be too direct with Mr. Vinh," says Anh. "He was acting on directions from the publisher."

"You should also know that your book is a living thing," says Giang. "It can be published again, with material that was cut in the first edition added back in later editions."

I assure Anh and Giang that I will do my best not to offend anyone. They know that an uncensored Vietnamese version of my book will be released soon on the web.

"Right now we have no standards in Vietnam," says Giang. "We don't know our rights, and we don't know from what direction the censorship is coming. But our system is changing. We hope you understand that we can improve. We can do better. We are learning how to function in the world of international publishing."

"If your book is republished, we want to put back in the details that were cut," he says. "You have a positive perception of Vietnam. People know this. So we're asking for you to be patient. Give us some time to work things out. People appreciate you as an expert on Vietnam, a critic, sometimes a tough critic, but a fair one. *Vietnamology*—maybe that's the right word for what you do."

"How many 'hard' books do you publish each year?" I ask.

"In our career we are always working with difficult books," says Anh. "This comes with the territory. But your book was a special case. It was the most difficult. I wanted to give up. I thought it was hopeless. I'm hot-headed, and this was just too hard. I threw up my hands. 'This book is never going to be published!' I said.

But my colleagues are more patient than I am. 'Wait,' they told me. 'There is still a chance.' It was thanks to Mr. Giao and Ms. Yen that your book saw the light of day. They were patient. They persisted."

"I felt like a hostage between two warring armies," says Anh. "I was being fired on from two directions. The author was resisting cuts. The censors were demanding cuts. There are authors who know how this system works—Milan Kundera, for example. He has lived under censorship. When we published his books, he understood our problems and agreed to let us do what we had to do. It would have been helpful if you had been more reassuring."

"On behalf of the publisher, we want to tell you that we're happy your book has been published," says Giao. I suspect he is feeling sorry about my having been compared unfavorably to Milan Kundera. Actually, I am amused that a refugee from communist Czechoslovakia would prove tractable to being censored in communist Vietnam.

"This is not the first time that Vietnam and the United States have engaged in difficult negotiations," I say. Anh and Giang appreciate the joke. "I'm glad we arrived at a happy conclusion." We shake hands, and then I am asked to sit at Anh's desk to sign copies of my book for members of Nha Nam's staff. Apparently, everyone in the company wants a copy—perhaps before the book disappears from the shelves. All throughout their lunch hour people keep drifting into Anh's office with yet more copies for me to sign.

Perfect Spy?

To date, there have been six books written about Pham Xuan An, three in Vietnamese, one in French, and two in English. The self-described "official" biography, Berman's *Perfect Spy,* was published in the United States in 2007 and translated into Vietnamese a year later. "We turned the book red," said someone knowledgeable about its publication in Vietnam. In other words, Vietnamese

Vu Hoang Giang, Nguyen Nhat Anh, and translator, Hanoi, 2014.

censors brightened the patriotic color in an already selective portrait of a national hero.

From the title alone, one understands that *Perfect Spy* portrays Pham Xuan An as a Vietnamese nationalist and patriot. The book also claims that he retired happily at the end of the Vietnam War in 1975. The problem with this narrative is that it appears to be false. Every spy has a cover, the life he hides behind while leading a double existence—or, in Pham Xuan An's case, a quadruple existence for, at one time or another, he worked for the French *Deuxième Bureau,* the CIA, and both the South and North Vietnamese intelligence agencies. His spying for the French was limited to moonlighting as a censor at the post office, where he trimmed Graham Greene's dispatches to *Paris Match*. His work for the Americans included being trained in psychological warfare in the 1950s by Edward Lansdale and other CIA operatives.

An's work for South Vietnamese intelligence, where he served as righthand man to the spy chief Tran Kim Tuyen, supposedly ended in 1962 when Tuyen was cashiered in a failed coup attempt. But An kept in touch with Tuyen, who remained an inveterate "coup cooker." He took him food and medicine while the master spy was under house arrest (undoubtedly passing messages during these exchanges). Then An did Tuyen one final service. He saved his life. The famous 1975 photo of the last U.S. helicopter lifting off from the roof of 22 Gia Long Street shows a rickety ladder leading up to the chopper. The last man climbing that ladder, thanks to the intercession of his former righthand man, is Tran Kim Tuyen. Why did An help the long-time head of South Vietnamese intelligence escape from the communists? "I knew I would be in trouble," An told me. "This was the chief of intelligence, an important man to capture, but he was my friend. I owed him." Who knows what bonds of loyalty were served or embarrassing questions avoided as Tuyen flew off to exile in England?

For twenty years An maintained his cover as a journalist, but when this was blown at the end of the Vietnam War, he developed a second cover—that of a happily retired global strategist who spent his days shooting the breeze with Western journalists and other visitors. Recently I saw film footage of An being interviewed in 1988 by the Vietnamese refugee and Hollywood actress Tiana Alexandra-Silliphant. Tiana was gathering material for her documentary *From Hollywood to Hanoi*. While being interviewed, An sits casually on the front steps of his house, with not one but two German shepherds guarding his back. Tiana asks him straight away about the people he betrayed and the friends who died as a result of his spying. An goes bug-eyed and shifty. He seems to be making up his answers on the spot, beginning to spin the story that will develop into his second cover. "I retired from the military a few weeks ago," he says. "I never betrayed anyone."

An is on record as saying that he retired from the military in 1988. He is also on record as saying that he retired in 2002 and again in 2005, when a visitor noticed a large flat-screen TV in his living room, with a card attached saying that it was a retirement present from his "friends" in Tong Cuc II—Vietnamese military intelligence. It is more likely that An never retired, that he remained a member of the intelligence services until the day he died. Under his first cover, as a journalist, he worked as a spy from the 1950s until the end of the Vietnam War in 1975. Under his second cover, as a retired strategist, he worked as a spy for another thirty years—even longer than his first career. What he did as an intelligence agent in active service remains unknown, but he undoubtedly wrote reports about his visitors and offered the kind of political analysis for which he was famous. With his humorous quips about how the communists had failed to "reeducate" him, An deflected any suspicions that he was still working as a spy. This aspect of his life was revealed only after his death, when General Nguyen Chi Vinh, who was then the head of Tong Cuc II, delivered the oration at An's funeral. General Vinh's speech about An's "extraordinary military achievements," accomplished while living "in the bowels of the enemy," included a list of An's military medals, including several awarded *after* the end of the Vietnam War.

In a glancing reference, *Perfect Spy* mentions that Pham Xuan An won eleven military medals. He actually won sixteen, and six were awarded after 1975. Fourteen of the total number of medals, and four of those awarded after 1975, are combat medals given not for strategic analysis but for specific military actions. An won medals for his *tactical* assistance in battles ranging from Ap Bac in 1963 and Ia Drang in 1965 to the Tet Offensive in 1968 and on to the Ho Chi Minh Campaign that ended the war in 1975. What An did to win four military medals *after* 1975 remains unknown.

The strategy of undercounting An's medals, ignoring their significance, and disregarding the dates when they were awarded has been part of the campaign to make him a "perfect spy," a benign figure, like Ho Chi Minh, removed from the staggering violence that marked Vietnam's anticolonial wars. Other aspects of An's career have been trimmed or suppressed in *Perfect Spy*. Softened in the narrative are his criticisms of communist incompetence and corruption, his acerbic comments about Russian influence in Vietnam, his attacks on Chinese meddling in the nation's affairs, his jokes about having been "reeducated" in 1978, and his opposition to the Chinese-influenced clique that currently runs the country. Also downplayed or ignored are the details that explain why An's wife and four children were sent to the United States in 1975 and then, a year later, recalled to Vietnam. In the version crafted for

Pham Xuan An, *Time* correspondent, whispering in the ear of Robert Shaplen, *New Yorker* correspondent, Continental Hotel, Saigon, April 17, 1971. Photograph by Richard Avedon.

public consumption, and as reported by An's "official" biographer, the spy remained in Saigon at the end of the war to care for his sick mother. In fact, the Vietnamese intelligence services planned to send him to the United States, where he would continue spying for the communists. Only when this plan was overruled by the Politburo was An forced to stay in Vietnam and recall his family. This information about his postwar activities reveals how Vietnam intended—and undoubtedly succeeded—in placing spies in the United States at the end of the war. It also reveals a rift between the country's intelligence services and the Politburo, a rift that Vietnamese propaganda would like to paper over with a story about a sick mother.

Once the shadows are put back into Pham Xuan An's life, the censors are bound to object to his less-than-perfect narrative. In fact, they will spend five years rewriting the story and struggling to get it as close as possible to the official version. Nha Nam's gambit was flawed. Because one book about Pham Xuan An by a westerner had been translated and published in Vietnam did not mean that a second book would follow easily. In fact, as we learned recently, even the "red" version of An's life had been a hard sell. This was revealed in a U.S. State Department cable of September 2007, which was released by Wikileaks in 2011. The cable, by a consular official in Ho Chi Minh City, describes how the Vietnamese translation of *Perfect* Spy, although it was published by a government-owned company, was nearly pulped at the last minute by censors in the Ministry of Public Security. They objected "to the numerous quotes from Pham Xuan An lamenting that Vietnam had simply traded one overlord for another—the Soviet Union—and his criticism of post-war policies." The editors were in trouble for "supporting the publication of a book in which one of the country's most renowned heroes unleashes broadside attacks on post-war GVN policy and the closed nature of Vietnamese society." According to the consular memo, "the pro-reform faction within the GVN" got "the upper hand" over "the counter-reform faction" only when the president of Vietnam himself gave his approval to publish the book.

One can see in these stories about Vietnamese censorship how the rule of law has been replaced by the rule of the jungle. Powerful people will do everything possible to protect their prerogatives. I am alarmed by these stories, but many people yawn when I talk about censorship in Vietnam. "What do you expect?" they say. "There's nothing surprising here." Even my Vietnamese friends have succumbed to fatalism and the strange belief that they can read around corners. "I can tell where a book has been cut," novelist Bao Ninh assured me. "We know what's missing. We just can't talk about these things."

It is hard to argue against censorship in the face of rampant cynicism, but the Nobel laureate Amartya Sen, an economist who did his award-winning work on the theory of famine, has recently made a worthy effort. In an essay written for *Index on Censorship* in 2013, he chastises his native India for thinking that it should emulate China as a model for how authoritarian governments can swap personal freedom for economic growth. Sen argues the opposite position, that "press freedom is crucially important for development." Free speech has "intrinsic value," he says. It is "a necessary requirement of informed politics." It gives "voice to the neglected and disadvantaged," and it is crucial for "generating new ideas." China seems to be doing all right at the moment, says Sen. He then reminds us what can happen when propaganda replaces news.

"There is an inescapable fragility in any authoritarian system," Sen writes. The last time this phenomenon revealed itself in China, during the botched agrarian reforms of the Great Leap Forward, the country suffered one of the world's most devastating famines. "The Chinese famine of 1959–1962 . . . killed at least 30 million people, when the regime failed to understand what was going on and there was no public pressure against its policies, as would have arisen in a functioning democracy."

"The policy mistakes continued throughout these three years of devastating famine," says Sen. "The information blackout was so complete with censorship and control of the state media that government itself came to be deceived by its own propaganda and believed that the country had 100 million more metric tons of rice than it actually had. Eventually, Chairman Mao himself made a famous speech in 1962, lamenting the 'lack of democracy,'" a lack that, in this case, had proved to be lethal. India and other parts of the world might be tempted to emulate China, in light of its double-digit growth, but people would be foolish, says Sen, to adopt the anti-democratic measures that weaken totalitarian systems and make them susceptible to believing their own lies.

Literary Seismometer

These are dark days in Vietnam, as the courts decree long prison terms for writers, journalists, bloggers, and anyone else with the temerity to criticize the country's rulers. The brief efflorescence of Vietnamese literature that followed the collapse of the Berlin Wall in 1989—known as *doi moi,* or Renovation—is long gone. After twenty years of black pens and prison, the censors have nearly succeeded in wiping out an entire generation of Vietnamese writers, driving them into silence or exile.

This is the reality I discovered when I accepted the offer to have *The Spy Who Loved Us* translated into Vietnamese and published in Hanoi. Based on a *New Yorker* article published in 2005, the book tells the story of Pham Xuan An, the South Vietnamese journalist, whose remarkable effectiveness and long-lived career as a spy for the North Vietnamese communists—from the 1940s until his death in 2006—made him one of the greatest spies of the twentieth century. Trained in the United States as a journalist and using his profession as his cover, An worked as a correspondent for *Time* during the Vietnam War and served briefly as the magazine's Saigon bureau chief. Charged with drawing battlefield maps, following troop movements, and analyzing political and military news, he leaked invaluable information to the North Vietnamese Army.

After the war, the victorious communists made An a Hero of the People's Armed Forces and elevated him to the rank of general. He is a natural subject for a biography, and, indeed, six have already been published, including Larry Berman's *Perfect Spy* (2007). The book characterizes An as a patriot, a strategic analyst who observed the war from afar until he happily retired to his living room, where he entertained a stream of distinguished visitors, from Morley Safer to Daniel Ellsberg.

My own account of An's life is more troubling. I eventually concluded that this brilliant raconteur had developed a second cover as a spy. Claiming to be a friend of the West, an honest man who never told a lie (although his whole life was based on subterfuge), An had worked for Vietnamese military intelligence, not only throughout the Vietnam War but also for thirty years after the war. At the same time, Vietnam's northern power brokers distrusted this wise-cracking southerner who was outspoken in his attacks on the corruption and incompetence of the country's communist government. An's rise in military rank was slow and begrudged, and he had been kept under police surveillance for years. The Vietnamese government might initially have been pleased by the prospect of publishing two American-authored books about their "perfect spy," but the longer the censors squinted at my version of An's life, the more nervous they got, and the more the story had to be chopped and rewritten before it could be approved for publication.

After rejecting several publishers' offers to translate my book, including the People's Public Security Publishing House (an official arm of Vietnam's Ministry of Public Security) and the Ministry of Culture, Sports, and Tourism (one of the country's largest censors), I sign a contract in July 2009 with Nha Nam, a respected publisher whose list of translated authors ranges from Jack Kerouac and Annie Proulx to Umberto Eco and Haruki Murakami. Nha Nam is an independent publisher, one of the few in Vietnam not affiliated with a ministry or other state censor. Nha Nam is occasionally fined for publishing "sensitive" books, and sometimes their titles are pulled from the shelf and pulped. Only later do I learn that Nha Nam's status as an independent publisher does not guarantee its independence, but to its credit, the company is scrupulous in honoring our contract and keeping me apprised of every move to censor my book.

Many authors ignore their books in translation. They delegate the sale of subsidiary rights to their agents and barely glance at the texts that arrive later in German, Spanish, or Chinese editions. I have planned something different for my Vietnamese translation. Because I suspect it will be censored and want to track the process, I ask my agent to write into my contract a clause stating that the book will not be published without my prior consent and that I have to be consulted about changes made to the manuscript. I want to record the work of the censors, to register their preoccupations and anxieties, so that by the end of the day I will know what the Vietnamese government fears and wants to suppress.

The process of translating my book into Vietnamese begins in March 2010, when I receive an email saying, "I am Nguyen Viet Long of Nha Nam company, now editing the translation of *The Spy Who Loved Us*. I should like to correspond with you in regard to the translation."

Mr. Long then asks if I know the correct diacritical marks for the name of Pham Xuan An's grandfather. These are missing in English but important in Vietnamese, and I appreciate his attention to detail. Unfortunately, the rest of his email adopts a more aggressive tone. "You make some mistakes," he writes, before mentioning a laundry list of items. Many of these mistakes are not really mistakes but questions of interpretation or judgment or matters of dispute in the historical record. They are the Vietnamese equivalent of inside baseball, arcane tidbits good for keeping scholars dancing on pinheads.

For example, did Jean Baptiste Ngo Dinh Diem (the first president of the Republic of Vietnam) become a provincial governor at the age of twenty-five? This depends on the day he was born, which is not an easy question to answer. People in Vietnam customarily fudge their birth dates, a practice recommended for scaring away demons, improving astrological signs, and attracting younger mates. An obscure item for an American author is apparently a big deal for the Vietnamese. If one assumes that Ngo Dinh Diem was an American puppet, a running dog for the imperialist invaders, then the last thing one wants to do is credit him with being the youngest governor in Vietnamese colonial history. Hence, one denies that he was born in year x and insists that he was actually born in year y. This complicates the issue so extensively that it becomes easier simply to drop the claim.

Responding to a query from my literary agent, Mr. Long on March 15 writes, "There will be (absolutely) censorship, the book is sensitive. But please do not worry. We will keep talking to the author and will do our best to protect as much as possible the wholeness of the book."

Mr. Long is trying to rush the book into print by April 30—an auspicious day marking the end of the Vietnam War. After my agent reminds him that he is contractually obligated to show me the translation of the book before it can be published, Mr. Long misses the first deadline, and then he misses more deadlines until, finally, six months later, in September 2010, I receive a copy of the galleys. The first thing I notice are numerous footnotes scattered throughout the text, in a book that originally had no footnotes. I have enlisted a number of friends—academics, translators, an ex-CIA agent, an editor at Voice of America, and a former U.S. diplomat and his Vietnamese wife—to review the translation. They come back to me with sobering news. The footnotes generally begin by saying, "The author is wrong." Then they correct my "mistakes."

Clearly, I have misunderstood the function of Vietnamese editors. Even before my book goes to the real censors—the chaps who control Vietnam's publishing licenses—it has to be massaged in house. Mr. Long will do the first whack, and the more efficiently he prunes, the more appreciated he will be by the state officials who can cap their black pens and turn to censoring more important items.

Fighting Hand to Hand in the Hedgerows of Literature

I write to Mr. Long, asking him to remove his footnotes. The poor man is now the mouse in the middle, caught between an exigent author and equally demanding censors. As we descend into the fine points of Vietnamese history and geography, my editor and I embark on a voluminous correspondence. The nature of this correspondence is exemplified by the Swamp of the Assassins, which is the first item that Mr. Long has tagged for a footnote.

Southeast of Saigon, bordering the city's main shipping channel to the sea, the Swamp of the Assassins, or Rung Sat, as it is called in Vietnamese, is the tidal mangrove swamp that for many years was home to the Binh Xuyen river pirates. The pirates had aided the French in managing their colonial operations in Vietnam. Bay Vien, the head of the pirates, had been elevated to the rank of general and given Saigon to run as a personal fiefdom. He owned the Hall of Mirrors, the largest brothel in Asia, with 1,200 employees. He ran the Grand Monde casino in Cholon and the Cloche d'Or casino in Saigon. Bay Vien's lieutenant was named the chief of police in the capitol region, which stretched for sixty miles from Saigon to Cap Saint Jacques. Bay Vien's most lucrative operation was the opium trade that stretched all the way from Laos to Marseille, with a share of the proceeds going to the French government. The Swamp of the Assassins also served as a communist staging area during the Vietnam War, and the river pirates had briefly doubled as communists before switching to the other side.

Until he retired to Paris, where he could be seen strolling down the Champs-Elysées with his pet tiger on a leash, Bay Vien used to hide in the Rung Sat swamp when things got too hot in Saigon. This was the case in 1955, after the legendary spook Edward Lansdale arrived in town. Intent on knocking the French from their colonial perch and replacing them with a client government loyal to the United States, Lansdale launched a military campaign against the Binh Xuyen. Vietnamese army troops fought the pirates house to house for control of Saigon. More soldiers were involved in this week-long battle than in the famous Tet Offensive of 1968. Five hundred people were killed, 2,000 wounded, and another 20,000 left homeless. This proxy battle between France and the United States marked the transition from the First Indochina War to the Second. Pham Xuan An claimed that he learned everything he knew about spying from Lansdale, who was An's patron as he began his career in military intelligence and who recommended that An study journalism in the United States.

Because of the swamp's importance to colonialists, communists, river pirates, and spies, I had done a lot of archival work to verify its position in Vietnamese history. This is why I am surprised to find a footnote saying, "The author is wrong." It is not called Rung Sat but Rung *Sac,* says Mr. Long, thereby turning the Swamp of the Assassins into the Forest of Seacoast Shrubs. (*Rung* means "forest," but when dealing with wet mangrove forests, one might plausibly call them "swamps." *Sat* is a Sino-Vietnamese combining word meaning "death," as in *am sat,* "to assassinate.") Mr. Long explains that the Vietnamese government has renamed the Swamp of the Assassins the Swamp of Seacoast Shrubs because the Swamp of the Assassins was never its correct name. And why is this? Because the people of southern Vietnam have been distorting the country's language and inadvertently displaying their ignorance for centuries. Southerners pronounce words ending in t as if they ended in k or a hard c. Thus, Rung *Sac* mistakenly became Rung *Sat* because southerners can't spell correctly and are often confused by two words that sound the same. Undoubtedly, the communist officials behind this renaming were also sensitive about the fact that Rung Sat had served as a communist staging area during the American war. They didn't want noble warriors confused with swamp-dwelling assassins.

The issue might plausibly have been resolved by saying that the area used to be called X and is now known as Y. But Vietnamese censors don't work this way. They have a totalizing view of history. They reach back through time to correct errors retroactively. Even in quoted speech, Bay Vien and Lansdale would be forced to talk about the Forest of Seacoast Shrubs. One can imagine the stilted prose this produces, as anachronisms and communist terminology are inserted into the historical record.

The situation leaves me no choice but to mount a campaign proving "The editor is wrong." I send Mr. Long a variety of French and Vietnamese maps, including a 1955 Vietnamese map showing military operations against the Binh Xuyen river pirates. I send maps from U.S. naval operations in the area, a copy of President Richard Nixon's citation to the Rung Sat Special Zone Patrol Group, and a 1974 U.S. Academy of Sciences research report on Rung Sat. I send a 2010 Google satellite map, with the area marked as Rung Sat, and I even send a photo of a bus leaving Ho Chi Minh City, with its scheduled destination clearly marked as Rung Sat.

Mr. Long returns the salvo with his own "proof and evidence," including the website for the Rung Sac Resort and Restaurant and some real estate prospectuses for housing developments that are financed, I presume, by local Communist Party officials. I press the argument through more emails until Mr. Long eventually writes, "I agree to remove the footnote about Rung Sat entirely."

With each successive footnote, Mr. Long and I return to fighting hand to hand in the hedgerows of literature. Every email exchange becomes the Swamp of the Assassins Redux until, finally, Mr. Long proposes "to remove wrong footnotes or footnotes concerning your mistakes." I graciously accept his offer. (These footnotes will reappear at the end of this saga, but for the moment I am lulled into thinking that I have won the battle.)

Next we turn to discussing the title of the book. *The Spy Who Loved Us* could be translated as *The Spy Who Loved America* or, more poetically, as America's Best Enemy, except that the censors reject these titles. As Mr. Long explains, "'America's Best Enemy' is good, but somewhat sensitive. Why 'best enemy'? Is this implying that Pham Xuan An was not entirely loyal to the revolutionary cause?" After further reflections on "the right viewpoint," Mr. Long admits that "the issue proves to be more intricate than we initially thought." Later I receive word that The Spy Who Loved America has been "immediately rejected" by Vietnam's "publishing authorities."

By this time, the people helping me review the manuscript (all of whom wish to remain anonymous) have compiled a list of phrases, sentences, and paragraphs that have been bowdlerized or pruned from the text. When I send this list to Mr. Long, he replies, "I assure you that the translator did not omit any sentences or paragraphs. He only highlighted sensitive phrases. The omissions or modifications are mine."

In October 2010, Mr. Long writes to say that he is "tired of this project" and discouraged by having the book rejected by two state-owned publishing companies. He is trying to secure a publishing license from a third company, but people are telling him that the upcoming Eleventh Communist Party Congress in the spring of 2011 makes it a "sensitive time" for publishing in Vietnam. This is a delicate moment "when everybody takes non-action to avoid complexities," he notes.

Writing to my agent in December 2010, Mr. Long says, "We understand the impatience of our author! But the situation is worse than you imagine. Another state-owned publisher has refused to issue a publishing license for our translation. Clearly, it is a highly-sensitive book at this moment in time. Everything is now hanging in the wind."

When Mr. Long writes to tell me that another batch of publishers has refused to give him a license, I imagine the process as something akin to Random House having to clear each book it publishes through the Pentagon Publishing Company. If Pentagon Press won't ink the deal, then Random House has to go to publishers owned by Homeland Security or the FBI. These negotiations must be prolonged and humiliating, and, in a gift-giving culture like Vietnam's, they must also be expensive.

I cool my heels through 2011, waiting for the Communist Party to shuffle a new set of rulers into place. In February 2012, I write to Mr. Long, wishing him a happy Water Dragon Year and asking if he would kindly provide me with a list of all the governmental bodies that have so far been involved in censoring my book.

A month later, he writes back to apologize for being out of touch. He says he has left Nha Nam to work as an editor at a company that publishes math books for children. I feel a twinge of conscience, fearing that I might have driven him to change jobs. "About the license to publish *The Spy Who Loved Us*," he writes, "Nha Nam has been applying and still continues to apply to several publishers for a publishing license, not stopping at any time as you maybe think. I have asked for the latest information and was told that officials at Nha Nam still hope that the book will be published."

"Officially, only state publishing houses are permitted to produce printed books," Mr. Long explains. "So a privately-owned (non-state) company like Nha Nam must participate in so-called joint publication, in order to publish a book under the aegis of a state publishing house and pay a publication fee to this publishing house."

"Technically, there is no censorship in Vietnam," he says, "but directors or editors-in-chief of the publishing houses are sometimes required to remove sensitive items, or even are timid enough to let the book go unpublished (this is our case). This kind of action we call self-censorship, and it is the Gordian knot of the Vietnamese publishing industry."

Mr. Long attaches to his email a copy of Vietnam's *Law on Publishing,* a twenty-two-page document that does indeed say plainly in article 5.2, "The State shall not censor works prior to their publication." The rest of the document is devoted to contradicting article 5.2 as it enumerates what is "prohibited during publishing activities." This includes "propaganda against the Socialist Republic of Vietnam (Article 10)," the incitement of war and aggression, and the "spread of reactionary ideology, depraved life styles, cruel acts, social evils and superstition, or destruction of good morals and customs." Other sections are devoted to the protection of party, military, defense, and other kinds of state secrets. Also forbidden is the "distortion of historical facts," particularly those "opposing the achievement of the revolution."

Mr. Long tells me that my new editor at Nha Nam is Ms. Nguyen Thi Thu Yen, who appears to be doing double duty as the person who negotiates foreign contracts. After our months of emailing back and forth, Mr. Long and I had prepared a second set of galleys, stripped of footnotes and corrected, at least as far as my advisors and I could push it. The manuscript is still bowdlerized and rewritten in dozens of places. All criticism of China has been removed. So, too, have any references to reeducation camps, graft, corruption, mistakes made by the Communist Party, and other "sensitive" subjects. Unfortunately, Mr. Long's text will soon be supplanted by another, officially licensed version. Again, I have misunderstood the nature of Vietnamese publishing. After all these months, my book has not yet been censored. It has undergone a kind of pre-censorship review, but the serious work of scrubbing sensitive material from the text has yet to begin.

Hostage Trade

In June 2012, I receive an email from Ms. Yen notifying me that *The Spy Who Loved Us* (or whatever the book is going to be called) has finally been approved for publication. "After a very long time of applying for publishing permission, we finally got a positive result from Lao Dong (Labor) Publishing House," she writes. Lao Dong is owned by Vietnam's Ministry of Labor, Invalids, and Social Affairs. As a hex against other, less powerful censors, Lao Dong's name will appear on the title page. The deal involves certain concessions, Ms. Yen admits. "In order for your book to be published, there are cuts and changes that cannot be otherwise. However, the good points are that they edited rather well in terms of Vietnamese language in writing and literature."

No page proofs are sent with her email. Ms. Yen offers instead a description of the censored text. "Given the highly sensitive content of your book, I do hope you can see these changes in the most supportive aspect, as necessary for your book to come to our readers."

Attached to Ms. Yen's email is a twelve-page document listing no fewer than 333 additional cuts to the book. Sentences, paragraphs, and entire pages have disappeared. The cuts begin with the title and carry through to the final acknowledgments. Historical facts are airbrushed out of the text and so are various people. Vo Nguyen Giap, the great Vietnamese general who won the battle of Dien Bien Phu, is no longer a quotable source. Colonel Bui Tin, who accepted the surrender of the South Vietnamese government in 1975, has been scrubbed from the text and even from the acknowledgments. Scenes describing Pham Xuan An's interaction with the party, the military, the Chinese, and the police have all hit the cutting room floor. Forbidden also are any attempts at cracking a joke or being the least bit ironic.

"You can't write the truth in Vietnam," says one of my advisers, a former professor of literature who is now living in the United States. "My country is lost to lies. Your book had a human being at the center of it, but now it is stripped of all the details that made the story specific and compelling."

"The communists want the words to come out of your mouth," she says. "Their official propaganda will look more authentic if it is authored by a Westerner. You are their tool. You can protest and negotiate what look to be small concessions, but in the end, they are going to win. They always win."

"Even the language in your book is now ugly," she says. "It is opaque rather than clear. Many terms have been borrowed from the Chinese. Other words are what the French call *langue de bois,* bureaucratic jargon. The communists think they are superior when they use these words. They want to control everything, even your thoughts."

"There is so much the censors don't like. They just cut, cut, cut," she says, after comparing the Lao Dong version of my book to Mr. Long's manuscript. "I get a big headache just looking at this text." Pham Xuan An is not allowed to "love" America or the time he spent studying journalism in California. He is only allowed to "understand" America. His quip that he never wanted to be a spy and considered it the "the work of hunting dogs" is gone. His claim that he was born at a tragic time in Vietnamese history, with betrayal in the air, is cut. The Gold Campaign organized by Ho Chi Minh in 1946, when he solicited contributions for a bribe large enough to induce the Chinese army to withdraw from northern Vietnam, is erased.

Pham Xuan An's family is not allowed to have "migrated from north Vietnam to the south." Nor is he allowed to have participated in the *nam tien*. This is the historic southward march of the Vietnamese, taking place over hundreds of years, as they worked their way down the Annamite Cordillera, occupying territory formerly held by Montagnards, Chams, Khmers, and other "minority" people. Praise for French literature is gone. An is not allowed to say that France created the map of modern Vietnam. His description of communism as a utopian ideal, unattainable in real life—cut. His praise of Edward Lansdale, as the great spy from whom he learned his tradecraft—cut. Throughout the text, North Vietnamese aggression is played down, South Vietnamese barbarism played up. The communists are always in the vanguard, the people always happily following. Pham Xuan An's attempt to distinguish between fighting for Vietnamese independence and fighting for communism—cut.

We have only got to page 38 when my friend says, "They want to kill this book. They don't like it at all." Discussions of communist land campaigns and collective ownership—cut. The communists are no longer responsible for ambushing and killing An's former high school teacher in 1947. Instead, "there was an ambush" by unnamed agents. A description of John F. Kennedy and his brother Robert visiting Vietnam in 1951—cut. References to Vietnam's offshore islands and oil fields, which are currently being fought over with the Chinese—cut. Claims that the river pirate Bay Vien fought for the communists before switching sides—cut. "These people are getting more paranoid every day," she says.

There is also a long list of errors in the translation, words that my Vietnamese editors have either misunderstood or refused to understand, words such as *ghost writer, betrayal, bribery, treachery, terrorism, torture, front organizations, ethnic minorities,* and *reeducation camps.* The French are not allowed to have *taught* the Vietnamese anything. Nor the Americans. Vietnam has never produced *refugees*. It only generates *settlers*. References to communism as a "failed god"—cut. An's description of himself as having an American brain grafted onto a Vietnamese body—cut. His analysis of how the communists replaced Ngo Dinh Diem's police state with a police state of their own—cut.

The story of the first American casualty in the Vietnam War, the Office of Strategic Services officer A. Peter Dewey, who was accidentally assassinated by the communists in 1945, is gone. Vietnamese army officers are written out of campaigns. The Tet Offensive is not allowed to be described as a military failure. Dogs are no longer barbecued alive. Sexual peccadilloes, mistresses, forced marriages—all disappear when communist officials are involved. Descriptions of Saigon in the weeks immediately following the end of the war, including food shortages and the tightening noose of state security—gone. Even the ban on cockfighting becomes unmentionable. That Boat People fled the country after 1975—cut. That Vietnam fought a war against Cambodia in 1978—cut. That

Vietnam fought a war against China in 1979—cut. Pham Xuan An's last wishes, that he be cremated and his ashes scattered in the Dong Nai River, have been cut. (Instead, he receives a state funeral with the eulogy delivered by the head of military intelligence.) By the time we get to the end of the book, entire pages of notes and sources have disappeared. So has the index, where so many words would have had to somersault into their opposites.

"Thank God we have come to the end," says my friend. "This has given me white hairs and nightmares."

The Lao Dong manuscript presents a conundrum. How does one respond to something as nefarious as this? My advisors suggest two solutions. Kill the project, or work out a hostage trade. Nha Nam and Lao Dong will be allowed to proceed with publishing the book, but only in exchange for giving me an unlocked version of the manuscript that can be restored to its original form and published on the web.

To prepare for these negotiations, I review the contract I signed with Nha Nam three years earlier. The publisher will make only "slight modifications in the original text of the work," and these modifications "shall not materially change the meaning or otherwise materially alter the text." I ask my agent in New York to send notice to Nha Nam alerting them that they are in breach of contract for substituting a work of propaganda for a translation.

Along with paying me for translation rights—a delay occasioned by "accidental oversight"—Nha Nam begins backtracking on the "cuts and changes that cannot be otherwise." They had wanted to call the book *Perfect Spy*, but now Ms. Yen agrees to restore an earlier title that Mr. Long and I had negotiated. "This translation being censored is what both parties have seen from the beginning," she writes to my agent in July 2012. "The extent to which the translation has been censored may have shocked the author (as well as us). But we are in here, all the time now, and we know the situation in our country. We have gone to seven different state-owned publishing houses, and, in the end, only Labor Publishing would give us a license, with cuts and changes."

My canceling the publishing contract would be "the most easy-way-out-solution," Ms. Yen concludes, but "this would be unfair to us and our honest intentions. We would be *very* disappointed."

My hostage negotiations are not going well either. Ms. Yen demands the right to censor the book on the web, thereby extending Vietnamese hegemony throughout the universe. Eventually she retreats to demanding a six-month delay between publication of the book in Vietnam and its release on the web. We also agree that a disclaimer will be printed on the copyright page saying, "This is a partial translation of *The Spy Who Loved Us*. Parts of the text have been omitted or altered."

By the end of the year, when I have yet to receive a copy of the galleys to review and our publishing license is about to expire, Ms. Yen writes, "Why have you agreed to work with Nha Nam if you don't trust your Vietnamese editor? Are we less trustworthy than your friends?" I imagine her lacquered nails scratching the keyboard as she types. "We would like no more opinions from outsiders. It is not professional."

In June 2013 Ms. Yen sends me a note announcing that Nha Nam is trying to secure another publishing license (the last one having expired), and she hopes soon to be writing with good news. She admits that editors in Vietnam are "scared" of the project. The following week I receive a request from Ms. Yen to "friend" me on Facebook.

Not Worth Being Killed For

In a blog post released in June 2013 by *Irrawaddy Magazine*, the Vietnamese reporter Pham Doan Trang describes how censorship works in Vietnam. As she explains, every week, the Central Propaganda Commission of the Vietnamese Communist Party in Hanoi and the commission's regional officials in Ho Chi Minh City and elsewhere throughout the country "convene 'guidance meetings' with the managing editors of the country's important national newspapers."

"Not incidentally," she writes, "the editors are all party members. Officials of the Ministry of Information and Ministry of Public Security are also present. . . . At these meetings, someone from the Propaganda Commission rates each paper's performance during the previous week—commending those who have toed the line, reprimanding and sometimes punishing those who have strayed."

Instructions given at these meetings to the "comrade editors and publishers" sometimes leak into the blogosphere (the online forums from which the Vietnamese increasingly get their news). Here one learns that independent candidates for political office, such as the actress Hong An, are not to be mentioned in the press and that the dissident activist Cu Huy Ha Vu, charged with "propagandizing against the state," should never be addressed as "Doctor Vu." Also buried are reports on tourists drowning in Halong Bay, Vietnam's decision to build nuclear power plants, and Chinese extraction of bauxite from a huge mining operation in the Annamite Range.

The weekly meetings are secret, and further discussions through-out the week are conducted face to face or by telephone. "Because no tangible evidence remains that . . . the press was gagged on such and such a story, the officials of the Ministry of Information can reply with a straight face that Vietnam is being slandered by 'hostile forces,'" Trang says. These denials were strained in 2012, when the BBC released a secret recording of one of these meetings.

The Propaganda Department considers Vietnam's media to be the "voice of party organizations, State bodies, and social organizations." This approach is codified in Vietnam's Law on the Media, which requires reporters to "propagate the doctrine and policies of the Party, the laws of the State, and the national and world cultural, scientific and technical achievements [of Vietnam.]"

Trang concludes her report with a wry observation. "Vietnam does not figure among the deadlier countries to be a journalist," she says. "The State doesn't need to kill journalists to control the media, because by and large, Vietnam's press card-carrying journalists are not allowed to do work that is worth being killed for."

Another person knowledgeable about censorship in Vietnam is David Brown, a former U.S. foreign service officer who returned to Vietnam to work as a copy editor for the online English-language edition of a Vietnamese newspaper. In an article published in *Asia Times* in February 2012, he describes how "the managing editor and publisher [of his paper] trooped off to a meeting with the Ministry of Information and the Party's Central Propaganda and Education Committee every Tuesday where they and their peers from other papers were alerted to 'sensitive issues.'"

Brown describes the "editorial no-go zones" that his paper was not allowed to write about. These taboo subjects include unflattering news about the Communist Party, government policy, military strategy, Chinese relations, minority rights, human rights, democracy, calls for political pluralism, allusions to revolutionary events in other communist countries, distinctions between north and south Vietnamese, and stories about Vietnamese refugees. The one subject his paper *is* allowed to cover is crime, and he notes that the press is not toothless in Vietnam. In fact, journalists can prove quite useful to the government by exposing low-level corruption and malfeasance. "To maintain their readerships, they aggressively pursue scandals, investigate 'social evils' and champion the downtrodden. Corruption of all kinds, at least at the local level, is also fair game."

Another expert on censorship in Vietnam is the former BBC correspondent Bill Hayton, who was expelled from Vietnam in 2007 and is still banned from the country. Writing in *Forbes* in 2010, he describes the limits to political activity in Vietnam, where article 4 of the constitution declares that "the Communist Party of Vietnam, the vanguard of the Vietnamese working class, the faithful representative of the rights and interests of the working class, the toiling people, and the whole nation, acting upon the Marxist-Leninist doctrine and Ho Chi Minh thought, is the force leading the State and society." In other words, what the party wants, it gets, and what it fears, it suppresses. "There is no legal, independent media in Vietnam," says Hayton. "Every single publication belongs to part of the state or the Communist Party."

Lest we think that Vietnamese culture is frozen in place, Trang, Brown, Hayton, and other observers remind us that the rules are constantly changing and being reinterpreted. "Vietnam . . . is one of the most dynamic and aspirational societies on the planet," writes Hayton. "This has been enabled by the strange balance between the Party's control, and lack of control, which has manifested itself through the practice of 'fence-breaking,' or *pha rao* in Vietnamese." As long as you "don't confront the Party or pry too deeply into high-level corruption, editors and journalists can get along fine," he says.

In certain circumstances, even journalists who pry more deeply can get along fine, depending on who is controlling the news leaks and for what end. Geoffrey Cain, another observer of censorship in Vietnam, describes this process of controlled leaks. In his master's thesis, completed in 2012 at the School of Oriental and African Studies at the University of London, he writes that the Communist Party in Vietnam uses journalists and other writers as an "informal police force." They help the central government keep regional officials in line, limit their bribe taking, and patrol aspects of public life that otherwise might remain in the shadows. This represents "soft authoritarianism," which is characterized by "a series of elite actions and counter-actions marked by 'uncertainty' as an instrument of rule." What is often described in Vietnam as a battle between "reformers" and "conservatives" is actually the method by which an increasingly market-oriented society can be "simultaneously repressive and responsive." In this interpretation, journalists and bloggers lend themselves to the "informal policing" of free-market profiteers.

The "legal" mechanisms for the arrest of journalists and bloggers who overstep the boundaries or accidentally get caught on the wrong side of shifting rules include article 88c of the criminal code, which forbids "making, storing, or circulating cultural products with contents against the Socialist Republic of Vietnam," and article 79 of the criminal code, which forbids "carrying out activities aimed at overthrowing the people's administration." Other grounds for arrest range from "tax evasion" to "stealing state secrets and selling them abroad to foreigners." (This was the charge leveled against the novelist Duong Thu Huong when she mailed one of her book manuscripts to a publisher in California.)

Other repressive measures lie in the Press Law of 1990 (amended in 1999 and updated in 2016), which begins by declaring, "The press in the Socialist Republic of Vietnam constitutes the voice of the Party, of the State and social organizations" (article 1). It continues, "No one shall be allowed to abuse the freedom of the press and freedom of speech in the press to violate the interests of the State, of any collective group or individual citizen" (article 2.3). Then there is the Law on Publishing of 2004, which prohibits "propaganda against the Socialist Republic of Vietnam," the "spread of reactionary ideology," and the "disclosure of secrets of the Party, State, military, defense, economics, or external relations."

On goes the list of laws and regulations through various decrees and circulars, including decree 56, on "Cultural and Information Activities," which forbids "the denial of revolutionary achievements"; decree 97, on "Management, Supply, and Use of Internet Services and Electronic Information on the Internet," which forbids using the internet "to damage the reputations of individuals and organizations"; circular 7, from the Ministry of Information, which "restricts blogs to covering personal content" and requires blogging platforms to file reports on users "every six months or upon request"; and the 2012 draft decree on "Management, Provision, and Use of Internet Services and Information on the Network," which requires foreign-based companies that provide information in Vietnamese "to filter and eliminate any prohibited content."

The draft decree was codified the following year as decree 72, which outlaws the distribution of "general information" on blogs, limiting them to "personal information" and making it illegal for individuals to use the internet for news reporting or commenting on political events. Condemning this statute as "nonsensical and extremely dangerous," the organization Reporters Without Borders, in an August 2013 press release, said that decree 72 could be implemented only with "massive and constant government surveillance of the entire internet. . . . This decree's barely veiled goal is to keep the Communist Party in power at all costs by turning news and information into a state monopoly." The 2016 revision of the Press Law triples the number of prohibited acts.

Vietnam has borrowed many of these techniques for monitoring the internet from China, its neighbor to the north. China has imprisoned dozens of authors and journalists, including the Nobel laureate Liu Xiaobo. Like China, Vietnam falls near the bottom in rankings of press freedom. Freedom House calls Vietnamese media "not free." In 2017, Reporters Without Borders ranked Vietnam 175 out of 180 countries in press freedom. (It fell between Sudan and China.) In 2016, the Committee to Protect Journalists ranked Vietnam as the world's sixth-worst jailer of reporters, with at least eighteen journalists in prison. Human Rights Watch estimates the total number of political prisoners in Vietnam at 130. Recently, a draconian crackdown against bloggers and anti-Chinese protestors sent dozens more to jail, for terms as long as twelve years. Pro-democracy and human rights activists, environmentalists, writers, bloggers, investigative journalists, land reform protestors, and whistleblowers are all being swept up in Vietnam's totalitarian dragnet.

Literary Control Mechanisms

Sometime in March 2014—no one can tell me for sure, and, in fact, the book's publishing license was not issued until May 2014—a Vietnamese translation of *The Spy Who Loved Us* appeared in Hanoi. By this point, even the title of my book had been censored. It was reduced to Z.21, a code name for Pham Xuan An, as if the book itself, like its hero, would try to travel unnoticed through the shifting terrain of Vietnam's culture wars.

I had been sent a final list of censored passages and was settling down to review these cuts when I received the email telling me that the book had been published. This was a breach of contract, but I decided not to press the point because I was now contractually free, in six months, to release my own uncensored version on the web. The web is the arena to which Vietnamese literature has moved as the gray net of police surveillance, fines, exile, and prison is cinched ever more tightly around the country's journalists, bloggers, artists, musicians, writers, and poets. Yes, even Vietnam's poets can get in trouble, as I will learn later during a visit to Vietnam.

I use the minor stir occasioned by my book's publication (including a cover story in *Communist Youth* magazine) to schedule a trip to Southeast Asia. I want to meet the censors with whom I have been sparring for five years, or at least the ones who will talk to me. I arrive on the night flight from Paris to Hanoi at the end of May and begin swimming through a miasma of tropical heat and humidity before taking refuge in the Church Hotel, near St. Joseph's Cathedral in Hanoi's old quarter. From here I schedule a meeting with Nguyen Viet Long, my original editor at Nha Nam. I then learn that two other people who played a role in this affair are willing to speak with me. They include Nguyen The Vinh, an editor at Hong Duc, the state-owned publishing company that produced the final list of passages to be censored and then issued my publishing license, and Duong Trung Quoc, a historian and elected member of Vietnam's National Assembly. Vinh and Quoc seem to have negotiated the political deals required to get my book—or at least a version of my book—published in Vietnam.

The original translator of *Z.21*—the chap who produced the first manuscript that Mr. Long began to edit—is a Hanoi journalist named Do Tuan Kiet. Judging from his work (unfortunately, he is out of town during my visit), he speaks Vietnam's dominant northern dialect, which today is larded with Marxist-Leninist terms borrowed from the Chinese. This language grates on the ears of southern Vietnamese. It was not the language spoken by Pham Xuan An, the hero of my book, who, in fact, mocked this speech. He dismissed the ten months he spent in 1978 at the Nguyen Ai Quoc National Political Academy outside Hanoi as "reeducation"—a failed attempt to teach him this jargon. "I had lived too long among the enemy," he said. "They sent me to be recycled."

As Mr. Long began editing Kiet's translation, and as one state-owned company after another refused to grant the book a publishing license, more and more changes were made to the text. By the end, I imagine, the project had grown ripe with the odor of danger. It was not a book that people who valued their careers as editors at Police Publishers or the Ministry of the Interior wanted to touch. Mr. Long himself, before he left trade book publishing and began editing math texts for schoolchildren, must have begun to look a bit suspicious.

On the afternoon of our meeting, Mr. Long rings the bell of my hotel suite and nervously enters the room. He sits on the edge of the sofa, apologizes for being late, and finally agrees to drink a beer. In his fifties, with dark hair framing his square head, he is dressed in the uniform of a Vietnamese cadre: owlish eyeglasses, short-sleeved white shirt with a pen in the front pocket, metal watch flopping around his wrist, gray slacks, and sandals. He glances around him, as if he is looking for listening devices, and begins answering my questions with the kind of guarded indirection one develops in a police state.

Trained as an engineer in the former Soviet Union, Mr. Long specialized in cybernetics or control systems for nuclear reactors, particularly the one in Dalat that the victorious North Vietnamese seized from the retreating Americans in 1975. A graduate of the Moscow Power Engineering Institute, he taught himself English during his five years in Russia.

After chatting about his move from cybernetics to publishing, we begin talking about my book. "There was a serious battle to edit your book," he says. "I was caught in the middle, being pressured by the author and my superiors. The regime has declared this a sensitive book. You can get in a lot of trouble for handling this kind of project improperly. That's all I can tell you."

"By law, there are no private publishing houses in Vietnam," he says. "So Nha Nam has to ally itself with a state-run publisher every time it releases a book. We took your book to a lot of publishers, and they all turned it down. Finally, Hong Duc agreed to give it a publishing license. They're a powerful publisher."

"Why are they powerful?" I ask.

Mr. Long laughs nervously. "Let's just say they're powerful. That's all I can tell you." Later I learn that Hong Duc is run by Vietnam's Ministry of Information and Communication, one of the country's major censors.

"What about the material that was cut from the book?" I ask.

"The translator translated the entire book," he says. "Then we removed the passages that had to be removed. We couldn't leave them untouched. Publishing your book was a very hard process. A lot of subjects had to be censored, and there was no choice about removing them."

When I ask for examples, he mentions Colonel Bui Tin, who defected to France in 1990 to protest Vietnam's lack of democracy, and General Giap, who, before his death in 2013, wrote letters opposing China's influence in Vietnam. "Nothing about these affairs can be written," he says. "Everyone knows about them, but you can't get a publishing permit if these things are in your book."

"How do you know what has to be censored?"

"We must know. We observe. Maybe some people have different ideas, but we know what we're supposed to do. A lot of it depends on timing," he says. "We published a book by the Dalai Lama against China. Then, when the authorities noticed what we had done, we were forbidden from publishing more books by the Dalai Lama. In general, we couldn't publish anything bad about China. For example, the 1979 border war between Vietnam and China was something we weren't allowed to write about."

Mr. Long has a nervous cough at the back of his throat. He declines a second beer. Again he glances around the room, finding nothing to make him look less glum.

"The censorship is often silent," he says. "Without formally being banned, all the books that have been published can suddenly disappear from the shelves."

"Publishing your book was a very hard process," he says again. "It was the most difficult book for me."

I ask Mr. Long if he is a member of the Communist Party. "I am not a party member," he says, "but my brother is. There are political benefits from joining the party. It helps you rise in state-run institutions."

He again declines another beer and says it's time for him to retrieve his motorbike and ride home. He congratulates me on the publication of my book.

"It is not really my book," I say, mentioning the four hundred passages that were cut or rewritten.

"Four hundred is not so many," he says. "We have an expression in Vietnamese, 'If the head goes through, the tail will follow.' In the next edition, maybe some of these passages will be restored."

As Mr. Long slips out the door, he looks worried about having said too much during our brief encounter. I wish him well in his new job. "The pay is better," he assures me.

Habits of War

Mr. Nguyen The Vinh, the editor at Hong Duc publishers, is the next censor I meet on my Vietnamese publishing tour. I am scheduled to appear at a Hanoi book fair to sit on a panel discussing my book. Flanking me are the sober Mr. Vinh, who, like many editors, seems to prefer books to authors. On my other side is Duong Trung Quoc, the historian and politician who also played a role in getting my book published. I don't know what kind of history he writes, but, as an elected member of Vietnam's National Assembly, Mr. Quoc—a hearty fellow who resembles a Vietnamese Bill Clinton—is obviously a successful politician.

I try to hide my annoyance when most of the evening is devoted to discussing Pham Xuan An as a "perfect spy." Remember, Mr. Vinh has edited—and censored—both the "official" biography of An and my own work. I have been advised to curb my tongue and not jeopardize the continued sale of my book. The ordeal continues over dinner, where I am still holding my tongue, while Mr. Vinh and Mr. Quoc tuck into a multi-course feast. By the time our meal has moved from sautéed vegetables to steamed fish, my tongue has slipped enough to broach the subject of censorship.

"By law there is no censorship system in Vietnam," says Mr. Vinh. "Mainly what we have is self-censorship."

Mr. Quoc the politician agrees with his literary friend. "Here in Vietnam censorship is inside the brain of everyone," he says. "It was your editors who cut your book, not the government."

I ask them to elaborate on how a country without censorship manages to censor so many writers. "Publishers belong to the state," says Mr. Vinh. "Everyone who works in the system understands this. For the higher purpose of the nation, they have to sacrifice something. We have an expression here in Vietnam: 'It is better to kill an innocent man than let a guilty one escape.'"

Mr. Quoc allows a smile to spread across his face before gently chiding his friend. "You are speaking like a political commissar," he says.

Later in the evening Mr. Quoc will hint at why my book was finally published after having been blocked for five years. "The authorized biographies on Pham Xuan An were works of stenography," he says. "People printed what he told them to print. Your book is something different. It is documented and researched, but, more importantly, it captures his personality. This is why I thought it should be published."

I take the compliment but note that my book has not actually been published in Vietnam. A promotional teaser is for sale, while a complete Vietnamese translation can exist only outside the country. This will happen when the book is retranslated and released in Berlin as an electronic file stored on computers hardened against attacks from Vietnam's censors. The fact that Vietnam has censors trying to reach across the world and disable computers in Berlin makes these agents far less benign than Mr. Vinh would have me believe. In this case, the censors are working not as freelance gardeners, shaping literary topiaries, but as political operatives executing orders to attack people in foreign countries.

As we move from fish to grilled meats, Mr. Quoc indicates that he is going to give me an important scoop. Not only did Pham Xuan An continue working as a spy after the end of the Vietnam war, but he did so at the highest levels. "He was *hieu truong,* or dean, of the postwar military intelligence school in Ho Chi Minh City." An's eight-month stint in 1978 at the Nguyen Ai Quoc National Political Academy in Hanoi had prepared him for this important assignment.

I have seen no evidence supporting this claim, and I suspect it is part of the propaganda campaign designed to make An into a perfect apparatchik. The claim is even more improbable because, earlier in the evening, Mr. Quoc had confessed that An, as a southerner who had worked for the Americans, was always distrusted

Pham Xuan An, Ho Chi Minh City, 2005. Photograph by James Nachtwey.

by his northern colleagues. "People in Pham Xuan An's position were not trusted by the government," he says. "There were a lot of questions about him." Apparently, these questions will remain unanswered for a long time. "It takes at least seventy years for documents in Vietnam to be declassified," he says.

Later, to verify Mr. Quoc's claim that An was the dean of Vietnam's spy academy, I visit Bui Tin in his one-room garret in Paris. Tin is another famous journalist spy. He was the deputy editor of *Nhan Dan,* Vietnam's Communist Party newspaper, when he penned an editorial in the spring of 1990 praising the collapse of the Berlin Wall and the introduction of democratic reforms into the communist world. He was about to be cashiered by the Politburo, which was preparing to sign a secret agreement allying Vietnam with China. ("The Thanh Do agreement in September 1990 was the beginning of the Chinese colonization of Vietnam," he says.) To avoid being arrested, Tin left his wife and two children in Hanoi and flew to Paris for a meeting of communist newspaper editors. After the meeting, he didn't fly home. He thought the situation would reverse itself in a year or two, that Vietnam's progressive forces would regain the upper hand and reintroduce democratic reforms into the country. Twenty-seven years later, Tin is still in Paris, while his wife, whom he has not seen since 1990, remains "under close surveillance" in Hanoi.

As an army colonel and a confidante of General Giap, and as a fellow journalist who befriended Pham Xuan An when the two men met in 1975, Tin is a reliable source for double checking Mr. Quoc's information. "Yes, Pham Xuan An wrote reports on his visitors," Tin confirms, "and every once in a while he was asked to give lectures to the spies being trained in Saigon by the Ministry of Interior. But he was nothing as grand as the dean of a spy academy. The government treated him like an interesting artifact. He was a bauble they toyed with and admired. He was good for propaganda, but they never trusted him."

Bui Tin, Paris, 2014.

In spite of his dubious pronouncements, I warm to Mr. Quoc as we plow through a steady round of beers and end the evening with toothpicks propped in our mouths, a sign of having eaten well. He has surprised me with another confession. Unlike the old days, he says, the Vietnamese government is not run by intellectual giants and military geniuses. "Today the government of Vietnam isn't smart enough to allow a Pham Xuan An to do what he did. It requires bravery and intelligence to run a spy like that. What is your expression in English? 'The first victim of war is truth.' Here in Vietnam, we have the habits of war."

By this point in the evening, as convivial friends at the end of a good meal, agreeing on almost everything, my censors and I have begun toasting each other, bottoms up.

CHAPTER IV

Wandering Souls

With the censor's boot on their necks, a generation of Vietnamese writers has been forced into silence or exile. To report on their plight, I met with three of the country's best-known authors: Bao Ninh in Hanoi, Duong Thu Huong in Paris, and Pham Thi Hoai in Berlin. Each had his or her own story to tell about censorship, arrest, banishment, or silence—realities that are becoming increasingly dire in Vietnam.

Bao Ninh (whose real name is Hoang Au Phuong; Bao Ninh is the name of his family's native village) was a seventeen-year-old student when he enlisted in 1969 as an infantryman in the Fifth Battalion, Twenty-fourth Regiment, Tenth Division. He would spend six years fighting his way down the Ho Chi Minh Trail, surviving some of the war's deadliest battles, before his regiment captured Saigon's Ton Son Nhut Airport in 1975. Of the five hundred men who joined his military unit in 1969, Ninh is reported to be one of ten who survived.

The son of Hoang Tue, a former director of Vietnam's Linguistics Institute, Bao Ninh went back to school after the war and finished college in 1981. He worked briefly for Vietnam's Science Institute and then decided to become a writer. In 1984, now age thirty-two, he enrolled in the second class of students admitted to the Nguyen Du Writers School, named after the celebrated Vietnamese poet who wrote *The Tale of Kieu*. For his thesis, Ninh wrote a novel about his wartime experience. The manuscript, then titled *The Sorrow of War*, began circulating around Hanoi in Roneo form in the late 1980s. One of these stenciled duplications, similar to a mimeograph's, was published in 1990 under the anodyne title *Fate of Love*. The original title was restored in a 1991 edition and then removed again when *Fate of Love* was reissued in 1992. The book won a major literary award and became instantly famous—too famous, apparently, because a denunciation campaign was launched against Bao Ninh, his literary award was retracted, and his book went out of print for a decade. "The time is not right" to republish it, he was told. *Fate of Love* reappeared in 2003, but it was not until 2006—fifteen years after its original publication—that *The Sorrow of War* reappeared in Vietnam. The Vietnamese use a variety of euphemisms to describe this gap in Bao Ninh's literary career, but the correct term is *censorship*. He was not thrown into prison or banned. In fact, he was rewarded for his silence, but he was censored nonetheless.

Translated into English by the Vietnamese poet Phan Thanh Hao and the Australian journalist Frank Palmos, *The Sorrow of War* became a literary sensation when it was published in London in 1993. The book revealed that Vietnam's veterans on the winning side suffered the same trauma and disillusionment as the losers had. Hailed as a great novel, comparable to Erich Maria Remarque's *All Quiet on the Western Front*, *The Sorrow of War* has been republished in a dozen languages, and the Society of Authors has named it one of the fifty best translations of the twentieth century.

While the book was becoming a best seller in the West, it reverted in Vietnam to being passed hand to hand in pirated editions. Bao Ninh stopped publishing. He took a government job, and his son was allowed to leave the country to study economics at the University of Massachusetts. *The Sorrow of War* is currently widely available in Vietnam, but its two successor volumes remain unpublished.

During my first meeting with Bao Ninh in Hanoi in 2008, we talked about his unpublished books. He assured me the works had been written, gave me their titles, and described their plots. I have to say that I have not personally verified the existence of these manuscripts, which have assumed a status in Vietnamese literature comparable to Captain Ahab's great white whale—doubted by many, believed by some, seen by few. The subversive nature of Bao Ninh's trilogy becomes apparent only after one confronts the shock of the first volume. *The Sorrow of War* may be a great war novel, but it holds a double surprise for readers in the West by revealing the bitterness of NVA soldiers, the soldiers who *won* the war. They were betrayed by incompetent commanders and self-serving politicians. They were scorned by a postwar generation that wanted to forget the incredible suffering inflicted on Vietnam during thirty years of war and turn instead to making money. The survivors of the war are ravaged by guilt and attacked by bad dreams. They drink too much, brawl too much, and drift all too often from failure to suicide. They display all the symptoms of post-traumatic stress disorder, shell-shock, battle fatigue, or whatever we call the soul-sucking misery that invades a soldier's bones at the sight of men killing other men.

The "friendly, simple peasant fighters . . . were the ones ready to bear the catastrophic consequences of this war, yet they never had a say in deciding the course of the war," writes Kien, the narrator of the novel, who, like its author, spent a decade fighting Americans in Vietnam's Central Highlands. "We have so many of those damned idiots up there in the North enjoying the profits of war, but it's the sons of peasants who have to leave home," Kien explains in a manuscript that turns out to be the book we are holding in our hands.

At war's end, the former infantryman is detailed into recovering the corpses of his fallen comrades. "Over a long period, over many, many graves, the souls of the beloved dead silently and gloomily dragged the sorrow of war into his life." He returns to his native Hanoi in 1976 to find the city consumed by careerism, graft, corruption, and all the other ailments of an emerging Asian Tiger. The political propaganda is ham-fisted. His former fiancée is a prostitute. He joins the ranks of the "traumatized misfits" who survived the war, works as a journalist, and writes a novel that sits abandoned on his desk until the pages blow away in the wind.

"Those who survived continue to live," writes Kien. "But that will has gone, that burning will which was once Vietnam's salvation. Where is the reward of enlightenment due to us for attaining our sacred war goals? Our history-making efforts for the great generations have been to no avail. What's so different here and now from the vulgar and cruel life we all experienced during the war?"

"In this kind of peace it seems people have unmasked themselves and revealed their true, horrible selves," Kien says to a fellow veteran. "So much blood, so many lives were sacrificed—for what?"

"I'm simply a soldier like you who'll now have to live with broken dreams and with pain," his colleague replies. "But, my friend, our era is finished. After this hard-won victory fighters like you, Kien, will never be normal again."

Kien is wracked by the kind of survivor guilt that comes from knowing "that the kindest, most worthy people have all fallen away, or even been tortured, humiliated before being killed, or buried and wiped away by the machinery of war." He is left with the "appalling paradox" that "justice may have been won, but cruelty, death, and inhuman violence have also won."

On the two occasions when Bao Ninh was allowed to travel to the United States (he visited Boston in 1999 and Texas in 2005) he gravitated to the war veterans in the crowd. They swapped reticent greetings, established whether they had carried guns or flown airplanes, and then started drinking, letting the silence fill with the ghosts of departed friends. Bao Ninh had more dead friends than the Americans did, and they died more gruesome deaths, but dead is dead, and he bore no grudges as he sat among his fellow soldiers. "Soldiers never say 'sorry' to each other," he told me. "They have nothing to apologize for."

When Wayne Karlin, a former U.S. marine, met Bao Ninh at a hotel café in Hanoi in 2007, he was reminded of another Vietnam veteran turned writer, Tim O'Brien. "Both men are compact, their faces not so much sharp as sharpened, their eyes bright, at times with a flare of pain, at times with a gleefully malevolent intelligence, a sardonic, challenging grunt's stare. And they both smoke like hell," wrote Karlin in his book *Wandering Souls* (2009).

I am not a former soldier who fought in Vietnam, but the war was the cloud under which I came of age, and I seized the chance to begin traveling to Vietnam when the country opened to outsiders in the early 1990s. I met Pham Xuan An on my first trip in 1991, when the journalist-spy was still under police surveillance, and I kept returning to see him as I wrote my *New Yorker* profile and then my book, both titled *The Spy Who Loved Us*. After An's death in 2006, I visited Vietnam again two years later to talk to sources reticent about speaking while he was alive, and it was on this trip that I first met Bao Ninh.

Eyes in the Back of His Head

It is a steamy night in June when I meet Ninh at his house in Hanoi, where we will spend the evening chatting and sweating over green tea. Located in an old part of the city, the house has the usual barred gate opening into a covered patio filled with motorbikes. Behind the bikes is a narrow room with yellowed walls lit by neon tubes. The room is furnished with a black couch, a couple of chairs, and a coffee table holding lychees, biscuits, and our bitter tea. I am accompanied by my Vietnamese assistant and another young woman who is serving as our translator.

Bao Ninh strikes me as hyper-cautious, with the kind of wariness one develops after many years spent trying to avoid people who want to kill you. Curled in a chair, ready to spring, his body looks as if its muscles have forgotten how to relax, and I can't shake the idea that he has eyes in the back of his head. It is a large head, bristling with silver hair. Ninh's eyebrows sweep over glancing black eyes, above sunken cheeks and a drooping mustache. Wearing a brown short-sleeved shirt and black trousers, he chain-smokes Camel Lights, lighting one after the other with nicotine-stained fingers. A fan blows on us as we sit in the yellow gloom.

The next thing I notice about Ninh are his feet. He is barefoot, with wide, spatulate toes gripping the linoleum. Sunburned and flat, these are the feet of someone who spent years walking in rubber sandals made out of old truck tires, traveling down jungle paths with a backpack on his shoulders and an AK-47 in his hand. These are the feet of a peasant warrior whose physical needs have been stripped to a bare minimum. As he stares at me through his narrowed eyes, I realize that I am traveling heavy, with notebooks, digital recorders, and two assistants, while Ninh is still traveling light.

My first visit falls on National Journalists Day, which is celebrated mainly through bottoms-up drinking with one's fellow cadre. Ever since his career as an author got derailed after the denunciation campaign that began in the early 1990s, Ninh has supported himself by writing a column for the newspaper *Literature (Bao Van Nghe)*, published by the Vietnamese Writers Union. "In principle, I have to go to work every day, but I am an old man, so I stay at home instead of going to the office," the fifty-six-year-old author tells me. "I write an article a week. My last piece was on the countryside, about illiteracy among rural kids who are so poor that they have never been taught how to read."

After years of penning inoffensive columns for *Literature,* Ninh was allowed to publish a short story collection in 2002 and another in 2005 called *Daydreaming During a Traffic Jam*. "As is usual in Vietnam, the publisher printed two or three thousand copies of *Daydreaming* and then allowed the book to go out of print," he says. "You will have a hard time finding it now. I don't even have a copy." One story in the volume was translated and published in English as "Savage Winds." "The title refers to the wind that blows in the Central Highlands," he tells me. The rest of the stories remain untranslated. When I ask if he minds his literary obscurity, Ninh shrugs. "I only care about the royalties," he says.

In 2006, Ninh was allowed to release a Vietnamese version of *The Sorrow of War,* for which he was paid a few thousand dollars. "The book has been translated and published in ten countries," he says. "I don't know anything about these translations. People tell me that sometimes parts of the text have been left out." Again, he tells me how much he appreciates the royalties from these foreign publications.

"I have written two unpublished novels," he says when I broach the subject of censorship. "I do not intend to publish them." The first, called A Plain of Grass (Thao Nguyen), is about a platoon of soldiers who capture a Montagnard village in the Central Highlands. Here they find a white missionary who has filed down his teeth like a Montagnard and gone native. What do the soldiers do with their half-white, half-Montagnard captive—kill him, set him free, or ship him to Hanoi? The question divides the unit, and they begin fighting among themselves. "The central character is a Catholic priest," says Ninh. "The story is set during the war, when times were very different than they are now. We were ardent communists back then."

"The second novel is about the interrelation of cultures and people, about the mixing of cultures. It, too, is about the war," he tells me. This, the final, yet-to-be-named volume in Ninh's trilogy, is the most incendiary. It tells the story of South Vietnamese prisoners of war who have been sent to a POW camp in the north. (I have been told that the camp is located in Nghe An, Ho Chi Minh's natal province.) Since most of the village men have died in the war, the local women mate with the southern soldiers and produce a new Vietnamese race blended from Ho Chi Minh northerners and defeated southerners.

"The novel deals with soldiers, President Thieu's soldiers," says Ninh, referring to soldiers in the Army of the Republic of South Vietnam. "After the war they are arrested and sent to the north, to undergo a kind of brainwashing. Ten years later they are released."

"My son has a girlfriend who is the daughter of a Republican soldier," he tells me, confirming that the new blended Vietnam is already in existence. At the time we are speaking, his son is working in Hanoi for an American investment firm. "It is safe to have money now," says Ninh. He mentions that his son appeared recently on a TV program about Vietnamese youth and that he is helping to organize a film festival in Hanoi. "It's strange to me how Vietnamese youth like American movies," he says. "Americans and Vietnamese have something in common. We Vietnamese are often mistaken for Chinese, but we are very different. We are more open than the Chinese, more like Americans."

Ninh returns to narrating the plot of his novel. "The soldiers are brought to the north."

"To Nghe An province?" I ask.

"I didn't say that," Ninh says, narrowing his eyes and retreating behind a cloud of cigarette smoke. Everyone knows that if he mentions Nghe An province, the book will be read as a commentary on Ho Chi Minh. He wants to drop the subject. "It is too difficult to understand," he says. I urge him to continue.

"They are sent to a labor camp, in a residential area. Some northern women get pregnant. The soldiers are released and go to America. Then they return from America, to visit the women and their children."

"So at this point the soldiers are *viet kieu*," I suggest, using the term for exiled Vietnamese.

"You are right, but the Vietnamese people don't like the term *viet kieu*," he says. "This originated from the Chinese, and now you

Americans use the term, but we prefer to say *nguoi viet hai ngoai,* 'foreign Vietnamese,' which is more precise."

"Do the soldiers stay in Vietnam?"

"Are they happy?" Bao Ninh replies. "It depends. Life in America is easier. They keep their American nationality. This is a fable about the history of Vietnam. It was written a couple of years ago. I do not intend to publish this now. For me, writing is more important than publishing. This is a story from the past."

"Usually I never talk about my books, only with my closest friends," he says. "I wrote the novel from my personal interests. I wrote about Vietnamese soldiers who worked with Americans. I tried to find out special things about Republican soldiers. I tried to understand them."

"Did you succeed?"

"No one can understand another person fully," he tells me. "I believe I understood them. It took me a long time, actually from the end of the war until now. I have traveled to the south a lot. I stayed in the south for several months after the end of the war. Many of my relatives live in the south. My younger sister, a teacher, lives there. It's easier to earn money in Saigon than in Hanoi."

As if to skirt away from a sensitive subject, Ninh says, "I haven't finished writing the book yet. I spend most of my time drinking with friends."

"Drinking what?" I ask.

He leans over and writes in my notebook *"bia hoi"* (draft beer) and then jokingly gestures toward my colleagues. "This is not a suitable subject for your translator," he says.

"Middle-aged people like me are undisciplined," he says. "I write at night, for three to four hours, starting after 10 p.m. I was born in the Year of the Cat, and cats don't sleep at night. Writing is not an occupation here in Vietnam. It is a hobby. You don't earn any money for it."

My final question concerns Duong Thu Huong, one of whose books, *Novel Without a Name,* contains a number of passages resem-

Bao Ninh, Hanoi, 2008.

bling his own work. Ninh avoids the question. "There's a lot of false information about her, saying she isn't respectable, which isn't true," he says. "I have read all of her books, even those not allowed to be published in Vietnam because she is anti-communist." To get my question answered, he suggests I go to Paris and ask Duong Thu Huong herself.

Black Cloud

I meet Bao Ninh again in 2014, when I am visiting Hanoi after the publication of *The Spy Who Loved Us*. I arrive at his house at seven in the evening, again with a translator and an assistant (both of whom wish to remain anonymous). The evening heat wraps around us, and I feel like a clay pot baking in Hanoi's summer oven. Ninh uncorks a bottle of Chilean red wine and welcomes us into the living room, which looks cheerier than it did the last time I was here. The neon tubes on the wall are not quite so pallid, and a new sofa is angled next to his chair, now placed to look out toward the front door.

Ninh's wife, Thanh, has skipped her exercise class to come home and cook dinner for us. She is a former secondary school teacher with a wary smile, and tonight she has fried up a few dozen egg rolls, which are laid out on the coffee table along with bowls of hot sauce and *nuoc mam* fish sauce. I have brought soft drinks, pastries, and beer. Ninh urges us to begin eating. He sticks to drinking wine while Thanh flutters in and out of the kitchen. We chat about his son, who now works in Saigon for Vina Capital, an investment company.

"It's a different world from the one I know," Ninh says. He himself has retired from writing his weekly column for *Bao Van Nghe Tre*. Now he works for himself, rising at midnight to write through the night and then shredding his work at dawn, or so he says. Even when relaxing over a glass of wine, he is reticent about discussing his work.

When I broach the subject of his two unpublished novels, Ninh tells me that I have the wrong titles for his books and that he never wrote one of them anyway, except for a short piece that was published somewhere. (He says he can't remember where.) He has a way of shaking his head from side to side and grinning under his moustache when he disagrees with me or wants to avoid talking about something. So forget about discussing censorship, internal exile, or other sensitive subjects. He is not going to retell his story about how a thousand South Vietnamese POWs were brought north to impregnate a thousand widows in Ho Chi Minh's natal village—even if this tale summarizes in one allegorical masterstroke the history of postwar Vietnam.

Ninh complains about the heat, and then he starts complaining about the Chinese, who are currently the number one topic in Vietnam. On April 30, a national holiday marking the unification of north and south Vietnam, China moved a billion-dollar oil rig into

Vietnam's offshore waters and started drilling for oil—in other words, choosing the day you pick if you want to kick your enemy in the nuts and then spit in his eye. China surrounded the rig with an armada of ships and chased off any Vietnamese boats that dared to approach. The Chinese rammed Vietnamese coast guard vessels. They sank fishing boats. They fired water cannons that looked like medieval dragons spouting blue flames. Despite their silly appearance, they proved quite effective at destroying electrical gear on the Vietnamese boats, which were forced to flee.

Following this Chinese aggression, 30,000 Vietnamese rose up in protest and started sacking Chinese textile factories around Saigon. Mobs burned at least fifteen companies and damaged another five hundred before police got the area locked down. Speculation abounds about the cause of these riots. Were they orchestrated by government agents or by antigovernment agents or by criminal gangs or by the Chinese themselves, given that the looted factories turned out to be owned by Taiwanese and Koreans?

"We are experts on China," says Ninh. "We just don't talk about it. They are always smiling, but their smile is dangerous. They will be the nightmare of the world. By 2030, China will be far stronger than the United States. Our civilization will be threatened. I'm pessimistic. I see no light at the end of the tunnel," he adds, using a phrase that Richard Nixon employed during the Vietnam War. "I see only darkness. The younger generation should prepare. I feel a black cloud coming. Danger is approaching."

Now that the red wine is gone, Ninh fills his glass with white and urges us to eat more egg rolls. He has a thatch of salt-and-pepper hair, more salt than pepper, and his Fu Manchu moustache gives his face the look of a window hidden behind Venetian blinds. He has kicked off his sandals and is cooling his feet on the linoleum as he settles back in his chair to ponder the dark cloud floating over Vietnam. It is quiet out on the street, save for the occasional motorbike rolling down the lane, but Ninh tells us how, during the day, he hears a constant din from the loudspeaker attached to a pole outside his door. The party directives and propaganda become increasingly strident around holidays, the worst being April 30, which commemorates the day in 1975 that Bao Ninh and his fellow soldiers captured Saigon.

"They talk about the old victories over and over again," he says. "Even as a soldier I don't like it. It's like telling a beautiful girl she's beautiful. She already knows she's beautiful, so all you're doing is annoying her. Next year, which marks the fortieth anniversary of the end of the war, it's going to be *really* annoying."

I have given Ninh a copy of my newly published book. He keeps fingering it, flipping through the pages, stopping now and then to study a passage. "I don't like intelligence agents and the police," he tells me. "Maybe I'll like them better after I read this."

He pours himself another glass of wine. "I never met Pham Xuan An," he says. "He was a big general. I was just a soldier. Now that the government has made him a hero, they've started telling young people to act like him, which is really stupid. It's like telling American teenagers they should grow up to be like Lyndon Johnson."

Ninh stops to read the opening paragraph. "This is how you can tell if a translation is worth reading," he says. "It looks pretty good." Later he will send me an email praising the book and telling me how much he enjoyed reading it, even with the missing passages.

Ninh's face is animated by the thick eyebrows that sweep over his black eyes. He windmills his hands through the air and slaps the back of his head. Then he pushes his hands in front of him like a surf swimmer heading for deep water. "The more we understand the Chinese the more we fear them," he tells me. "Hitler was able to come to power because he was helped by Britain and France. They took care of him. The same is true with the United States and China. The Americans built up China's industrial capacity. You moved your factories to China. You made the Chinese strong by doing business with them, but this strategy is going to fail in the end, just like it failed with Hitler."

I nudge the conversation back to writing. "We have to follow the Communist Party line," he says about censorship in Vietnam. "Every writer knows this. You're hired for a reason, so don't talk back. If you don't accept the censorship system, then don't be a writer."

"They want to make Pham Xuan An into a political commissar," he tells me. "This is why they censored your book. A good intelligence agent is like a priest. He keeps his secrets to himself." The secrets of Pham Xuan An can be revealed only after the war and only selectively, after having been shaped into a heroic tale.

"For Vietnamese readers, a book without any cuts is a surprise," says Ninh. "People will know where your book was cut. I prefer to read the printed version, but young people will go online to learn what you really wrote. This is becoming second nature for us, and soon we won't have any printed books at all."

He tells me he is writing a new novel, but he won't say what it's about. "We have to work quietly and not talk about it to anyone," he says. "My time is over. I just write. I don't publish."

I ask him what Vietnamese writers I should be reading. "There is no generation of young writers," he tells me. "There are just some individuals, one or two that I read."

Next we talk about the movie version of his novel. Film rights to *The Sorrow of War* were sold to a young American producer, Nicholas Simon, who also wrote the screenplay, but the project unraveled a few days before filming was to start. "We didn't understand each other," says Ninh. "We're both stubborn people. He was young. He knew nothing about Vietnam. The script was so far from reality that it was ludicrous. I kept editing it, but it never got better. I yelled at him in Vietnamese. He yelled at me in English. The translator cried. Finally, the main investor, who was a friend of mine, fled after seeing our inability to get along. A movie has to be easy. My book is too hard to make into a movie."

Before saying goodnight, Bao Ninh offers his final word on the subject of censorship. "Some guy who grew up as a peasant has the right to mess with your work? No one has the right to censor a book. When politics enters the room, ethics flies out the door. Other countries have laws protecting writers. In Vietnam, we have nothing. There are no rules to follow. The politicians make the rules."

The Struggle

On a sunny morning in July 2012, my daughter Maude and I set out to meet Duong Thu Huong, Vietnam's best-known novelist, who is currently living in exile in the thirteenth *arrondisement* of Paris, the city's Chinatown, southeast of the Seine. I know from talking to her on the telephone that Huong speaks heavily accented French, rich in vocabulary but weak in grammar. She says she learned French in prison during seven months of solitary confinement in 1991. After falling out of favor as the "fille bien aimée par le Parti" (the darling of the Communist Party), she was arrested for "selling secret documents to foreigners," the documents being, in this case, the manuscript for her fourth work of fiction, *Novel Without a Name*. Allowed to have one book with her in prison, Huong chose a French dictionary—hence the rich vocabulary and wobbly grammar.

My daughter lives in Paris and speaks fluent French. She will help translate, but I have also brought her along as a witness in case the interview gets tricky. Huong lives alone in a two-room apartment on the ninth floor of a modern building that has a car dealership on the ground floor. She works at night, writing from midnight to six in the morning, sleeps until noon, and then spends the rest of the day on *la lutte*—the French term for "the struggle." La lutte usually connotes a political platform on the left, but in this case it describes Huong's fight against the Communist Party of Vietnam. Huong refers to herself as a *sans papiers*, an "illegal immigrant." Her passport was stolen in Marseille a few years ago, and neither the Vietnamese nor the French government has offered to replace it. During the "Sarkozy mandarinate," as she dismissively refers to the rightwing government of Nicolas Sarkozy, she was afraid to leave her apartment for fear of being picked up on the street and deported. For Huong, one of the benefits of voting Sarkozy out of office was the fact that the new government gave her a French *carte d'identité,* although she still has no passport.

Huong is a lively woman, with flashing black eyes and shoulder-length hair, dyed blue—the same color as her eye shadow, the pillows on her sofa, her blouse, and her jeans. Her round face is smooth and even-featured; she has tattooed eyebrows, and her rouged lips break often into a winning smile. She has the hands of a musician, although her long tapered fingers have begun to curl with arthritis, but her girlish charm and colored hair make her look younger than someone born in 1947. Seated in the *salle de séjour* that doubles as her office, she plies us with cherries, sliced pineapple, tea, and chocolate.

Huong is a natural-born storyteller. She answers my questions in discursive loops that reach back through hundreds of years of Vietnamese history. We begin by talking about her family, a common way in Vietnamese narratives to set the scene and dictate everything that follows. As a "beloved daughter of the Communist Party," Huong might be expected to have working-class roots, but in fact she was born in a village north of Hanoi and is the granddaughter of a mandarin landowner. Her family lost its wealth and status by getting into trouble—first with the French, for manufacturing rice wine without paying the necessary fees to the colonial government, and then with the communists, for being bourgeois landowners during the agrarian reforms of the 1950s.

Huong's grandmother, Le Thi Cam, sold half the family land to bail an alcoholic uncle out of prison. (The hapless male saved by a noble female is a common trope in Huong's fiction.) Her father fought in the *maquis* against the French and led a troop of engineers in General Giap's signal corps, but the general did nothing to save him during Vietnam's Maoist-inspired land campaign. In 1954, her father was sent to a labor camp in the mountains. (This has become another trope in Huong's fiction: party ideologues protecting their own prerogatives, while throwing their loyal followers to the mob.)

After losing their land, Le Thi Cam and three of her four sons moved to southern Vietnam. Huong's father, the youngest, remained in the north and worked for the post office after he got out of prison. Her mother taught in a primary school. In spite of the ardor with which Huong joined her communist classmates in chanting, "Down with the landowners!" she was penalized for her class background. Not allowed to learn foreign languages or go to university, she enrolled in art school and then dropped out in 1967, at the age of twenty, to join a communist youth brigade. She played accordion in a troupe of female singers and dancers who were sent to the military front to raise morale. Huong tells us that out of her art school class of eighty students, only she and two others survived the war, one with no arms and the other crazy from shellshock.

Huong spent seven years in the jungles and tunnels north of the seventeenth parallel, the dividing line between the opposing armies and the most heavily bombed part of Vietnam. A girl crouching next to her was killed by a bomb that left Huong deaf in her right ear. Her fiancé was also killed. In 1968 she married a fellow student from the Ministry of Culture Arts College. She gave birth to a son, Minh, in 1970, and a daughter, Ha, in 1972. "He was not talented enough to perform at the front," she says dismissively of her husband, whom she divorced in 1982. (Her unhappy marriage provided her with another theme that runs through her writing: wars are fought by good men who die young. Meanwhile, the party hacks with special privileges survive, while the unlucky women who marry them will either suffer in silence or revolt against these men who oppress them.)

After the war Huong began writing screenplays for propaganda films and working as a *nègre*, a "ghostwriter," for communist generals penning their memoirs. The Hanoi Fiction Film Studio made five of her scripts into forgettable movies. She wrote anti-Chinese tracts while serving as a combatant-reporter during Vietnam's war with China in 1979. She was admitted to the Communist Party in 1985 and traveled to the Soviet Union the following year in a delegation of screenwriters. She also began publishing fiction, beginning with a short work called *Journey to Childhood* (1985). Her first full-length novel, *Beyond Illusions* (1987), tells the story of a woman's disillusionment with her marriage, which parallels her falling out of love with the Communist Party. In bed, in government, unworthy men plague women everywhere. The novel sold as many as 100,000 copies before it was banned.

According to Nina McPherson, who for a decade worked as Huong's English translator, the artist first tangled with Vietnam's censors in 1982, when one of her screenplays was suppressed. Huong protested at a Writers Union congress, but banning orders against her work remained in place until 1985. Perhaps as a result of joining the Communist Party, Huong was allowed to publish her writing for the next two years, until her novel *Paradise of the Blind*, an attack on Vietnam's Maoist land reform campaign, was banned in 1988. *Paradise*, which was also the first Vietnamese novel published in English in the United States, tells the story of a young woman who labors as a guest worker at a textile factory in the Soviet Union. The book attacks party hacks who use their political connections to traffic in consumer goods as well as the government officials who implement Ho Chi Minh's disastrous agrarian campaign. Equally radical was Huong's redefinition of the Vietnam War, which, by this time, she had come to see not as a holy crusade against Western invaders but as an internecine struggle among north and south Vietnamese family members.

Huong published one more novel in Vietnam, *The Lost Life* (1989), before the censors began moving against her with increasing ferocity. She was expelled from the party in 1990 and arrested in 1991. This ended her career as a novelist publishing in her own country. Her next three books, *Novel Without a Name* (1991), *Memories of a Pure Spring* (2000), and *No Man's Land* (2002), have appeared only in foreign editions. Today, none of her books is legally sold in Vietnam, with the exception of a few stories that the government bowdlerized and republished in 1997. (This allows them to claim with a straight face that the author is not censored in Vietnam.) The dance of the censors, with works allowed to appear in print and then removed from bookstore shelves and then reprinted in altered form, shadows all of Vietnam's writers, but none more than Duong Thu Huong. Beginning with *Novel Without a Name*, she has published her works in French, English, and overseas Vietnamese editions, but not in Vietnam. The sole exception is her eighth novel, *The Zenith* (2009), which she allowed to be released in a Vietnamese edition on the web. The book is about the 1958 murder of Ho Chi Minh's mistress by operatives of the Vietnamese Communist Party who wanted the father of the country to preserve his purity. It has been read online by a half million readers, she says.

"My British agent tells me I shouldn't release any more books on the web," Huong tells me during our visit. Apparently, he was displeased by the lost sales. "My life is dedicated to the fight against communism. Writing is in second place, and I leave everything having to do with that to my agent." Yet for someone who dismisses her own writing, she is remarkably prolific. Her ninth novel, *Sanctuary of the Heart,* published in France in 2011, tells the story of a Vietnamese gigolo kept in a luxurious villa by a wealthy businesswoman. Her tenth novel, *The Hills of Eucalyptus,* published in 2014, is the story of a homosexual man imprisoned and sentenced to forced labor.

Today Huong has an international and generally appreciative audience. In 1991, for example, she was awarded France's Prix Femina. In the words of one critic, "She is unmatched in her ability to capture the small, telling details of everyday life." Other readers are more critical. The reviewer Brendan Wolfe calls her style "intensely sentimental and unfashionably melodramatic." The Vietnamese American poet Linh Dinh, who appreciates "Huong's literary gifts sans soapbox," notes that her "fine descriptive passages are perverted by a heavy-handed political subtext. Its bias can be traced to the war, in which both North and South demonized each other."

Huong would say that Linh Dinh and her other critics have missed the point. She cares more about politics than literature. Her life is dedicated to the struggle for social justice and democracy, a global campaign that employs novelists but values them foremost as propagandists. "We want to see a democratic government in Vietnam," she says. "Our example is Korea. Here you have the same people, the same history, until the people are cut in half. In the north, under communism, the people live like wild animals in caves. In the south, you have a relatively powerful and prosperous country. This is how you liberate people, how you change society for the better. Our struggle in Vietnam is similar. It is very difficult, but one must not abandon hope."

Phan Huy Duong, an exiled Vietnamese writer living in Paris, was for a decade Huong's translator into French. He says that the author "was the first writer who dared to criticize the Vietnamese land reform campaigns and the degradation of intellectual life in Vietnam under the communists." The Maoist campaigns, lasting from 1951 to 1953, were followed in 1956 by the repression of intellectuals and artists—a dark period in Vietnamese history that ended, albeit briefly, with the onset of the *doi moi*, or Renovation movement, in 1986.

Unfortunately, *doi moi* quickly gave way to the paranoia of today's censorious regime. "Vietnamese literature is in a grave state," says Duong. "The people in power have developed a mafia of corruption" that allows only for the publication of propaganda and third-rate authors imported from the West. "It is the old resistance fighters like Bao Ninh and Duong Thu Huong who frighten the government, because they speak the language of the people," he says. "These writers are the only ones who can bring Vietnamese literature and culture back to life."

"Duong Thu Huong shows that the power of the communists resides solely in violence," Duong concludes. "First, the popular violence against colonialism. Then the violence against the Vietnamese people themselves. . . . Duong Thu Huong is respected because she says out loud what everyone else in Vietnam only says to themselves."

Apart from her novels and speeches at Party congresses, Huong's most politically subversive act was a film, *The Sanctuary of Despair*, which she began shooting in 1986. She had discovered in the mountains near Tan Ky, at the narrow waist of Vietnam above the seventeenth parallel, a concentration camp holding seven hundred North Vietnamese soldiers. This "gulag-style psychiatric camp," as Nina McPherson describes it, was filthy with excrement and filled with disease-wracked prisoners who looked like walking cadavers.

Huong began filming in the camp. "It was a movie about soldiers driven crazy by the war," she says. "They were thrown in a concentration camp in the forest to hide the fact that they had been driven crazy. They were treated like criminals. The authorities are hypocrites. They want to hide these facts. The soldiers were pissing and crapping everywhere. The place was filthy. The nurses and doctors had become crazy along with the soldiers. They, too, were prisoners."

"This was the most atrocious, the most stupid war in our history," she says. "This is why everything written about the war by the Vietnamese is nothing but propaganda, while the real history is hidden. All my friends were killed in the war. Others were driven insane. I am the only one who has returned to bear witness."

"We are a people deprived of hope," Huong tells me. "We yearn for freedom and are given only enough to survive. We are condemned to unhappiness. This destiny weighs on me. It crushes me. This is why I made this film. I would finish it and wait for the right moment to release it."

Huong's film was being processed at a lab in Saigon when government agents broke into the facility in 1988 and destroyed the negatives with acid. Officials moved to expel her from the Communist Party, and, by the time she was arrested in 1991, the party's secretary, Nguyen Van Linh, was referring to her as *"con di cua dang,"* or "the party's whore," thus denigrating everything she had done since working as a female performer at the front.

After spending seven months in solitary confinement in a high-security prison for political prisoners, Huong was released through the intercession of Danielle Mitterrand, the wife of the former French president. "The French government also paid the Vietnamese a large bribe," Huong tells me. Made a *Chevalier des Arts et des Lettres* in 1994, she was given political asylum in France in 2006. This was also the year she appeared on stage at the 92nd Street Y in New York. Praised by the war novelist Robert Stone and cheered by the crowd, Huong began by introducing herself as a "criminal" and then launched a fierce attack on governmental stupidity and corruption.

By the time we meet in Paris's Chinatown in 2012, the French government has shifted from right to left, but her scorn for the French president ("that little mandarin Sarkozy") is as piquant as her scorn for the communist rulers back in Vietnam. "I was like a dishrag, a prisoner in my house," she says of her life as an immigrant in France. Now that the government has given her an identity card, "I'm as good as the street sweepers," she says. "I have my working papers. I can circulate in France, but I can't leave the country."

Her feud with the French government is part of a larger feud that Huong has been waging with former friends and colleagues. "I detest Vietnamese men," she says at the end of a story about why she has fallen out with her French translator, Pham Huy Duong. She has also fallen out with her American translator, Nina McPherson. Huong tells us that she is a member of no political party and is not close to her fellow refugees or her French hosts. Her friends, she says, are Americans or Australians, who, unlike the French, are not "too sophisticated." "I am sorry for your daughter who has to work here," she says.

Now that she has broken with her former translators and friends, Huong has nothing to do but write. She has been producing a book every couple of years and is becoming almost as quirky and famous as that other great Franco-Vietnamese writer, Marguerite Duras. By now the biographical details of Huong's life are indistinguishable from the recurring tropes of her novels. Through "the drug of love," women are ensnared by men unworthy of them. Sexual jealousy divides the world into possessed and possessors. Instead of existing in socialist harmony, we live in a fallen state of greed and hypocrisy. The solitary hero is the author speaking truth to power. To comfort herself in the loneliness of this struggle, Huong tells herself stories, late at night, when the ghosts of her dead friends return to talk to her. Expelled from her country, cut off from the translators who made her famous, disillusioned with the French political mandarins, she sits in front of me, a lonely woman with blue hair and tattooed eyebrows—a brave, even heroic, figure who is creating out of her loneliness a partial, one-sided, but also noble vision of what Vietnam could be.

We are headed into our third hour of conversation when I broach the subject of plagiarism. Especially in their first twenty pages, Bao Ninh's *The Sorrow of War* and Duong Thu Huong's *Novel Without a Name* are remarkably similar. Both novels tell the story of a twenty-eight-year-old soldier fighting in the Central Highlands. One book opens in the Jungle of Screaming Souls, the other in the Gorge of Lost Souls. The infantryman hero encounters innocent girls mutilated by marauding troops, a dead orangutan with human characteristics, and narcotic flowers blooming in a hallucinatory forest. Yet while Ninh's novel burns with the intensity of lived experience, Huong's often falls into set pieces with soapbox dialogue.

Roneo copies of *The Sorrow of War* began circulating around Hanoi in 1989. A year later, what McPherson calls the "hastily titled" *Novel Without a Name* was sent to small overseas publishers in France and the United States. Huong, the best-selling author of three novels, was rushing her fourth book into print, while Ninh, a thirty-seven-year-old former soldier, was trying to finish his thesis at the Nguyen Du Writers School.

"Scenes in your novel resemble scenes from Bao Ninh's book," I say. Before I can continue, Huong sits bolt upright on the sofa. Her face hardens. She adopts the formal French that inserts *monsieur* into its declarations. "Yes, this is true," she says about the similarities between the two texts. "We were writing our books at the same time. Each of us was approaching the same subject from different directions."

"But you wrote your book after the appearance of Bao Ninh's novel," I say, mentioning the date at the end of her manuscript, which reads, "Hanoi, December 11, 1990."

"I don't know," she says. "I only read his book many years later, here in France. I never read it in Vietnam. I am not close to Bao Ninh. We live in different worlds. I am a committed dissident, while he leads a normal life."

Then Huong tells me a story about meeting Bao Ninh. The story is composed of her customary elements. It reveals a weak man overwhelmed by fear, but it has a surprise ending. She begins, "When Bao Ninh visited me in Paris last year, I asked him, 'Why is this book the only thing you have written in your life?'

"'It is because of my wife,' he said. 'She was worried about the safety of our family.' To protect his son and allow him to study in the United States, he rejected his other son. Literature is a child also. We give birth to it. He had to refuse this child out of fear for his family. It's sad. This may be hard for you to understand, but he had to turn his back on his own book. The police tortured him by threatening his family.

Duong Thu Huong, Paris, 2012.

"'This was a mistake,' he confessed. 'It was wrong of me to do this. I regret it. I should have done things differently. You have to forgive me. I did it for my wife, so my son could finish his studies and travel overseas.'"

"This is the inevitable bargain for every Vietnamese writer," Huong says.

After talking for more than four hours, after drinking endless cups of tea and being plied with cherries and cashews, we visitors are given as a parting gift not one but two boxes of chocolates. I am reminded of the fact that in Vietnam a gift is not a gift. It is an obligation.

"I believe you are a true journalist, a journalist who can interview gangsters and criminals," Huong says. "I myself feel like a sort of criminal who has just had her past history examined."

"I'm sorry for making you feel like a criminal," I tell her.

Back on the street, my daughter and I begin searching for a florist. I will be the next man in Duong Thu Huong's life to send her his apologies, along with a large bouquet of flowers.

Cyberspace Country

A few weeks after talking to Duong Thu Huong, I arrange another meeting with a writer whom Vietnam's censors have driven into exile. This time, I travel to Berlin to meet Pham Thi Hoai. Born in 1960 in Hai Duong, east of Hanoi, Hoai did her graduate studies in archival science at Humboldt University in the former East Berlin. She returned to Vietnam to write stories and novels and translate into Vietnamese the works of Kafka, Brecht, Tanazaki, Amado, and other writers, before being exiled back to Berlin in 1993. Hoai has long presided over Vietnam's intellectual community-in-exile. For thirteen years, she produced, edited, and wrote two electronic journals of culture and politics, *talawas* and its successor *pro&contra. These* were key sites for anyone interested in discovering what was really happening in Vietnam. From her place of exile, forbidden from returning home, Hoai became the sibyl delivering the final word on her benighted country's fate. This work would end, she promised, at the stroke of midnight on December 31, 2014, when she would stop publishing her journals.. "I will return to being a writer, but perhaps not to fiction," she tells me during our meeting. "I am not really interested in fiction."

We agree to meet on a Saturday at 6:00 p.m. for dinner at her apartment in Prenzlauer Berg in the former East Berlin. Hoai will be cooking. The menu, discussed in several emails, will blend East and West in a medley of flavors. Even before the first bite, I am impressed by the logic and rigor of her planning.

I ride the S train to Bornholmer Strasse and exit onto the bridge where thousands of East Berliners gathered on November 9, 1989, to demand access to the West. That was the first border crossing to fall. Soon the wall itself would come tumbling down, and then all of East Germany, and then the Soviet Union, as forty years of Cold War came to an end. Today the last vestige of this war can be found only in a few states such as Vietnam that are still propped up by Marxist-Leninist ideology.

I walk down a wide boulevard with a trolley running down the middle. The street is lined with modest five-story buildings, a few small cafes and billiard parlors, a bookshop, and several stores selling vegetables, beer, and coffee. I ring Hoai's bell and walk upstairs to the apartment that she shares with her German partner. I am greeted at the door by a trim woman with a round face, a pixie haircut, and a lustrous smile. The first thing I notice on entering the apartment is a blinking array of lights and switches—an industrial-strength security system that she installed after death threats and attacks on her computers.

Walking down a hallway, we pass a bathroom with a Japanese soaking tub, then a modern kitchen, and finally arrive at a large room that opens onto bedrooms and studies and conceals yet more doors behind Japanese sliding screens. Hoai tells me that the unusual layout is due to the fact that she and her partner recently knocked down the walls and put together two separate apartments. The room holds a dining room table, decorated with a bouquet of freshly cut daisies, and a bookcase filled floor to ceiling with a neatly archived collection. In Hoai's office next door, more shelves are filled with clasp binders in serried ranks.

Seated at the table are Andreas, Hoai's companion, and Dan, her son from her former marriage. A handsome man in a blue work shirt,

Andreas runs a ten-person electrical engineering firm that specializes, among other things, in installing alarm systems. The apartment is his handiwork, and so is the security system at the front door. There is an ironic tug to his smile, and he seems to be the kind of solid fellow one would want to consult after receiving death threats.

Dan, age nineteen, is a slender young man who will be studying applied computation and mathematics at Jacobs University in Bremen in the fall. He lives nearby with Hoai's former husband, a German whom she married in 1991. Hoai speaks English quite well, but Dan is fluent, and he is being pressed into service tonight as his mother's translator.

Hoai explains that the meal will be running from spicy to not-so-spicy, from hot to cold, "the opposite direction from normal." The thought enters my mind that the meal will be retracing her steps into exile, moving from the spicy East to the temperate West. While Hoai busies herself in the kitchen, I chat with Andreas about Prenzlauer Berg, a bohemian enclave that is rapidly being gentrified. "In this building we have Italians, Argentineans, Russians, Americans, and Vietnamese," he says. "I am the only German."

"The reason this part of the city still exists is because the East Germans had no money to destroy it," he tells me. "The area is full of artists. The poor ones live in the basement. The rich ones live on top." Bemused by Berlin's newfound prosperity, Andreas entertains himself by spending his weekends cycling pedicabs full of tourists around the city.

The table is set with a full assortment of crystal glasses, fish knives, and three forks for each upcoming course. We start drinking a Gewürztraminer Riesling and later switch to a Spanish rioja. During our first course—papaya salad with shrimp, a Thai dish—I get a closer look at my hostess. Nam, as she is known to her friends (her full name is Pham Thi Hoai Nam), has the classic features—flat nose, golden skin, and high cheekbones—of a north Vietnamese. Dressed in jeans, a white blouse, and a light wool sweater, also white, she wears wire-rimmed spectacles with tortoiseshell highlights and a pair of silver earrings holding a dark stone, maybe an emerald. The conversation flows through English, German, French, and Vietnamese, whichever is the sharpest tool for the concept at hand.

"I am not sure of my exact birth date," Hoai says, when I ask about her family. "It was sometime in 1960, during the war, when people didn't register births until weeks or months after they occurred."

"During Ho Chi Minh's version of the Chinese Cultural Revolution, in the 1950s, my parents were sent from Hanoi to the countryside, to work as schoolteachers," she says. "My grandfather had been Minister of Education in Thanh Hoa province, but my father, revolting against his bourgeois background, had left at the age of twelve to fight with the Viet Minh. His big dream was to become a party member, but he was never allowed to join."

Her father's uncle was Pham Quynh, a journalist and the publisher of the largest Vietnamese newspaper in the French colony. Quynh was the minister of education and then the minister of the interior in the government of the last Vietnamese emperor, before he was kidnapped and killed by the communists in 1945.

"The first generation of communist leaders all came from bourgeois families," Hoai says. "But after the party was formed, they closed the door behind them. No one else from the bourgeoisie could rise into the ranks. They needed followers, not leaders. They needed useful idiots.

"Ho Chi Minh is the perfect example. He eliminated all the intellectuals around him, thereby removing the competition. Since then, the idiots have reproduced themselves so successfully that in the present government not a single official speaks a foreign language, and this is in spite of the fact that eighty percent of them have 'Ph.D.' in their title."

Excelling in school, Hoai was chosen in 1977 as one of 130 students sent to the Eastern Bloc to be trained as archivists by the

Stasi and other communist police agencies. "This was paradise for us," she says, recalling her feelings about leaving war-torn Vietnam for Europe. For the first fifteen years of her life, the war had existed in her world "like clouds in the sky," and after the war came the "reign of hardline ideology," a period of "poverty, backwardness, and repression."

One day, one of her professors at Humboldt University saw her waiting at a bus stop reading a book. On another day, he cracked a joke in class about Robert Musil's *Man Without Qualities*. "I was the only one who laughed, because I was the only one who had read the book," she says.

"He sent me on an internship, first to the Goethe archives, then to the Schiller and Brecht archives, where I wrote my master's thesis. These were happy days for me, spent reading and living among the papers of these great writers. My professor did me a big favor," she tells me.

After six years in Germany, Hoai moved back to Vietnam in 1983, where she worked as an archivist at the Institute of History and began, in her spare time, to write short stories and novels. "When I was twelve, I thought I was born to be a writer. Now I think I may not have been correct. One is not *born* to be anything. One *chooses* what to do."

"I went back to Vietnam because I was disappointed by life in East Germany," she says. "It was just like Vietnam. There was no freedom or human rights, and the East German food was horrible. I thought I had a debt to Vietnam, for having sent me here to be trained. But on my return, I was classified as 'untrustworthy,' because of the time I had spent abroad."

In 1988 Hoai published *The Crystal Messenger*, the novel that made her famous in Vietnam and pushed her to the forefront of *doi moi* writers. It also got her censored and eventually banished from the country. Vietnamese censors, with what Hoai describes as "a twinge of idiocy," will block books from publication if there is too much interest in them or ban published books if they become too successful. This is what happened with *The Crystal Messenger*. It was pulled from the shelves after selling 50,000 copies and winning the Frankfurt Book Fair's LiBeraturpreis for best foreign novel.

Told through the interwoven stories of several young women, *The Crystal Messenger* is an allegory about the reunification of North and South Vietnam in an age of careerism and consumerism. One strand of the novel tells the wry tale of a beautiful Vietnamese Amerasian with Texan blood who conquers the hearts of the uptight men of Hanoi. In their banning order, the censors charged Hoai with "salacious" writing, said that she had an "excessively pessimistic view" of Vietnam, and accused her of abusing the "sacred mission of a writer."

Hoai went on to publish literary essays, the short-story collections *Me Lo* (1989) and *Man Nuong* (1995), and another novel, *Marie Sen* (1996). At the same time, she was producing numerous translations from German into Vietnamese. But none of her work since *The Crystal Messenger* has been published in Vietnam, except for a few stories that were quickly suppressed. "The censors never tell you when a book is withdrawn from circulation. I consider myself lucky if I even learn that something has been published in the first place."

"The same thing happened all the time in East Germany," says Andreas. "Here we had lots of films that were made, and then the censors got scared and never released them."

"One day I received in the mail an article that I had written," recalls Hoai. "It had been heavily censored, and it even had someone else's name on it. Everyone in Vietnam accepts this level of corruption. It doesn't even surprise me anymore."

Now she posts all of her writing online. "I'm not writing books for money," she says. "I write to make myself happy. Every author I deem important is publishing his or her works online rather than allowing them to be censored. Some let their work be published in hard copy—censored—and then send it to *talawas* to be published in its original form." She suggests that I do the same thing with *The Spy Who Loved Us,* and I tell her that I will be pleased to accept her offer.

At dinner we have moved on to a German recipe: our next course is celery-apple soup. Dan is working hard as his mother's translator, while Andreas sits listening, sometimes offering a humorous story of his own.

In 1993 Hoai returned to Berlin, where she had lived as a student a decade earlier. The city had been transformed in her absence, with the wall coming down and West Berliners flooding into the ramshackle neighborhoods of the former East Berlin. Hoai settled in the city and married. "I made several trips back to Vietnam when Dan was small, but, since 2004, I have been banned from traveling to Vietnam," she says.

In 2001 she began publishing the censored news out of Vietnam on her *talawas* website. "*Talawas* is a Dadaist name," she says. "It was created by putting *ta la* ('we are') together with *was,* as in '*Was ist los?*' ('What's up?'), which gives you a *double entendre* meaning either 'What are we?' or 'We are something.'" Her "journal of culture" became a target for government hackers who tried for years to close the site with denial-of-service and other electronic attacks. Hoai kept outsmarting them behind ever-more-elaborate firewalls, and she is proud of the fact that *talawas* was closed only twice, each time briefly. Electronically, she was following in the footsteps of her great uncle Pham Quynh.

"It lasted nine years, as long as Vietnam's war with the French," she says about her decision to close the site. "It took an entire day to put it out. It was updated several times a day. No one was volunteering to do the work; so I decided to put an end to it."

"Ten years ago I stopped writing fiction," she tells me. "Now, in two years' time, I plan to write fiction again." In the meantime, she has begun publishing a more personal journal *pro&contra.* "I want to use the next two years to return to writing. I want to get an inventory of what I am able to do and my strengths. This is a transitional phase for me to learn to walk again."

"When I get back to writing, I will be writing a combination of fiction and nonfiction," she says. "Pure fiction is too boring. The Vietnamese reality is more interesting than any fiction I could imagine."

While running her websites, Hoai has supported herself as a simultaneous translator, rejecting only the most odious clients. "I watch the delegations of high Vietnamese officials," she says. "They come to Germany to learn, but they learn nothing. They are people with no education. This is why they hire me. They don't even know who I am."

"She is seldom at home," says Dan, speaking of his mother's busy schedule as an interpreter.

After a salad of radish sprouts, tomatoes, and carrots, our next course is baked codfish served with rice. "While talking, I forgot to turn on the oven," Hoai apologizes. "Cooking is like prose writing, not poetry. It takes the same attention to creative detail."

We return to talking about censorship. "The governments of China and Vietnam are not afraid of anything," she says. "This is linked to U.S. tolerance of their oppression. The U.S. does nothing to oppose them; so they have nothing to be afraid of."

"Before their economies boomed, they weren't sure of the western response, but now they know," she says. "If business is booming, then they have nothing to fear from the West. Whenever I criticize human rights in Vietnam, the government refers to the prisoners in Guantánamo. 'If the Americans can do it, why can't we? We aren't doing anything different.' Whenever I criticize corruption, they start talking about Lehman Brothers. Whenever I criticize the economy, they say, 'Look at Spain or Greece.' The pool of bad examples they draw from is just too large."

"The government in Hanoi was lucky," she believes. "During the Cold War they had a lot of support from Western countries, especially from leftist movements. Now they have the support of the global capitalists. Standing in this good light, they don't need to fear anybody. They have always found support in the West, whether during the Cold War or now."

Andreas opens another bottle of wine for our next course, a fruit and cheese tray, and Hoai excuses herself to go smoke a cigarette.

"When I first started writing, I had no money for cigarettes," she says when she returns. "A friend said, 'I will give you one cigarette per page.' As time went on, to fill up the pages faster, my letters got bigger and bigger. I still write for cigarettes. But now I allow myself to smoke after every line."

Hoai tells me a story about how censorship destroys even successful writers. "One day in Vietnam a writer came to me, asking for my advice 'How can I write about the war?' he said. He had written books about the war, but they were not working anymore, and now he had no clue what to write.

"This is a story about a writer who has died as a writer, who has been eliminated. A serious writer would not consider what people wanted to read. He would look at his own perception of the war. This writer had been writing in a style approved by the government. He had voluntarily adopted this style, which made the work of the censors superfluous. It also made him susceptible to every new way of being censored, including censorship through the market, which allows you to write only what you're expected to write, and which is happening more and more."

Hoai tells me the Vietnamese are borrowing their approach to censorship from the Chinese. "We always look to the Chinese and copy them, but when we copy them, we do it even worse than the Chinese, several orders of magnitude worse and in even more minute detail."

"It is mandatory for every high Vietnamese official to get training in China once a year, just as it was in the time of the Cold War," she says. "It is no accident that every campaign and law adopted in

China is introduced into Vietnam six months later. Right now the press is filled with the Bo Xi Lai scandal—a high official accused of corruption. In Vietnam the sides are set for a similar struggle for power. I am certain that a Vietnamese official will soon be suffering the same fate."

"Your story about the writer who came to visit you reminds me of Bao Ninh," I say. "Without consulting anyone, he wrote the great novel about the war."

"I don't think it's a great novel," she says. "I am not fond of the romantic style, and the way it's written in Vietnamese is very romantic. The English translation is different from the original, and perhaps this explains why the book is more popular for English readers than Vietnamese. The English translation was inevitably—because of the nature of English—more direct."

"I prefer Franz Kafka to Thomas Mann," she tells me. "I prefer a clear, crisp, intelligent use of language, which dispenses with any decoration or superfluous elements."

"This is the language she uses to boss me around," says Dan. All of us, including his mother, laugh at the joke.

I ask about the two novels Ninh wrote after *The Sorrow of War*. "He has retreated because of censorship, gone into internal exile," Hoai says. "Everybody who hasn't migrated from Vietnam suffers from this."

"The best thing for Bao Ninh would be live his life, after writing his one book," she says. "At the end of his life he can publish his last, best work. Then he will have two books in his life, one at the beginning and one at the end. This is the best thing for a writer."

She explains that it is getting rarer for artists to leave Vietnam for the West. "Artists and writers live better than ever before in Vietnam. With today's media, the people who can write, who can create things for radio, TV, and the internet are at a premium. Intellectuals and artists who have spent time abroad find that life is so expensive that they are not able to create anything. You can't be creative and write under these circumstances, so you return."

"I am no longer a Vietnamese citizen," Hoai says. "I have a German passport. It is my trauma to be Vietnamese. My son has been spared this trauma. Why am I still confronted by Vietnamese problems? They stopped worrying about human rights and losing the support of the West when they realized that all the West cares about is making money."

The major exception to the banalization of Vietnamese literature is Duong Thu Huong. She is a throwback to the days when exiled authors were politically potent. When I mention her name, I can tell from Andreas's and Dan's raised eyebrows that Huong has already been a subject of conversation. "I admire her courage and bravery," Hoai says. "She can be very disagreeable, but that's all right. She is very honest and frank. If she could get beyond propaganda and make use of her skills, she could be a fine writer."

In some ways, Pham Thi Hoai is the polar opposite of Duong Thu Huong. Her writing is concise and elegant. Her stories are deftly crafted. She is conducting an intellectual conversation, not with the ghosts of dead combatants but with Kafka and the other writers whom she has translated into Vietnamese.

In other ways, though, Pham Thi Hoai is very much like Duong Thu Huong. Both decided to place the fight against Vietnam's authoritarian government above their work as writers. Both are committed militants, fearless opponents of a regime they consider to be corrupt and oppressive. Hoai runs the most important websites for Vietnamese dissidents, and her writing is required reading for tens of thousands of Vietnamese, both inside and outside the country. She is one of the axes around which Vietnam's artistic community turns, a commander leading the attack on Vietnam's censors.

When I ask Hoai about Huong's *Novel Without a Name*, she says, "I read only twenty pages and put it down." So who is she reading today? Hoai mentions Mo Mieng, the "Open Your Mouth poets," who have not been translated into English because their writing is "difficult." Mo Mieng began as a quartet of poets who

Pham Thi Hoai, Berlin, 2016

set out in the early 2000s to shock the niceties of Vietnam's Confucian norms. They use the language that people speak on the street and publish their work in samizdat photocopies passed from hand to hand. "We want to avoid the state censorship that often cuts the life out of literary works," one member of the group, the poet Ly Doi, told the BBC in 2004. Since then, a dozen other Vietnamese artists have begun writing "dirty" poetry, and Hoai recently released on her website the dirtiest of Vietnamese literary transgressions, a work called "Di Thui" ("Stinking Whore") by Nguyen Vien, which retells Vietnam's national epic, *The Tale of Kieu*, as an attack on the Communist Party.

I ask Hoai if she sees any signs of hope for Vietnam.

She clears her throat for an oracular pronouncement, and Andreas laughs. "Twenty years from now the ocean will be much higher than it is today, so the coastal area won't exist anymore," she says. "If the coastal people are gone, the mountainous people will remain. If Vietnamese literature succeeds in moving from the coastal areas to the mountains, it will survive. It might also learn to swim."

"The internet does not know the flooding of oceans, so the internet is a space where one can survive," she tells me. "Maybe Vietnam will become the first cyberspace country—a country that exists only in cyberspace."

By then Vietnam's literature and culture, maybe all of Vietnam itself, will be updated daily and living online, and cyberspace will be the only space in Vietnam free of censorship.

CHAPTER V
Stabbing People in the Back with My Pen

After the censored version of my book was published, I commissioned an uncensored translation, to be released outside of Vietnam, and wrote an article about my experience. The article was translated into Vietnamese and published online in the fall of 2014, along with side-by-side comparisons of the censored and uncensored versions of my book. I was surprised by the howl of protests that greeted my efforts. My first article was pulled down, as was a longer version—also translated into Vietnamese—that I released in February 2015. Facebook comments and blog postings weighed in heavily against my "treachery," and the only Vietnamese who stepped forward to praise my efforts were a ragtag collection of former political prisoners, dissidents, students, and exiled authors.

Thus began my final instruction in Vietnamese censorship. The charges against me were numerous. I had allegedly "betrayed" my sources by naming them and using real quotations in my article, thereby "stabbing people in the back with my pen." I had taken "confidential" conversations and printed them for financial gain.

Because my article had been translated into Vietnamese and published on a Vietnamese website before being published in English, it was inauthentic, unverified, and unverifiable. It was the work of an outside agitator meddling in Vietnamese affairs. It was neocolonialist. It denied agency to my Vietnamese editors, and what was I complaining about anyway, given that my book had been published in Vietnam with only "minor changes"?

To understand these reactions, one also has to understand the peculiar nature of authorship in Vietnam. The country has never had a free press. Truth telling has been a deadly enterprise throughout its history Indirection and conflict avoidance are built into the very structure of the Vietnamese language, which is loaded with syntactical ambiguities while inscribing everyone into a familial relationship. There was no free speech in the royal era of kings and mandarins. There was none in the colonial era or during the First and Second Indochinese wars. There is none now, unless one is willing to face prison or exile. The muscle for free speech is undeveloped in Vietnam because few have had the chance to exercise it. Those few include imprisoned authors, journalists, bloggers, and human rights activists, but people willing to defend these outspoken critics are in short supply. Freedom of speech is seen as an attack on social solidarity, a dangerous import from the West, a treasonous activity meriting multiyear prison terms.

A similar situation pertains in Vietnam's neighbor to the north. In 2013, the Chinese government issued a secret directive known as Document Number Nine. Later leaked to the press, it revealed a government campaign to suppress threats posed by universal values, civil society, and press freedom. In this context, censorship is seen as a *positive* force working to defend Chinese values, the party hierarchy, and propaganda campaigns. Censorship is not something to be ashamed of, to hide or fight against. It is a tool of government to be supported and perfected, like military hardware or industrial espionage. If *Index on Censorship* and other human rights organizations think that exposing censorship will have the salutary effect of exposing mold to sunlight, they might want to rethink their strategy. The Chinese government is proud of its techniques for surveillance and social control. After originally borrowing them from the West, the Chinese have now perfected these techniques and have begun selling them to repressive regimes around the world.

Since it was promulgated, Document Number Nine has been developed into a propaganda campaign targeting professors and journalists. In January 2015, the Chinese education minister banned from Chinese universities "textbooks promoting Western values" and other material "slandering" party leadership. Journalists in China, after being forced to take classes in Marxist-Leninist propaganda, must now pass multiple-choice exams on Communist Party slogans. Provincial propaganda officials have been put in charge of Chinese journalism schools, and old-line Maoists at the Chinese Red Culture Institute are warning "those who smash the Communist Party's cooking pot . . . [that] we will take away their bowls."

Vietnam is following close on the heels of Big Brother China. It, too, relies on journalists who are members of the Communist Party of Vietnam and who receive weekly instructions on how to implement propaganda campaigns and governmental directives. Yet Vietnam also strives to outdo China, arresting more bloggers per capita and giving them longer prison terms. As the gray net of state security settles ever more tightly around them, the Vietnamese are left with free access to online sex and commerce but not to ideas. The country's long history of censorship has led to some peculiar journalistic practices. People mentioned in articles have the right to approve quotations or kill stories entirely, even after the articles have been published. Journalists customarily refer to people by their initials rather than their given names. For instance, "BTN" will be quoted as complaining about police corruption and having to pay bribes at traffic stops, but because no one can verify BTN's statements, journalists are presumed to have manufactured them. This labor-saving device—accomplished without ever having to leave the office—is considered the norm in Vietnamese journalism, and it helps explain why my article's use of real names and quotations shocked so many people.

The gentleman who translated my essay into Vietnamese demanded that it be removed from the internet. He was succumbing to one of the more unusual charges leveled against me, that my article had not been published "publicly." Apparently, being published in Vietnamese was not good enough. If the article had not appeared first in English, it did not really exist. The order of publication was explained by the fact that my story was originally commissioned by Pham Thi Hoai, who, at the time, was still running her Vietnamese website in Berlin. I saw nothing wrong with allowing an exiled author to get first dibs on an article that would later be expanded and published in English.

Only when I stopped to think how censorship works in dictatorships did I understand how my piece had not been "properly" published. If you want to break the news about a scandal in country X, you send the story to country Y and then comment on the already published story back in country X. (At least this is how it used to be done, before Julian Assange and Edward Snowden turned the internet into a supranational country of its own.) For example, under the Ben Ali dictatorship in Tunisia, a Tunisian journalist reporting a sensitive story would leak the news to *Le Monde* in Paris and then, after the story had been published, comment on the news in *La Presse de Tunisie*. The French call this practice "hiding behind your finger." It is not possible, of course, to hide behind a finger, but everyone appreciates the effort, and it is difficult to arrest someone for merely repeating the news out of Paris or cyberspace. In my case, because my essay, although written in English, had appeared first in Vietnamese, my translator had no finger to hide behind. He was not repeating the news out of New York. In fact, he could be mistaken for doing something more dangerous: helping to author an original report on Vietnam's sorry literary state. So at his insistence, my essay was taken down, while my publisher and I scrambled to find a hardier soul to undertake a new translation. This time the job went to Pham Hong Son, a confirmed dissident who had already spent five years in prison for translating an essay on democracy and another seven years under house arrest. One can see why even the few people who had spoken up in my defense were now edging toward the exits.

The Country That Never Existed Rejects the Freedom It Never Had

I was in Oregon, attending a conference called "Engaging with Vietnam," when the first part of my article was published in Berlin on Hoai's *pro&contra*. The Vietnamese internet lit up on its release, with thousands of Facebook comments and blog postings pouring in, most of them negative. Some of these attacks were generated by *du luan vien,* public opinion agitators on the government payroll. Others came from respected writers and journalists who seemed to be truly shocked by the kind of investigative reporting I was doing. At the conference, the atmosphere around me stiffened. Everyone knew what was going on, but no one mentioned it. The western academics and independent scholars wanted to steer clear of Vietnamese politics. The Vietnamese, many of them graduate students allowed to study in the United States because they were Communist Party members or children of the country's ruling elite, were equally wary about commenting on censorship and other forms of social control.

The most interesting talk at the conference was the keynote address delivered by the American scholar Christopher Goscha, who teaches at the University of Quebec. A widely published historian, whose latest work is *The Penguin History of Modern Vietnam,* he debunked the idea that Vietnam is a unified country whose history was temporarily interrupted by French colonialism and war with the United States. In reality, said Goscha, before the end of the American war in 1975, Vietnam had been a unified country for no more than forty-three years, in the early nineteenth century, under Emperor Gia Long. During the rest of its 5,000-year history, it was a mosaic of people, languages, and cultures from more than fifty ethnic groups. Vietnam was a hodgepodge of countries, kingdoms, empires, warlords, fiefdoms, tribes, sects, river pirates, and migrants battling each other as the Khmers and Chams pushed in from the west and the Viets descended from the north. "There has never been one Vietnam," said Goscha. "Even under Gia Long. it was not a unified country." Vietnam's national holiday, Reunification Day, which commemorates North Vietnam's victory over the south on April 30, 1975, actually marks the *unification* of Vietnam in its current S-shaped form. "Vietnam has existed for a shorter time than the United States has," said Goscha. "No wonder the country is so anxious about its history" . . . and so anxious to censor lapses in the official narrative of this history.

I had originally heard this view during one of my conversations with Pham Xuan An. "The map of Vietnam was made by the French," he said. "Before they arrived we had no nation. The high plateaus belonged to the Montagnards. Other parts belonged to the Cham and Khmer."

Goscha agreed that French colonialism had created the idea of a unified Vietnam, and he said that it "is still not all that unified. Vietnam is the product of its own colonial expansion southward," which has shaped what he calls "an empire state." The dominant Viets rule over the country's various peoples and territories, keeping a wary eye on dissidents, defectors, critics, and anyone else brazen enough to challenge the party line. "Vietnam is a historical construction," Goscha concluded, before challenging his audience to acknowledge the existence of "Asian colonialism."

On the last day of the conference, a Vietnamese graduate student at an Ivy League university approached me to talk about my article. I suspected he was on assignment. A report would be filed. The conversation quickly veered into an interrogation. By using real names and quotations, had I had put people's lives in jeopardy? Was I responsible for what the Vietnamese government might do to my sources? If they got fired, arrested, locked up, or tortured—at what point would I beg forgiveness and withdraw my article? My interlocutor did not condemn the Vietnamese government for doing these things; he simply assumed it would. This threat system is what keeps censorship in place. Even if no one were harmed by my piece—and so far, to the best of my knowledge, no one *has* been—the threat that they *could* be harmed keeps people from supporting my efforts. In this view, all that matters is my humanity—or lack of it—in condemning my sources to the whims of the Vietnamese government.

The Invisible Wall

At roughly the same time as my interrogation, the Norwegian author Karl Knausgaard was publishing an essay on censorship called "The Invisible Wall." "Everyone who writes, be it novels, newspaper articles, Facebook posts, will sooner or later run up against the limits of what cannot, shall not, should not or must not be written," writes Knausgaard. "This limit is like an invisible wall, and to force one's way across it is painful, it is felt in the body as anxiety, an inner clenching, a feeling of dread. If I cross the boundary, it will have consequences, something will happen to me or someone else because of it. . . . If one wishes to speak about freedom of expression, and to really understand what kind of a right it is and how important it is, it is this boundary that one has to speak about, it is this invisible wall that must be localized and defined."

After my conference, while flying from San Francisco to New York, I found myself reading the *New Yorker* writer Janet Malcolm's 1990 book *The Journalist and the Murderer*. I had assigned the book to students in a class I was teaching on narrative journalism. Malcolm's book is about the encounters that lead people to sue journalists for libel, slander, breach of contract, and other charges related to feelings of betrayal. Malcolm is no stranger to these encounters. She describes herself as "a kind of fallen woman of journalism" and in fact was herself being sued for libel while writing this book about another journalist who was being sued for breach of contract.

In the book's famous opening paragraph, Malcolm describes a journalist as "a kind of confidence man, preying on people's vanity, ignorance, or loneliness, gaining their trust and betraying them without remorse. Like the credulous widow who wakes up one day to find the charming young man and all her savings gone, so the consenting subject of a piece of nonfiction writing learns— when the article or book appears—*his* hard lesson." Malcolm says that "journalists justify their 'treachery' in one of three ways. The more pompous talk about freedom of speech and the public's 'right to know'; the least talented talk about Art; the seemliest murmur about earning a living."

Even if a subject's views are correctly represented, even if his likeness is not unflattering, "what rankles and sometimes drives him to extremes of vengefulness" is the loss of control that comes from realizing that he is no longer the author of his own story. "The disparity between what seems to be the intention of an interview as it is taking place and what it actually turns out to have been always comes as a shock to the subject," writes Malcolm. The subject of a journalistic investigation is often on a "narcissist's holiday" before confronting a "dehoaxing" that resembles "love affairs that ended badly." If it goes so far as to be dragged into court, this "story of seduction and betrayal" falls into the legal conventions of libel law, defamation of character, false statement of facts, or reckless disregard of the truth.

None of these legal issues pertained in my case. Everyone admitted that my facts and quotations were correct. But still, among my Vietnamese subjects and readers, there existed this feeling of betrayal. I had used real names and quotations from people who, if I had been playing by Vietnamese rules, would have been allowed to suppress my essay, remove their names, ban the piece, or take it down from the web. I was riding roughshod over their sensibilities. I was embarrassing them. They were losing face. I could cost them their jobs, close down their publishing companies, or get them tortured or killed.

Anyone who thinks that opposition to censorship is a universal value, ardently supported by everyone in the world, should rethink this position. In Vietnam, opposition to censorship is a minority view, at least as regards those who are willing to address the issue in public. Opposition to censorship does not have a long history. It is not legally supported. On the contrary, censorship is enforced by a large and effective governmental apparatus. It is considered a social good, a necessary part of governance, and a benefit to the nation. Censorship is incorporated into the culture. It helps avoid conflict and, most insidiously, is incorporated into the watching agent of self-censorship that is implanted deep within everyone's mind.

I stumbled into these realizations belatedly. I thought revulsion toward censorship was universal, that no one would want cultural commissars telling them what to think. But lots of people are happy with this arrangement, and not just the public opinion agitators, government boosters, hall monitors, and paid informants. Following is easier than leading. Weakness appreciates strength. Tucking oneself into a defensive crouch while fighting off attacks from "outsiders" is always a popular move. When I corresponded with people who objected to my essay, such as my interrogator in Oregon, I found myself saying the same things over and over again until I concluded that my Vietnamese critics and I had fallen into a "cultural divide." They had been taught to avoid "sensitive" subjects, while I was an investigative reporter trained to get the facts and report them.

Robert Templar, in *Shadows and Wind,* his 1998 book on Vietnam, talks about the revival in Asia of Confucianism, which he cites as a leading factor in the region's transformation from colonial backwater to Asian Tiger. "The teachings of Confucius—respect for family and authority, the emphasis of the community over the individual, a moral bureaucracy selected by merit—were the Asian equivalent to Max Weber's Protestant ethic that had transformed the West," writes Templar. Confucianism "lent some legitimacy to authoritarian regimes and justified minimal attention to the rights of the individual. . . . At worst it has been a fig leaf for despotism." When scrutinized through the optic of human rights, each of the values assigned to Confucianism is opposed to freedom of speech and aligned instead with censorship and state power. From a Confucian perspective, my story about how it took me five years to get a book censored and published in Vietnam is a tale told by an idiot.

As one reader of my essay commented, "*The Spy Who Loved Us* as it appears in the heavily—and quite thoroughly—censored Vietnamese version is like a human being with its heart removed—not even worth the effort to drag over to the garden and bury for its value as fertilizer. But what did you expect?"

I couldn't reply to all my critics—there were so many of them—but one letter is worth noting. In it, a long-time friend, who is an American, wrote to defend the Vietnamese practice of using initials in place of names and accused me of denying the Vietnamese "agency" in their handling of censorship.

"The convention of substituting initials for people's names was used in Victorian novels to lend them an air of verisimilitude," I replied. "It has no place in journalism, where it produces fake quotes in fictitious stories. In the censored translation of my book, the poet To Huu—even though long dead—has his name changed to TH. What does this accomplish? Nothing that I can see, other than whitewashing the fact that To Huu was the Dr. Goebbels of the Vietnamese communist party, a major purger and book banner, who limned odes about 'the love I bear you, Oh Stalin!'"

"Your other argument," I wrote to my friend, "which is really a non-argument, centers on the idea of 'agency' and my supposedly denying the Vietnamese the right to speak for themselves. Every

PEN, Human Rights Watch, Amnesty International, and U.N. report on human rights in country X is greeted with the same defensive snarl. 'What allows you outsiders to criticize our local practices?'"

"I am sorry," I told my friend, who is now a former friend, "but I support the right of PEN, HRW, Amnesty, and the U.N. to report on human rights abuses in Vietnam. I also support their right to report on human rights abuses in the United States. None of this denies 'agency' to anyone. In fact, the more agents the merrier. Let's all become agents and start reporting abuses."

Typical of the responses to my essay was a Facebook posting by Xe Nho, whose real name is Nguyen Van Phu, the managing editor of the *Saigon Times*. Mr. Phu received close to a hundred comments on his posting, as well as 20 "shares" and 596 "likes." He wrote that I wasn't "playing fair." I had been received by people who thought they were speaking confidentially, and here I was "betraying their trust." It was something of a mystery how Mr. Phu, in Saigon, could speak so authoritatively about events in Hanoi, at which he was not present, but he was quite sure of himself, and his position quickly coalesced into the party line about me. "This man did a bad thing, publishing names and sensitive information. His action is so disrespectful," wrote a Phu supporter. Phu himself at least had the grace to admit that my observations about censorship in Vietnam were "totally accurate."

By this point in the debate, Hoai wrote to me from Berlin about what we had taken to calling the "breach of confidence" affair. "You have written a masterpiece about Vietnamese sensitivities," she said, while explaining how I had offended these sensitivities—and continued to do so with every word I wrote. She then jumped into the debate with an essay of her own. "Can the American journalist tell his own story truly? Can he do this while hiding the names of the real people in the story? This doesn't make sense," she wrote.

"This is a documentary about real people and real events," Hoai said. Like Seymour Hersh's story about the My Lai massacre, it has "the uneasiness of truth." People may be used to the

Vietnamese context, in which you don't use real names, but this is not how the game is played among western journalists, where the watch words are verifiability and accuracy, truthfulness to one's sources and transparency in identifying them.

"In the Vietnamese situation, real names are not used. We talk about 'Comrade X,'" Hoai wrote. "But in this case we are not discussing Lord Voldemort. The characters are not so evil that their names cannot be mentioned."

"This is a habit among the Vietnamese," she said. "You use lots of nicknames, rather than people's real names and titles." She gives as an example the pen name used by Ho Chi Minh—CB—which he employed when attacking landowners during the Maoist land reform campaigns of the 1950s.

"Now that the American journalist has thrown his censorship bomb," it has produced a "culture shock between Vietnamese and American customs," Hoai wrote, before describing her own contretemps with Vietnam's censors. "The pendulum gets dizzy as it swings between the two competing powers in Vietnam—the government and the Party."

She described being summoned to meet her censors in 2004 on her final visit to Vietnam. Installed in a villa in the former French quarter of Hanoi, the party officials concerned with ideology and culture were urbane men who "used to play ping pong; now they play golf." She characterized these men as living in a "tropical forest, a jungle of censorship. If you get lost in this jungle, you feel gratitude for the guide who will rescue you from sinking into marshes or being killed by tigers." These men will "live on forever," she fears, minding the interests of those in power, defending them against the helplessness of those armed only with pens.

My Literary Episiotomy

The most extensive comments on my essay came in a letter to *pro&contra* from Nguyen Viet Long, my first editor—and censor—at

Nha Nam publishing company. I had fought for five years to get Mr. Long's communist jargon and footnotes removed from my text and to restore the passages that he had cut from it. In his letter, Mr. Long rehashed every one of these disputes before arriving at exactly the same conclusion that he had reached in his footnotes: "The author is wrong."

An episiotomy is the surgical cutting of the perineum, the muscular area between the vagina and the anus, to enlarge the birth canal and prevent unwanted tearing during childbirth. Mr. Long invoked the procedure in describing his role as my editor. He was responsible for easing the birth of my book into print through judicious cutting. I had rejected his help, which resulted in the prolonged labor I had suffered before my book was delivered. Mr. Long still bore a grudge against his willful patient, a blockheaded westerner who had refused the simple snips that would have made his and everyone else's lives so much simpler.

"An editor is a midwife who helps deliver a work," Mr. Long wrote. "I think about the pain a woman feels when she gives birth. This book had such a difficult delivery." My book could have been published many years earlier, Mr. Long maintained, if I had not insisted "on looking at the translation with a magnifying glass." I hate to contradict the man and risk resuming our literary agon, but the date he gives for my painless delivery—his initial attempt to publish my book—precedes my having seen the translation, much less having reviewed it with a magnifying or any other kind of glass. "The chance was missed and the birth pangs lasted for four more years before the work was finally delivered," Mr. Long wrote, "and even then . . . we still couldn't say that Pham Xuan An 'loved' America."

In minute detail, running to twelve pages when printed, Mr. Long revisited each of our editorial disagreements. Once again, I found myself in the Swamp of the Assassins, fighting hand to hand in the hedgerows of literature. I was hearing once more how this famous patch of pirate turf southeast of Saigon was really called the Forest of Seacoast Shrubs. Every footnote over which we had fought, every northern locution to which I had objected, was dragged back into service as proof of authorial error. How about the material cut from the book, the names and historical facts removed, along with An's jokes, his criticisms of the Chinese, his love for America, and so on? This was extraneous material, Mr. Long wrote. The book reads better without it. Here we have the perfect rationale for combining the roles of editor and censor. Mr. Long was not really enforcing the ideology of the state. He was merely adding to the enjoyment of my readers.

Mr. Long resorts in his essay to a kind of intellectual jujitsu. It was Thomas Bass, not the Vietnamese, who had done "hardcore censorship of the Vietnamese translation" of my book. How did I do this? While reviewing the translation, my "supporting group [of advisers] turned simple details into big problems at the government level." The editor, "facing two big cats," had been "caught between a hard-minded author and equally hard-minded censors."

My advisers, according to Mr. Long, were "overseas Vietnamese" who "spoke a language that was used half a century ago in South Vietnam and has been frozen in place since they left the country. They wanted to protect their obsolete language." They clung to "old words and forms of speech" rather than adapt to the current language spoken in Vietnam. What Mr. Long fails to mention is that my book is about a South Vietnamese who speaks the language of the south. An comes out sounding very silly when his voice is translated into the Chinese-inflected, jargon-filled language that Mr. Long prefers. An himself spoke about this problem during one of our conversations. "I was never able to learn the 'new' Vietnamese," he said about his experience of being "reeducated" in North Vietnam at the end of the war. "They didn't like me at all," he said of the cadre at the Nguyen Ai Quoc Political Institute, who tried to teach him Marxist-Maoist thought. "But I haven't made a big enough mistake to be shot yet."

That my book was reviewed and censored so vigorously was

also my fault. I should have done what other western authors do: sign off on the deal and not meddle in Vietnam's internal affairs. Only when I demanded the right to review the translation—as was stipulated in my contract—did red lights start flashing in the various bureaucracies in charge of censoring books. I had brought these troubles on myself. I had invited "strict censorship" by objecting to Mr. Long's footnotes and insisting on a "purely academic" debate over these matters.

Apart from a passing reference to "a few cuts" in my book, Mr. Long says nothing about what was removed from the text. The author was overreacting to "errors that in my opinion don't make much difference," he writes. As for what was added to the text—or would have been added, if I hadn't insisted that he remove his explanatory footnotes—Mr. Long contends these explanations were required "to correct the author's errors or explain other opinions on the same subject."

The censorship of my book, he concludes, was nothing more than "trimming little hairs, like the hairs on a sweet potato. There is no political force behind these changes." He gives as an example the fact that the censors would not allow me to report that Pham Xuan An's family originated in southern China and then emigrated from northern Vietnam to the south. "The paragraph was cut a little bit," Mr. Long confesses. "But these minor details about the history of Vietnam are unimportant."

Hue-Tam Ho Tai, a professor of Sino-Vietnamese history at Harvard, sent a comment on my article to the Vietnam Study Group. She wrote, "I had known something of the tight censorship exercised in works of history. But Bass's account of his experience is the most detailed and dispiriting. Thomas Bass's experience goes a long way toward explaining why history as a discipline is in such a sorry state in Vietnam. The past is a minefield, like the landscape."

Take It Down

The vice-chairman of Nha Nam publishing company was one of the people who wrote letters demanding that my essay be taken down. I replied to his letters and then replied again, until I sensed that the exchanges were becoming ritualistic. His outrage looked staged, his protests as empty as acts of contrition at a Russian show trial. I had tricked people, he wrote. I had not allowed them to remove their names. They regretted ever speaking to the treacherous Thomas Bass. The facts of what I had written might not be in dispute, but my betrayal of confidence was unpardonable.

In February 2015, the British publication *Index on Censorship* published the long version of my article, in English. The editor released the story in thirteen installments, but on the last day of the release, she removed two of the chapters. Nha Nam's vice-chairman had written again to complain that I was publishing "confidential" conversations. The editor of *Index* informed me that the journal intended to "investigate" these charges and, while doing so, would suppress parts of my essay. I argued that this was a presumption of guilt rather than innocence. "Taking down parts of my essay is a dog whistle of support for Vietnam's assault on free speech," I wrote to the editor and her board members, but nothing I said prevented the irony of my being censored by *Index on Censorship*. This seemed a strange state of affairs for an august organization devoted to publishing banned works by Aleksandr Solzhenitsyn, Milan Kundera, Václav Havel, Salman Rushdie, and others.

Sometime later, with no notice, *Index on Censorship* restored the full version of my essay to its website. Now that the honorable thing has been done, only the scoundrels remain to be heard from.

CHAPTER VI

Vietnam: Brave New World

On a warm night in July, Saigon is a madhouse of motorcycles whirling down the narrow streets. A river of red taillights flows in front of the white facades. People are outside catching the evening air, seeing the city, being seen in the city, spending money, making money. Rich girls rev their Vespas. Poor girls ride postilion on the backs of their boyfriends' bikes. Married couples wedge their children between them and roll in an endless parade around city hall and the municipal theater, which remain among the few colonial buildings preserved in modern Saigon, or Ho Chi Minh City, as it was renamed in 1975.

Beyond the honking motorbikes and Saigon's new tower blocks lies a more sober reality. A country that looks feverish with pleasure and wide open to sex and money is actually a police state adept at silencing authors, poets, journalists, bloggers, and anyone else with the temerity to criticize Vietnam's one-party rule. State control over the press and publishing has hobbled scores of writers over the past forty years, forcing them into self-censorship, exile, or prison. Vietnam's best fiction writer no longer writes fiction. Its best poet no longer writes poetry. Its journalists and bloggers are beaten, arrested, and incarcerated at a rate that places Vietnam among the world's leading jailers of prisoners of conscience.

Vietnam is conducting an experiment to see if a people denied history, memory, and information can content themselves with motorbikes and shopping. Is life worth living if you empty out the content of a country's culture and replace it with slogans? In Saigon's distracted whirl of traffic, the answer seems to be yes. But a handful of critics insists on saying no. They raise their voices, at great personal risk, to oppose the official narrative. They contest the creation of Vietnam's brave new world, where the country of no memory rushes into the future of no hope.

Losers

On July 7, 2015, when Nguyen Phu Trong, the general secretary of the Communist Party of Vietnam, visited the White House to meet President Barack Obama, he was greeted by a small group of Vietnamese-American protestors who shouted that Trong was a serial abuser of human rights. Waving the red and yellow flag of a country that had ceased to exist forty years ago, the protestors looked like losers. They brought up bad memories from an unsettled time. The media ignored them.

Unfortunately, the protestors were right. Trained at Moscow's Academy of Social Sciences and elevated into his current position in 2011, Trong is in fact Vietnam's preeminent abuser of human rights. He presides over the party's Central Department for Propaganda and Education, whose tentacles reach through the Ministry of Information and Communication into "security bureau" A87 and from there into every party cell that controls the media in Vietnam, including the distribution agencies, publishing houses, filmmakers, and so on. In his position as Vietnam's chief censor, Trong is responsible for running what Reporters Without Borders calls a "gangster state," replete with "waves of arrests, trials, physical attacks and harassment."

In 2012 alone, the year after Trong assumed effective leadership of Vietnam, the country prosecuted forty-eight bloggers and human rights activists, meting out 166 years in jail sentences and 63 years of probation. This muzzling of the country's intelligentsia, which includes sending writers into exile, seizing passports, and incarcerating critics in psychiatric hospitals, has continued unabated, even after Vietnam, in 2014, moved into a seat on the U.N. Human Rights Council. The final confirmation that Trong can torture whomever he wants came in January 2016, when he was reappointed to a second five-year term as head of Vietnam's Communist Party.

At the end of the Vietnam War in 1975, Vietnam indulged in a bloodletting instead of a blood bath. It imprisoned hundreds of thousands of people on the losing side and launched an exodus of boat people that drained a million refugees from the former South Vietnam. "Truly, they squandered their hard-won victory," says Colonel Bui Tin of his former colleagues in the North Vietnamese Army. "One of the most ironic and painful things for us to realize is that there has never been a true democracy in Vietnam," notes Tin, who currently lives in exile in a one-room garret on the outskirts of Paris.

Ice Age

Human rights organizations, nongovernmental organizations, U.N. agencies, and governmental observers yearly produce sobering reports on Vietnam's human rights record. Catholic priests are beaten and imprisoned. Writers are censored and exiled. Journalists are arrested. Bloggers are tried for criminal offenses. One can read any of these reports—they vary little from year to year—and find grim statistics about Vietnam's violence against its own citizens. Several hundred prisoners of conscience have run afoul of the thought police. More are hounded out of jobs or harassed by summonses to police interrogations. Traffic accidents are arranged by plainclothes thugs. Even Vietnam's psychiatric hospitals double as holding pens for dissidents. If this grey net of state security resembles life in the Soviet Union or China in the 1950s, that is because Vietnam's original tutors in totalitarianism were Stalinist Russia and Maoist China.

In a 2013 report titled "Vietnam: Programmed Death of Freedom of Information," Reporters Without Borders fingers Trong as chief enforcer in Vietnam's "gangster state." According to the organization, he is responsible for the "waves of arrests, trials, physical attacks and harassment" that have led to "Vietnam's ice age."

The report details one horror story after another about Vietnam's suppression of speech, inquiry, association, and authorship. Almost immediately after the internet was introduced into the country in 1997, cyber-dissidents were arrested for distributing pro-democracy articles or criticizing the government. "The state's grip on the print and broadcast media has never let up," says the report. "When arrests, trials, and torture" don't work, "the authorities have no qualms about using gangster-like methods, including beatings, abduction and even violence against close relatives of bloggers and dissidents."

The report goes on to describe how Trong and his minions meet every Tuesday with the editors of the country's major media outlets for "a briefing in Hanoi chaired by the heads of the party's Central Department of Propaganda and Education." Here the editors receive their marching orders for the week. The role of the media in this system is to act as a mouthpiece for the Communist Party of Vietnam, "which alone decides whether and how news is covered."

"Media bosses are in the service of the state," says the report. "Their job is to promote and defend the government." Numerous editors have run afoul of this arrangement and been forced to resign. In January 2009, Nguyen Cong Khe, the founder and editor in chief of *Thanh Nien,* and Le Hoang, the editor of *Tuoi Tre,* two of Vietnam's largest dailies, were fired for allowing their papers to report on government officials who were using development funds to place sports bets. A few months earlier, the two reporters who broke this story were sent to prison. The "thought police" mainly target "cyber dissidents and intellectuals, but it also monitors, harasses and arrests journalists," says the report, which currently describes Vietnam as an "enemy of the internet."

"Independent journalists and bloggers pay an incredible price for their commitment to freedom and information," continues the report. "They are kidnapped by the police, trumped-up charges are brought against them, they are held incommunicado, mistreatment is used to extract confessions, they are subjected to summary trials, they are confined in psychiatric hospitals, and they are confined in their homes when released from prison. At each stage in the judicial process, they are subjected to countless violations of their human rights."

"Vietnam has made no progress during the past four decades," the report concludes. It talks a good game. It has all the right provisions written into a constitution that it ignores, and it occupies—with no sense of irony—a seat on the U.N. Human Rights Council. The number of arrests goes up. It goes down. But Vietnam is resource-rich when it comes to the supply of political prisoners who can be swapped for normalized relations, favorable tariffs, trans-Pacific partnerships, or whatever else can be negotiated by trading dissidents for political advantage.

"Unfortunately, I can't see you. I am under house arrest."

The first person I try to contact on my trip to Vietnam is the distinguished novelist, essayist, playwright, and screenwriter Nguyen Quang Lap. Lap is also the founder of a widely read blog that covers Vietnamese politics, including the recent Sino-Vietnamese conflict in the South China Sea—or Eastern Sea, as the Vietnamese insist on calling it. He emails to say that he would be delighted to meet me, but unfortunately he is under house arrest. The government rarely arrests an author as distinguished as Lap. He is partially paralyzed from a motorcycle accident and in poor health.

International protests have been launched on his behalf, and bloggers have noted ironically that he was arrested three days before International Human Rights Day.

One odd feature of Lap's detention is the fact that he answers emails promptly. His access to the internet represents Vietnam's strange mix of brutality and incompetence. The country metes out long prison sentences to bloggers, while allowing one-third of its 90 million citizens to use Facebook. Introduced into Vietnam in 2009, Facebook may or may not be illegal, according to laws that are both contradictory and arbitrary, and access is sometimes blocked, although casually, with lots of workarounds. Vietnam currently ranks among the world's fastest-growing Facebook countries.

According to Sarah Logan, an Australian scholar who studies social media in Southeast Asia, "Vietnam was too late in censoring the internet, and it was ultimately doomed to failure, since it doesn't have physical control of the country's internet infrastructure, like China does." Logan also credits Vietnam's overseas diaspora with pushing the country into adopting western media that are "free," at least free of state control.

"Vietnam let Facebook in and let it grow until it was too late," says Anh-Minh Do, a tech analyst in Singapore. "And although the block has strengthened along with the political tides, this has served more to educate the population to self-censor than deterred use of Facebook."

Before he was removed from office in January 2016 in a reactionary coup by hardline party officials, Vietnam's prime minister, Nguyen Tan Dung, had admitted failure in the government's attempt to ban Facebook. "Everyone here has joined social networks," he told a meeting of senior government officials in 2015. "All of you have Facebook on your phones to read information. We can't ban it." So what solution did Dung propose? The government would hire thousands of fake commentators, known as "public opinion agitators," and flood social networks with propaganda "to spread the government's message."

Hanoi

Before heading into Saigon's whirling traffic, I begin with a visit to the country's more sedate capital in the north. I arrive in Hanoi near midnight in the middle of a torrential downpour. The city smells like a wet animal, with a feral humidity that knocks me torpid at first breath. A night ride from the airport into central Hanoi is always a bit grim. I stare from the highway down into concrete houses lit with no more than a dangling light bulb or neon tube. The gloom is pierced with sparks flying from workers welding rebar or a mechanic tinkering under the hood of a car, but mainly the light comes from signs advertising karaoke bars, massage parlors, and no-star hotels. The streets are rivers of mud. Under the bridges and overpasses huddle people in plastic slickers and flip flops. Trucks belching diesel weave from lane to lane, as if their steering columns have been repaired one too many times. I am headed into what are known as the thirty-six streets, the old part of Hanoi, where families descended from medieval guilds still trade in silk, silver, gold, conical hats, and funerary urns. My hotel backs onto the street of the money lenders. Here, all day long, I can watch people buzz up to the shop fronts on their motorbikes, dismount, kick off their shoes, and enter for a quick trade in cash or gold.

The sun returns the next morning. As I walk out of my hotel into the splash of color and bustle that marks Vietnam's capital, I pass a woman with squids wriggling in the panniers of her bicycle and a flower vendor squatting over a bucket of tight-budded roses. Perched on plastic stools lining the streets are groups of neatly dressed people eating breakfast, buying raffle tickets, chatting, and selling everything from electric fans to chicken soup. Songbirds brought out for a morning airing sing in their wicker cages. Vendors cycle down the street selling brooms, baguettes, bananas. Hanoi on a sunny morning is like a pointillist painting come to life, with the dots scurrying around the canvas, hailing each other in a whirl of rubber wheels and two-stroke Chinese motors.

Near St. Joseph's Cathedral, I turn into a trendy café filled with black sofas holding young professionals Skyping on their laptops. I order a coffee and sit for a few minutes before a woman with a noticeable limp and a creased brow slips into the seat across from me. She is carrying a backpack that looks like it holds everything she owns. We introduce ourselves, and Pham Doan Trang begins recounting her life as a journalist.

Trang was born in Hanoi in 1978. Her parents were high school chemistry teachers. Her mother worked in Hanoi, while her father was posted to the Central Highlands, where he spent fourteen years before hunger and malaria forced him back to the city. Trang graduated with a degree in economics from Vietnam's University of Foreign Trade. At the time she attended, the school was on the cusp of big changes. Instruction in Russian suddenly flipped to English. "Facebook is where we get our news," Trang says, "but very few of Vietnam's 35 million Facebook users know how to speak English. So I think the duty of journalists who speak English is to tell the world what's happening here."

In 2000, Trang began working as a journalist for *VNExpress*, Vietnam's first internet news site. Straightaway, she faced what she calls the "tragedy of the media" in Vietnam: censorship, self-censorship, government control, and the simple fact that "people are scared."

"We have 30,000 journalists in Vietnam," she says. "Fewer than a hundred are political journalists, and fewer than twenty are democracy supporters. I can count them on my hands and feet. They face administrative sanctions, reductions in salary, fines, physical assault. Journalists are victims of the police state," she tells me, before reminding me that every newspaper in Vietnam is state-owned. "If you include bloggers, every year there are hundreds of assaults on journalists, and lots of journalists have been put in jail for political reasons."

She mentions Anh Ba Sam, known as "Brother Gossip," who used to run the "Sidewalk News Agency," a popular blog calling for democracy in Vietnam. Anh Ba Sam is the pen name of Nguyen Huu Vinh, another person I was hoping to meet, until I was informed that he is currently in prison "to serve the investigating process." Charged under article 258 of the penal code, which outlaws "abusing freedom and democracy to infringe upon the interests of the state," Vinh, if convicted, faces seven more years in prison.

A fifty-eight-year-old former policeman and the son of a Communist Party Central Committee member who twice served as an ambassador to the Soviet Union, Brother Gossip fits the profile of a criminal only in a country as paranoid as Vietnam. The denunciation campaign mounted against him in the press says that Vinh specializes in "reporting and commenting on current social and political issues of Vietnam with a deliberately critical tone" and "trying to uglify Vietnam to make her as bad and ugly as he is."

Human Rights Watch estimates that as many as two hundred activists and bloggers are currently imprisoned. Vietnam Right Now, a Hanoi-based human rights group, lists 250 prisoners of conscience. "In 2013 I counted the number of political prisoners in Vietnam and came up with 326, to be exact," says Trang.

In November 2015, General Tran Dai Quang, Vietnam's minister of public security (the police), in an address before the National Assembly, explained how he used the country's vague national security laws to stifle dissent and arrest critics. Quang said that between June 2012 and November 2015, "The police have received, arrested, and dealt with 1,410 cases involving 2,680 people who violated national security." He went on to describe how he specifically targeted democracy and human rights groups, "which have about 350 participants from fifty cities and provinces."

While Brother Gossip is in jail awaiting trial, two of his three websites have been closed. This means the police have gained control of his passwords, but a third site remains open, run by supporters who have managed to keep their identities secret. Trang tells me that her own website, a blog set up in 2009, is currently blocked in Vietnam (although it, too, manages to keep publishing new articles).

I ask Trang what the word democracy means to her. "The democracy movement is hardly a movement," she says. "It's unorganized." The rest of her answer is straightforward. Democracy is the right to free and fair elections, organized political parties, majority rule with defense of minority interests, the rule of law, and freedom of speech and assembly. In other words, democracy is everything that we in the West take for granted and willingly compromise.

"In Vietnam, you can't enter politics unless you're a member of the Communist Party," Trang tells me. "Those of us who want to get people involved in government, actively, effectively, and meaningfully, . . . we are just waiting for the day they come to arrest us."

Trang has been "temporarily" arrested many times. A few days before our meeting, she was detained by the police for seven hours. "It happens all the time," she says. She had organized a seminar supporting victims of torture. "All the organizers were arrested, and the seminar was cancelled. 'This is an illegal social gathering,' they told us. 'You're inciting public disorder and disturbing the peace.'"

"The longest time they held me in detention was nine days," she says. Trang swipes through her phone to show me photos of police assaults and beatings. I stare at a young man whose hand was smashed with a brick when he was roughed up by plainclothes police. Trang is limping today from a recent attack that left her lying in bed immobile for two days.

Cyber Trolls

Trang describes how Vietnam stage-manages rigged elections, where 100 percent voter turnout is matched by similarly large margins of victory. "A police state never tolerates the press," she says. "The press is supposed to serve the interests of the Communist

Party. The difference is that now we have social media. With other sources beside mainstream media, the state has lost its monopoly.

"Change is coming not because the state is more tolerant, but because it has lost control. It has to control the press *plus* the blogosphere. It has to deal with services based in the United States. The law requires Facebook to provide information to the police, and sometimes they do it. Google refuses, but Facebook complies. They work for profit, not for human rights. I have a Facebook account, which is more accessible than my blog, but I am wary about Facebook being more 'cooperative' with the government than Google."

"In many ways, Vietnam is just a student of Big Brother China," Trang says. China spends billions of dollars blocking internet sites from the outside world and surveilling the communication of its citizens. Trang explains how China has mastered the art of reverse engineering global services and swapping them for Chinese copies. For Google, China substitutes Baidu. For Facebook and Twitter, it provides Weibo. For eBay, it offers Alibaba.

Unfortunately for Little Brother Vietnam, the country's attempts at emulating China in telecommunications and the internet have failed. Western technology arrived too suddenly and was embraced too enthusiastically to be blocked. None of Vietnam's imitation Googles (vinaseek, socbay, coccoc) has replaced the original. Nor have imitation Facebooks (go.vn) succeeded. People tell a joke about the Vietnamese prime minister. He searches online for "failed policies of Nguyen Tan Dung." Google retrieves a million articles. Vietnamese search engines find none.

"Vietnam is lost in the world technologically," Trang says. "It's way behind China."

China began blocking foreign services as soon as they were introduced, and the Chinese market is so big that even limited local services attracted large numbers of users. One unintended consequence of this reality is that Vietnam, unlike China, can block news only after it has been published. "This is why the Vietnamese government beats up so many bloggers and journalists," Trang says. "It's what happens when you can't block information at the source."

Instead of trying to ban Facebook and Google, the Vietnamese government has switched techniques. "They hack our accounts," Trang says. "They report us to Facebook so that we lose our accounts. They set up fake sites to attack us. They defame us. They steal our personal information and try to blackmail us with it."

According to Trang, the government has hired tens of thousands of "public opinion agitators" (*du luan vien*), who are paid per posting to spread propaganda and disinformation and lead attacks against internet users. "At the end of the month, when they are trying to meet their quotas, you can see comments from these cyber troops flooding onto websites."

"My phone is tapped," she says. "I hear agents talking in the background. You begin to fear for your safety. It becomes too dangerous to speak about human rights. This is why so few people do it."

"In the political culture of Vietnam, people don't want to be different from other people," she tells me. "You will be isolated from friends, family, community members. This is especially hard for women. Police pressure your employers to dismiss you. You can't find a job. You can't rent an apartment, or you find yourself being evicted in the middle of the night. Young activists have to sleep in the parks overnight. You can be attacked or arrested or sent to prison for a long time."

In January 2013, Ho Quang Loi, head of Hanoi's Communist Party Propaganda Department, confirmed that the department had hired nine hundred "rumormongers," whose job was "to fully exploit the power of propaganda." These internet trolls, "in obedience to orders from superiors in dealing with sensitive cases," are programmed to function like "button-pressing, rapid response journalists." Like China's 50 Cent Party, so named because participants receive fifty Chinese cents per posting, the rumormongers flooding Vietnam's cyberspace number in the thousands.

Not all the victories in the arms race between dissidents and the government go to the censors. "The good news is that in the past five years, some alternative media have emerged," Trang wrote in a recent blog posting. She listed the protest movement against bauxite mining in the Vietnamese highlands and several alternative news sites. She is also encouraged by the release of political prisoner Nguyen Huu Cau, whose "anti-revolutionary" activities had put him behind bars for thirty-seven years.

When the former army officer Dinh Dang Dinh was released from prison in 2014 and died less than a month later from cancer, 2,000 people showed up for his funeral. The event—a silent protest against the Chinese Aluminum Company being issued permits to strip mine bauxite in Vietnam's Central Highlands—was broken up by plainclothes police sent "to tear away commemoration banners from floral tributes" and disperse the crowd paying tribute to the "anti-state Dinh Dang Dinh."

Three other prisoners of conscience, including the legal scholar Cu Huy Ha Vu, were released in April 2014. Dr. Vu was flown directly from prison to exile in the United States, which suggested to Trang "that he may have been 'traded' by the Vietnamese government for some economic and political gains." Two months later, another trade seems to have netted the release of the labor activist Do Thi Minh Hanh.

Unfortunately, the good news was followed by another roundup of political prisoners, including the Sidewalk News Agency's Anh Ba Sam and the author Nguyen Quang Lap. Vietnam is happy to supply mice to the world's global cats, and, among its various shortages, Vietnam has never recorded a shortage of mice.

A Confession

Traveling to the Philippines does not require a visa for Vietnamese visitors, so in January 2013 Trang secretly left Vietnam and went there. During the following year, she received a fellowship from the German government to study public policy at the University of Southern California. After ten months in Los Angeles, she was offered political asylum in the United States but chose instead to return to Vietnam. In January 2015, she was arrested at the airport in Hanoi and told she was on a blacklist of people not allowed to leave the country.

"News about my detention went viral on Facebook," she says. "They released me that night but told me I was banned from leaving Vietnam for 'national security reasons.'" Today Trang, who is one of Vietnam's best political reporters, is basically unemployed and unemployable.

Back in 2009, when she was working as a columnist for *VietnamNet*, she and two well-known bloggers were arrested in a crackdown on dissidents. Held for nine days, she was accused of making "advocacy tee-shirts" and leading protests against Chinese bauxite mining.

"They confiscated my laptop when I was in jail and opened it to find private photos of me with my former lover," she says. "They tried to make me sign forty of these photos and confess to being in them. I refused to do this. Then they 'invited' my mother to the police station. With my mother seated at a table in front of me, they held up each photo and threatened to turn it around and show her the picture. My mother is a traditional Asian woman who doesn't believe in having sex before marriage. She looked miserable.

"They forced me to sign the photos and write a confession in front of my mother. 'This is my body. I am having sex with this man,' I wrote out forty times. Over the years, they have tried to silence me by threatening to use these photos."

Trang slumps in her chair as she tells me this story. Her face is grave and unsmiling. "In tears, before the Tet holiday, I wrote a confession telling everyone that I could do nothing to defend myself and them. I asked them to forgive me,'" she says.

Trang's "Confession" was published on her blog in February 2015. "I must admit that I am not in the best of moods as I sit down to write these lines right at this very moment," she warns her readers. "For the past six months, since the summer of 2014, when I was still completing my fellowship in the U.S., I have been regularly receiving threatening messages from unidentifiable Facebook pages with the same contents: they will disseminate to the internet private, sexual images of mine—Pham Doan Trang—if I continue with my works, [which] are described as 'subversive activities' by them."

Trang goes on to describe the "sad story of some six years ago," when she was arrested and the blackmail began. Often, in the middle of the night, she was "awakened by threatening and unidentified messages, harsh comments made by the government's internet trolls. I realized that, sooner or later, those pictures [would be] disseminated by posting on a website dedicated to 'war on dissidents' [or] by sending them directly to the people whom I would not want to be aware of this story. Worse yet, they could be photoshopped and disseminated with additional untrue and malicious information (this is how the internet trolls paid by the government have been treating dissidents) to create horrible tales about me.

"Even though it is truly heart-rending, I must write this 'confession' at the end of this lunar year because I simply cannot predict when my private pictures will be posted online with highlights and red circles, etc.

"I want to offer my apology to those who will be affected by this incident, if it happens the way I fear. I want to tell them that I do not have the power to defend myself and that it is impossible for me to take up the responsibility of securing those pictures once the security police have their hands on them."

Soon after Trang's return from the United States, her intimate photos began leaking onto the internet. "The police aren't using physical torture and imprisonment, but something more subtle," she says. "I suffered psychological trauma after that. I flash back to dozens of policemen staring at my photos, my body exposed before them. I cannot forget the way my mother looked that day—a traditional, soft-spoken woman who was then in her late sixties, wracked with misery and pain."

"That humiliation is still with me," she says. "My apartment is bugged. I can't change clothes in my room anymore. I have no more privacy."

"When I was offered asylum in the United States, I told the consular official, 'I don't want to be a burden. You have enough political refugees.'

"'You are not a burden. You are an asset,' he told me. I have never heard these words in my own country, where I have been arrested and beaten many times.

"On a national level, I see signs of hope in Vietnam. More and more young people want to build a democracy. Many others are declining to become members of the Communist Party. But here the phrase 'anti–Communist Party' means 'anti-state.' This is illegal. It is a crime.

"For myself I see no hope. I no longer have the chance to live a peaceful life. No more love life. No more family life. No more privacy. I have to live as a public enemy, with police repression."

"You can never take the prison out of someone's mind," she says. "It becomes part of your life. I can never get those nine days of detention out of my mind, with the police preaching to me in front of my mother about morality.

"My scandal has given me a slave mind. Fear is all around, and the police take advantage of this."

Sweet Virtues

Trang invites me to attend a journalism class that she teaches once a week at a café on the outskirts of Hanoi. "These are very brave students," she says. "Classes like this are raided by the police."

Later in the week, I give a taxi driver a piece of paper with an address written on it. We drive into Hanoi's western suburbs, and he drops me off on the shores of a small lake. The lake is surrounded by outdoor cafés full of people eating boiled crabs and drinking beer. I watch the festivities until I notice an alley leading away from the lake. I walk down the alley and turn left to discover a small café that doubles as a kind of community center. I leave my shoes at the door and walk upstairs to a carpeted room with low tables. At the far end of the room are seven young Vietnamese men, dressed casually in jeans and tee shirts, and one young woman in a skirt. Trang walks in behind me, still limping badly from her encounter with the police. She unslings her backpack and lowers herself to the floor with a wince. "Maybe tomorrow I'll go to the hospital for a checkup," she says.

We order iced coffee and tea and introduce ourselves. Among the students are a young man finishing a law degree, an "activist promoting civil society," a corporate accountant, a first-year engineering student, a specialist in mobile networks, another student studying economic law ("Vietnam doesn't train many criminal lawyers," he says), a hotel desk clerk, and the young woman, who has just finished medical school. They tell me they are studying journalism to understand what is happening around them. Many are political activists. For a Green Hanoi, a group that recently organized rallies to prevent Hanoi from chopping down its old trees, is one of their causes. One young man, a practicing Catholic, tells me about the lack of religious freedom in Vietnam, which has long been a political flashpoint.

Trang explains how public meetings in Vietnam are blocked. "You have to leave your apartment one or two days in advance to get to a protest. Otherwise, the police shut you in. The government is scared to see young people gather in groups," she says. "They're afraid of what they might do in the future."

The students begin asking me questions about journalism. "Are there occasions when journalists should not publish something?" "Is truth always the ultimate goal of journalism?" "Is there ever anything more important than publishing the truth?" They are polite, inquisitive, curious. They are doing nothing more than exploring the world around them, which, unfortunately, in Vietnam makes them criminals.

For these young people "democracy" is not a plot to overthrow the government. It is a request to vote in elections that aren't rigged. "Freedom of speech" is the desire to talk among themselves about Vietnam and the larger world. "The rule of law" is a wish to assemble in discussion groups, go to poetry readings, watch movies, and read books without being beaten and harassed. For someone like me, jaded by the hypocrisy laid on top of our basic values, it is a shock to be reminded of the sweet virtues of political freedom.

At the end of the evening, I wish the students luck in trying to do journalism in a country that fears it. We retrieve our shoes at the door and walk down the alley one by one pretending not to know each other. I stroll among the lakeside cafés, still filled with people drinking beer, before hailing a taxi back to the city.

Dragon Politics

Nguyen Huy Thiep arrives for our meeting in a long-sleeved white shirt open at the neck, dark blue slacks, and sandals. His face is slicked with perspiration, and he apologizes for being late, explaining that he has just ridden fifteen kilometers on the hybrid bike that he peddles around Hanoi for exercise, even on a day when the temperatures are in the nineties, with humidity to match. Thiep presents me with a couple of Vietnamese magazines, their pages open to articles he has written about how he came to publish his famous story "The General Retires." I sense that these articles represent a happy turn in his life. After thirty years of living in Vietnam's political deep freeze, he is finally seeing a ray of sunshine.

Thiep has the high cheekbones of a northerner, in a face that remains unlined and puckish at sixty-five. He smiles easily. He gets the joke. Imagine Picasso transplanted from the Riviera to

Hanoi and given brown, glancing eyes. Thiep speaks in rolling sentences that stretch back eight hundred years to the time when Cham slaves were brought north to Hanoi, where they settled in Thiep's ancestral village on the outskirts of the city and introduced the Buddhism that Thiep's mother and then Thiep himself began to practice. I notice that Thiep, under his thatch of silver-brown hair, possesses the large ropy earlobes that are known to Vietnamese as "Buddha ears."

Thiep was a leading figure of the Renovation movement of the 1980s. Although he may not be as well known outside the country as Bao Ninh or Duong Thu Huong, he is Vietnam's most famous author. He is the country's preeminent literary stylist and the creator of a kind of multifaceted storytelling that instantly catapulted Vietnamese literature from socialist realism to modernism. After Thiep appeared on the scene, no one could write the way they had written before. He redefined the canon, as month after month he published stories that became instant classics.

Thiep began his meteoric career in 1987, and already by 1988 he had published his collected works and celebrated what everyone was calling "the year of Nguyen Huy Thiep." In 1989, a film version of "The General Retires" was released, and by 1990 Thiep was installed as a member of the Writers Association. But that was also the year that copies of his works began disappearing from bookstores. *Nhan Dan,* the party newspaper, published two essays attacking Thiep, claiming that he had "betrayed the Vietnamese Revolution by toppling sacred heroes in Vietnamese history" and that he was "deceived by the chimera of pre-1975 Saigon." The denunciation campaign continued until 1991, when the police raided his house, carried off his books and manuscripts, and provoked a turning point in his life. The moment also marked a turning point in Vietnamese literature, when the country's brief, five-year experiment with Renovation reverted to the dark age that persists today.

"I want to lead a normal life," says Thiep, repeating what I have come to recognize as the mantra of every Vietnamese artist and writer who is hoping to avoid prison. "I am not comfortable with political figures. It is the tradition for people here to stay away from politics."

I have arranged to spend the afternoon with Thiep at Nhan Café, his favorite meeting place in the city. This hangout for artists and writers occupies a building near the Lake of the Redeemed Sword in the historic center of Hanoi. To recover from his twenty-minute ride from the suburbs, Thiep orders a mixture of kudzu powder and water, which is believed to be good for cooling overheated bodies.

"My family history was the inspiration for 'The General Retires,'" he says. "My grandfather had two wives. The second wife was cruel, like the wife in the story. She was so cruel that my father was forced to leave the north and move to Saigon. He worked for the Chinese community and then went to college to study engineering. He got a job as a supervisor on the colonial railroad, where he specialized in building bridges and roads. The French paid him well. He stayed in the south until 1945, when he joined the revolutionary forces and went to live in the northwest, where he worked for the court. He was a high-ranking official, who rode a horse and wore a white suit."

Thiep mentions that his father got into trouble for demanding that a chain gang of prisoners be released. This incident reappears in another one of Thiep's stories. His family is one of the oldest in Hanoi, he says. They can trace their lineage back eight hundred years but began losing their land, piece by piece, during Vietnam's twentieth-century wars. Eventually they had nothing left, until one parcel—a garden plot outside Hanoi, where the family used to go for breaks from the city heat—was returned to them in 1960. This is where Thiep lives today.

I realize that I am talking to an aristocrat on a bicycle, an old Hanoian who rolls around town like a market vendor, except that his bike is an expensive hybrid with pebbled tires. But none of the biographical material that I have read about Thiep mentions his father on horseback or the white suit. It discusses only his mother and how she was forced during the American war to leave the city and live as a peasant in the countryside.

Having seen a photo shot by a mutual friend, I know that a giant sculpture of Buddha presides over the garden at Thiep's house. "I built the Buddha in 1991," he says. "I built it when I got in trouble. It was my reaction to the government. It took three and a half months to build the statue and cost as much as a house. Religion helped me balance the conflicts that were swirling around me."

I ask him to explain. "In 1991 the police raided my house," Thiep says. "They took all my books and writings and accused me of destroying the success of socialism. I was interrogated for ten days in a row. They treated me like a dissident. I was shocked. This was a wake-up call for me."

Doi moi, Vietnam's brief experiment with *perestroika,* was over. "This is when the government started terrorizing authors in Vietnam," he tells me. "I realized my work might affect my family. They called me a traitor. They treated me like a political dissident. I decided to go slow. I would pause in my writing. The risks were too great.

"I didn't stop writing, but I stopped being naïve," he says. "I would write more cautiously. I would tame my writing. I would be more careful. I changed my subjects and my language. Before I was eccentric and arrogant. Now I would be more circumspect."

Thiep began writing obscure essays on Buddhism and cloaking his statements in esoteric thought. "I decided to write more upbeat stories, brighter stories," he says.

I ask if the culture police returned his books and manuscripts. "No, they did not. They were rubbish anyway," he says of his early writings.

I pause for a moment, before remembering that Thiep is speaking about his stories published before 1991—in other words, about the stories for which he is famous.

"Politics in the East is like a dragon," he says. "When it's happy, you can play with it, but when it gets angry, it may eat you alive."

He returns to talking about the Buddha in his garden. "Writing is like a religion. Writers sit in meditation. You have to keep your religious mind. You get hurt if you lose your contemplative mind."

When Thiep visited the United States in 1998, many people who turned out to meet the great author were disappointed. He was so arcane and convoluted in his philosophizing that his translators got lost. The deeper Thiep allowed his mind to float into Buddhist abstractions, the more the censors had won.

I steer the conversation back to his early career. "Before 1991 I wrote from instinct," he says. "I loved to write as a child, although my father opposed my becoming a writer." Thiep's literary background mixes Chinese classics with French literature and Vietnamese folktales, which Thiep heard during a decade spent living in Vietnam's northwestern mountains. "I wanted to combine eastern and western culture," he says of an *oeuvre* that includes fifty short stories, seven full-length plays, numerous essays, three films, and a novel published in French, *A Nos Vingt Ans*.

I Censored the Content Myself

Thiep was raised by a Buddhist mother, a maternal grandfather who introduced him to Chinese literature, and other teachers, including a Catholic priest and his professors at Hanoi's Teacher Training College, where he studied history. After graduating in 1970, he was sent to live among the Hmong and other ethnic minorities in Vietnam's northwestern mountains. He stayed there for a decade, teaching remedial classes to communist cadres. He enjoyed learning about the spirit-filled world of the mountain people, and apparently they appreciated learning about *his* mythic world. Thiep's teaching method consisted of borrowing books from a provincial library that had been evacuated to the mountains for safekeeping. He read widely in world literature and history and then told stories about these books to his students. In what must have been fabulous lectures, he mixed Dostoevsky and Camus with tomes on economics and philosophy. Thiep didn't need to borrow magical realism. He was living it.

In 1980, Thiep was driven out of the jungle by hunger and boredom. He worked for another seven years as a painter, a stonemason, and a black marketeer before getting his first story published in *Literature and* Art, the official journal of the Vietnam Writers Association. "In 1986, the social conditions in Vietnam were bad," he says. "Society was chaotic and poor. As it lost support from the Soviet Union, Vietnam opened to the outside world. It became easier to write. Before 1986, writers had been arrested. But after 1986 and the onset of *doi moi* there was an opening in society and writing became possible."

"I was lucky. My timing was right," Thiep says of his first story, published in 1987. "I hit at just the right moment. I wrote from instinct. I wrote for the joy of it. People waited for my stories to come out."

He is animated as he talks. He smiles and laughs and stomps his foot for emphasis. He seems smitten by my young assistant and quite pleased to spend the afternoon chatting with a charming young woman in his favorite café.

I ask Thiep if he had trouble getting his work published after his house was raided by the culture police. He answers, "Yes, after 1991 there was a secret command from the leadership. No one could mention my name or publish my work. My work had to be 'reviewed.' It took longer and longer to publish."

"I tried to adapt my writing to the social needs," he says. "I censored the content myself. Sometimes it was corrected by the editors. Often they were too enthusiastic or too creative, putting their comments on top of my stories. I had to accept that my stories would be censored by untutored people with no idea of what literature was about. Vietnamese literature was born in a revolutionary

Nguyen Huy Thiep, Hanoi, 2014.

era. It was used as a political tool, which makes it too ideological. It is not refined enough. It is very hard to be a writer in Vietnam."

Sharp Sword

As evening settles over the city, we decide to stretch our legs with a walk around Hoan Kiem Lake, which lies a few steps from the front door of the café. Thiep unchains his bike and pushes it beside him. The lakeshore is crowded with people at the end of the work day, meeting for lovers' assignations, playing Chinese chess, practicing Tai Chi, or strolling, like us, in the warm evening air.

As I stare across the water at a small temple that stands on the little green island marking the historic center of Hanoi, Thiep suggests that we cross the street. The traffic parts around us as we wade into the rush of motorbikes and cars. Thiep rolls his bicycle up to the door of a fancy new hotel, the Apricot, which is named after the Hanoi art gallery that financed this posh operation. The owner, who happens to be standing on the front steps, gives Thiep a royal welcome and invites us inside for a tour.

Thiep leaves his bicycle with the doorman. We enter a chandeliered lobby with a pianist tinkling at a grand piano and stroll past paintings of Vietnam's pastoral life. We ride the elevator to the second floor and walk back toward the front of the hotel. Here we find a series of glass display cases filled with dozens of white porcelain plates illustrated with bold blue drawings—self-portraits of Thiep, lines of poetry, pictures of people working in the fields, illustrations from Vietnamese myths and stories. A couple of plates show Thiep during a recent illness. One shows a woman burning books—an image from a folk tale about a doctor who has died and whose wife assumes that his writings are now worthless. Brushed onto the back of the plates in flowing cursive are excerpts from Thiep's journals or thoughts or comments on his everyday life.

Now I realize the source of Thiep's puckish grin. Blocked by the censors from telling stories, our local Picasso survives by making dishes. He has made other kinds of dishes as well. For many years, he owned a popular restaurant, Hoa Ban, on the banks of the Red River. Locals called the restaurant Kiem Sac, or "Sharp Sword," after one of Thiep's famous stories. But in Vietnamese slang, the term also means "to slash"—that is, "to overcharge."

I ask the owner of the Apricot if Thiep's porcelain plates are part of the hotel's permanent collection or if they are for sale. "That depends on the price," he says.

Remedial Classes for the Cadre

Nguyen Huy Thiep's most incendiary work is a trilogy of stories, set in the 1800s: "A Sharp Sword," "Fired Gold," and "Chastity." The stories animate characters from Vietnamese history. By reducing these figures to human scale, Thiep reveals their brutality and weakness. In "Fired Gold," Phang, the mercenary soldier who narrates the stories, concludes that Vietnam "is like a virgin girl raped by Chinese civilization. The girl simultaneously enjoys, despises, and is humiliated by the rape."

Phang tells us that the child of this rape is Nguyen Du, the famous poet who penned Vietnam's national epic, The Tale of Kieu which itself is a tale of rape. Kieu tells the story of a young girl who prostitutes herself in China to save her father from debtors' prison. "Nguyen Du is the child of this virgin girl, and the blood that flows through his veins is laced with the qualities of the brutal man who raped his mother," says the narrator.

This attack on Vietnam's national poet shocked Thiep's readers, but Thiep thought he was merely pointing out the obvious. Isn't it strange that Vietnam's national epic, which every Vietnamese schoolchild learns by heart, tells the story of a girl who is sold into prostitution in China? "The Vietnamese community suffers from an inferiority complex," says Phang. "How small it is next to Chinese civilization, a civilization equally glorious, vile, and ruthless."

Thiep's first and most famous story—"The General Retires," the one he published in *Literature and Art* in 1987—tells the tale of an old warrior, unfit for life in modern Vietnam, who returns to his military unit to die. The mercenary nature of contemporary Vietnam is exemplified by the general's daughter-in-law, Thuy, a character drawn from Thiep's own family history. Thuy is a "modern woman," a doctor at a maternity hospital, who spirits aborted fetuses out of her clinic to feed to the Alsatian guard dogs that she raises to sell on the black market. Caught in the middle of this domestic drama is the general's hapless son, who tries to navigate, unsuccessfully, between his wife's commercial instincts and his father's outdated moral code.

This provocative tale was published only because Nguyen Ngoc, the newly appointed editor of *Literature and Art*, found it in the magazine's slush pile and dared to print it. After working in obscurity for a decade, Thiep had several more stories ready to go, and Ngoc rapidly published as many as he could, until he was fired in 1988. This marked the beginning of the end for Vietnam's brief cultural efflorescence, and soon the cultural police came for Thiep himself.

In 2008, twenty years after he was sacked, Ngoc published an essay about contemporary Vietnamese literature in the *Journal of Vietnamese Studies*. He says that postwar Vietnam produced three great writers: Bao Ninh, who no longer publishes novels; Pham Thi Hoai, who lives in exile in Berlin; and Nguyen Huy Thiep, whose life is currently devoted to Buddhist philosophy and making porcelain plates. Until Thiep arrived on the scene, Vietnamese literature was stuck in an endless rerun of socialist realist tales about brave soldiers and noble peasants. The audience was too bored to purchase such stories, and, as a result, *Literature and Art* decided to suspended publication because it no longer had enough money to buy paper and pay the printer.

The first thing Ngoc did as the magazine's new editor was to reconsider stories that had been rejected because they came "too near the burning issues of life." As soon as it hit the stands, "The General Retires" shoved socialist realism offstage. It introduced into Vietnamese literature modern subjects and the ambivalence of modern life. No longer was there one central point of view or moral authority. Now there was ambiguity and all the shadings and compromises of the present moment. Thiep had gone back to the past in Vietnamese literature, reinterpreted it, and catapulted it so far forward into the future that he managed to invent, in one fell swoop, all the literary forms that characterized Vietnam's Renovation in the 1980s. He told stories of everyday life that pushed the frame akilter so that revelatory gaps appeared in accepted reality. He reinterpreted Vietnamese folktales with a modern spin. But most shocking of all were the three historical narratives that led the culture police to raid his house.

Thiep's "work stirred up public opinion," says Ngoc, who saw his magazine's circulation skyrocket. "All writers, though they may not have said so openly, realized something very important: they could no longer write the way they had before." The stories upstaged what Ngoc calls Vietnam's "epic literature full of revolutionary lyricism." They led to new genres were being invented or reinvigorated, including "novelistic reportage," memoirs, nonfiction reports, and "a bumper crop of short stories." With the exception of works by Bao Ninh and Pham Thi Hoai, "the power of the novel to generalize about society remained very weak," says Ngoc. "Literature chose another genre to do the work that the novel was not yet able to do, a genre that by itself, as a result of its distinguishing characteristics, demands generalization: the short story."

"The writer who stands out the most is . . . still Nguyen Huy Thiep, and next to him, Pham Thi Hoai," says Ngoc. "Very early he began writing from many differing angles, using an approach so multifaceted that it often left readers stunned. . . . In the process he initiated in modern Vietnamese literature what we can call *a literature of self-questioning*. As a result, a breath of new vitality spread through Vietnamese literature, and from literature it entered society. . . . One can say that this is the first time in literature that the Vietnamese people have become so decisively engaged in self-revelation."

Ngoc admires Pham Thi Hoai, describing her as being "armed with a literary knowledge that is as sharp as a knife," but he is more reserved in his praise for Bao Ninh. Nonetheless, he acknowledges that Ninh's *The Sorrow of War* "was the first novel to speak differently about the recent war in Vietnam," viewing it not as a collective triumph but as a personal disaster for the shell-shocked individuals who survived Vietnam's thirty-year struggle for independence.

"Bao Ninh was the first to move beyond the monologue of the epic and achieve the dialogue of the novel," says Ngoc. So shocking was Ninh's confession about the social cost of Vietnam's wars against the French and Americans that a special session of the Writers Association was convened in August 1991 to lead a denunciation campaign against him. Ngoc himself had been fired two years earlier, in a purge that included editors at other newspapers and literary magazine and attacks on writers themselves. Duong Thu Huong and Pham Thi Hoai were sent into exile, while Bao Ninh and Nguyen Huy Thiep were forced into a kind of internal exile.

"Suddenly there was a prolonged pause, as both those involved and not involved searched for an explanation," says Ngoc. Because he is unable to talk about censorship and Vietnam's police state, he can only confirm that the country is suffering. "As far as literary production is concerned, these have been, generally speaking, lean times," he says. Literature has returned to being "a mouthpiece for orthodoxy. The creative climate has become sluggish, exhausted, and disjointed and so the leanness, the mediocrity, of literature is an obvious result." Vietnam has replaced modern literature with the memoirs of former generals, ennobling art by government hacks, and romances imported from the West.

"Some writers who were outstanding a few years back now appear to be 'out of breath,'" says Ngoc. "Nguyen Huy Thiep keeps repeating himself, even in short stories, a genre of which he has been the commanding general, and his experiments with the novel have clearly been failures. Bao Ninh has been almost completely silent."

As he casts about for explanations, Ngoc focuses on Vietnam's "decline in culture" and "failures in our system of education." He decries the "shallow" cultural knowledge of Vietnamese writers and the fact that "Vietnamese literature has been cut off from world literature for many decades." What he fails to mention, because he not allowed to, is the crushing weight of Vietnam's censorship regime and the vicious attacks on the country's journalists and artists. Vietnam's single-party police state has spent the past twenty years engineering the country's cultural landscape.

It has created a featureless, sterile wasteland almost completely devoid of art, instead giving the country over to commerce, kickbacks, bribery, money laundering, and the buying and selling of commodities—people included. Welcome to Aldous Huxley's Brave New World, created, in this case, not by *soma* but by the kind of totalitarian control borrowed from Orwell's 1984. What you get is a sunny police state, a mirthless whirl of color, a land with no memory and no future save for the eternal joke that is communism's promised paradise.

"Considering the social atmosphere and the state of literature itself, I don't think there is any basis for optimism," Ngoc concludes.

Restricted Area

Pham Hong Son was a medical doctor, a businessman, and a pharmaceutical rep making good money when he came to the realization that Vietnam should transition from a one-party state to a democracy with universal suffrage, representative government, and free and fair elections. He found what he thought was a good essay on the subject published on the website of the U.S embassy in Hanoi. He translated the essay and sent it to the prime minister of Vietnam, the president, the chairman of the National Assembly, and the secretary general of the Communist Party of Vietnam. Son was arrested in 2002 and sentenced to thirteen years in prison. He appealed but refused to speak in front of the court. His sentence was reduced to five years, followed by three years under house arrest.

Son went to prison. He served his time and still lives under tight surveillance. He works at home translating essays on democracy into Vietnamese. Today only five communist countries remain in the world: China, North Korea, Laos, Vietnam, and Cuba. Throwing out the bums, controlling the treasury, instituting the rule of law, protecting human rights—Son believes that none of this is possible with one-party rule. If he would stop talking about these issues, he could lead a quiet life, but he wants to lead a better life.

When he was a successful businessman, Son built a four-story house in a wealthy neighborhood on the shores of West Lake. Because property in Hanoi is taxed on street frontage, the house, designed in the traditional tube style, is tall and narrow. Normally, these houses dedicate their ground floors to workshops and commerce, but here on West Lake Son enters his house through a small garden. The garden is approached through a narrow alley, which is usually filled with plainclothes agents and uniformed police, who stand behind two red and white traffic signs mounted in concrete blocks. One sign says, in English, "Restricted Area, No Trespassing!" The other, written in both Vietnamese and English, shows a camera covered with a red X and around it the words "NO PICTURE TAKEN."

On the morning I visit Son, the police are absent, and their signs have been dragged to the side of the alley. I walk up to his front gate and ring the bell. The gate is opened almost immediately by a slender man dressed in gray trousers and a pinstriped shirt open at the neck. Son has lively, glancing eyes in a fine-boned face, and he greets me in fluent English. We kick off our shoes at the front door and walk upstairs to a western-style living room, with wicker chairs, a sofa, coffee table, and air conditioning. We look out through French doors onto a balcony where birds flit among the flowering plants. Son's wife comes in to serve us tea and pomelo slices.

I present Son with the two books that I have brought to Vietnam at his request: James Bryce's *The American Commonwealth* and T. H. Huxley's *Evolution and Ethics*. The gifts are partial repayment for a favor. When one of my essays on censorship was translated into Vietnamese and published on Pham Thi Hoai's website in Berlin, the translator, fearing reprisals, demanded that his work be withdrawn. Son stepped in and redid the translation, in record time. Since then, he and I have exchanged emails and discussed the likelihood of my being able to visit him. He was recently prevented from meeting with U.S. congresswoman Nancy Pelosi, but today I walk in with no problem.

"The police are gone because this week the chief of the Communist Party is meeting Barack Obama," Son says. "Vietnam's human rights record has got better over the past year, but, still, they harass and beat people. If we look at specific cases, the situation is no different, but they want the Trans-Pacific Partnership finalized."

"Vietnam has two or three hundred political prisoners," Son estimates. "I myself am a political prisoner. I am talking about people who have suffered from political injustice."

"Vietnam has a democracy movement, but it is not well organized," he says. "We have no leaders, no established organization, and the founders argue among themselves. They have turned into credulous fame-mongers and bickerers. They neglect the importance of mutual trust, which has been broken down by the communist regime. Today, we exist only on paper or online."

Son describes how the movement grew from the ideas of Hoang Minh Chinh, an associate of Ho Chi Minh's. Because Chinh wanted to steer the Vietnamese Communist Party away from its allegiance to China, he was imprisoned several times, but he continued advocating for democracy as well as fighting against corruption.

"Why is Vietnam afraid of democracy?" I ask.

"The answer is simple," Son says. "All power must belong to the Communist Party of Vietnam. A multiparty system would have to accept political and social pluralism, including a private press. This goes against the interests of the government, whose ambition is to keep control of everything, especially the country's economic affairs.

"Is democracy going to destroy the communist system?" Son asks. "We never said such a thing. We have never called for the destruction of the government. We want to establish the rule of law and make the government tolerant to freedom of the press and association. We have no other choice but democratization if we want to save our sovereignty in the face of China."

I ask him to tell me about his time in prison. "I got into trouble in March of 2002 when I translated an article on democracy and tried to spread something considered dangerous," he says. "I didn't think it was dangerous, and I certainly didn't think it would lead to my arrest. Everything I was doing was legal. I just wanted to share these useful views with other people."

"I was summoned to police headquarters and interrogated about my behavior and attitude. I never accepted their authority," he says. "I told them, 'No, I cannot give up this work.' I said this because I hate deception and being two-faced. I had discovered that the police had been very cunning in playing games with me. One of them, pretending to be an ordinary young man, had become a friend of mine. He was actually an informant, checking on me through regular meetings. On realizing his deceit, I became indignant, and that's when I told the police that I would not stop translating documents and contacting other dissidents. I wonder now if it was the right response, but I was angry."

Son was following the example of other dissidents who have been arrested and refused to acknowledge the legitimacy of the state. "I was charged under article 80 of the penal code, which deals with espionage. It has three sections, and I was accused of violating the most dangerous of the three, relating to foreign espionage, because of my contacts with people in Australia, the United States, and France.

"I insisted that I wanted nothing more dangerous than to change my country by peaceful means. This is why I have been criticized by people, for being too soft in my dealings with the Communist Party.

"I had studied French philosophy and literature. I had attended a two-year MBA program with lectures given in French, mainly by French professors. I had prepared myself. I was ready to face my sentence. I knew the punishment would be harsh. I was thirty-four years old in 2002, and when I got out of prison, my young son

Pham Hong Son, Hanoi, 2014.

would already be in university. I pleaded my own case before the court. This was a message to the outside world that I was confident in my rights."

After his conviction, Son appealed and was put on trial for a second time. "My will was unchanged. I was in detention, cut off from the outside world, and I had only fifteen days to make an appeal. The hearing was held without me. I boycotted it."

Like other prominent dissidents, including the novelist Duong Thu Huong, Son was incarcerated in B14, a Hanoi prison that held American pilots during the Vietnam War. Then he was sent to two prisons south of Hanoi, where he was held in solitary confinement. "I was always isolated during my five years in prison, in a bare cell with no pen or paper."

Son's case was taken up as an international cause by many human rights groups. "In Vietnam there is no rule of law," he says.

"We have a lot of laws, but the enforcement is arbitrary. The government does only what is profitable for the government. Here people only play the game with each other."

Martial Arts

When I ask him about his family background, Son tells me that the two important people in his life were his father and brother. His father, born in 1926, was a revolutionary hooligan. "He was in charge of assassinating many people. Before 1956, his job was to kill opponents of the Vietnamese Communist Party.

"He faced his own irony," Son says. "Even though he had many medals from the Communist Party of Vietnam, he was sentenced by the government for his crimes to life in prison. I was five years old in 1973 when he was sentenced. I think my father was wrong. He was an alcoholic. He lost control and went on rampages. He was a man of impulse, trapped between his nature and the demands of the party.

"I decided to compensate for my father's faults He had done inhuman things to human beings. I would balance this out by becoming a doctor."

Son followed his older brother to medical college in Hanoi, but he found that he didn't enjoy the work and never practiced medicine. "Vietnamese doctors suffer from poor working conditions and poor wages," he says. "I couldn't care for patients under these circumstances." While he was figuring out what to do with his life, Son taught himself French. "In 1992, foreign companies began flooding into Vietnam. I went to work for one of them, a French pharmaceutical company. I lived quite well. I bought a motorbike. In two years I bought a house. I decided to go back to school and get an MBA. I got married. I got a much better job. Then I built this house."

Between the birth of his sons, in 1997 and 1999, Son taught himself English and opened a foreign language bookshop that he ran in his spare time. "I changed a lot when I saw how to manage a company in the western style," he says. "I was exposed to western freedom and democracy. Democracy is just a better way to manage corporate structures. I was exposed to human values about protecting the environment, saving energy, solving the problem of corruption, becoming more compassionate."

He tells a story about himself, about how, when he was young, he willed himself to become a better person. "I had a head injury when I was young. I stuttered and became a timid person. I practiced martial arts to change my personality, make myself more brave and confident. I overcame my fears."

When Son started translating essays on democracy and sending them to government officials, his friends and family thought he was crazy. Why would a successful businessman with a wife and children living in a nice house on West Lake put his life in jeopardy? Son thought he was acting for the public good, doing something quite normal.

"No one supported me when I took my stand for democracy— not even my wife," he says. "My family was very angry with me. My older brother was the most critical. Now he supports me," says Son. So do his wife and other family members, who eventually understood what he was doing.

"I haven't worked since I was arrested. The government has signaled people not to hire me. My wife supports me. She has a job with a French cultural organization, and I earn money from small jobs, such as translating. I can't live in fear. One has to live with confidence that one can raise one's voice."

We talk about the essay that Son translated for me and the firestorm of criticism that it provoked on Vietnamese websites. "I was quite disappointed that the people opposed to censorship chose to be silent," he says. "I thought more people would engage in the debate."

Son himself is backing away from his role as a public protestor involved in demonstrations and vigils. "A year ago I decided to withdraw from that activity. I will devote myself to more serious study. I must learn as much as possible about western cultures. The concept of freedom has come from the West, not from Asia. We have to study history. This might take my whole lifetime. I am nearly fifty. I may not have much time left."

Just as he overcame his head injury through martial arts, Son has managed to overcome his imprisonment. "I learned how to read books when I was in prison," he says. "When I was working, I had no time to read, but in prison I could finally read a book without distraction.

"At first I wasn't allowed to receive books, but I went on a hunger strike and the NGOs applied pressure, and finally I was able to get them. My most important book in prison was The *Oxford Advanced Learner's Encyclopedic Dictionary*."

Son walks to a bookshelf and pulls out a well-thumbed volume that he must have come close to memorizing during his time in prison. "I have to thank the wardens for allowing this book to be sent to me," he says.

We end the morning with a tour of his house, mounting floor by floor past bedrooms and his study before emerging onto a rooftop with a view over West Lake. We stare through the midday haze and chat with his wife, who is hanging the family laundry out to dry. Eventually, we descend into the garden. Son opens the gate and walks me down the alley that leads out to the street. We stop to look at the signs that barricade the entrance but that today are pushed to the side. I snap a picture of the sign saying "NO PICTURE TAKEN" and joke about taking another shot with Son in the frame. He shakes his head no. "People say the police in Vietnam are stupid. This is not true. They are very, very smart," he says, tapping his head, to show me that they play games with your mind.

CHAPTER VII

Shiva the Destroyer

Taking a break from Hanoi's summer heat, I travel to Hoi An, the old silk route entrepôt on Vietnam's central coast. I reach Hoi An by flying into Danang and driving twenty miles south. The route parallels what used to be called China Beach, a famous stretch of sand where the U.S. marines landed in 1965 to start the American ground war in Vietnam. The beach was equally famous for military R&R with its pliant mama-sans and hardworking bar girls.

Today I discover that the beach no longer exists. While the ocean and sand are still there, my view of them is blocked by miles of fencing covered with pictures of five-star resorts, condos, golf clubs, and casinos. The beach has been divvied up, sold, leased, or otherwise carved into public-private entities. Some of these schemes were in the midst of construction when Vietnam's housing bubble burst in 2010 and the money disappeared. The money might return someday, but in the meantime the fencing is falling down, and the pictures of luxury condos are flapping in the wind.

Vietnam recorded a serious downturn in tourism following anti-Chinese riots in 2014, but this is not apparent when I get to the sixteenth-century port of Hoi An, which is swarming with visitors. The lure of the city lies in its old temples and guild halls, but they are obscured behind layers of tchotchke shops selling popup postcards and conical hats. This is another reason why tourists are skipping Vietnam. They have begun to notice that it is a culture without culture. Amusement parks are built on top of natural wonders. Old structures are "restored" by tearing them down and building replicas.

Other than visiting China Beach and Hoi An, my goal in central Vietnam is to explore the Cham temple complex at My Son, which is dedicated to Shiva the destroyer. For a thousand years these temples were the center of Hindu culture in Vietnam. Here the Kingdom of Champa flourished between the fourth and fourteenth centuries at a site that was said to rival Angkor Wat. Driving from the coastal plains into the mountains, far from even the smallest hamlets, my guide and I begin a steep climb into a forested valley surrounded by mountains. These green beacons once summoned Cham faithful from as far away as India. We turn into an empty parking lot and step out of our vehicle to explore Vietnam's largest collection of ancient ruins. Walking up a steep path, we come to a red sandstone tower decorated with dancing girls and elephant gods. Much of the sculpture on the tower has been defaced or chipped away. Weeds sprout from the crumbling facades, and the rest of the temple consists of little more than mounds of red-brick rubble and atomized statuary.

As we walk among the trees, trying to locate My Son's seventy towers—twenty of which still resemble towers—we find rows of bomb craters showing that the site was targeted by B-52s and raked with artillery shells from the An Hoa firebase, ten kilometers to the northwest. The rest of the site was destroyed by airborne sappers who were dropped from the sky to dynamite any buildings left standing. As I stare into the craters, evenly spaced in bombing runs that blasted temple after temple, I wonder if this destruction was an act of revenge or cultural genocide. Was it meant to restart Vietnamese history from American Year Zero? Informed sources later assure me that the temples were used as a

Viet Cong arms cache, and a VC radio antenna had been mounted on top of the tallest tower. The site had to be destroyed to save it.

Pearl of the Orient

"Officially known as Ho Chi Minh City, Saigon is a mess," writes the poet Linh Dinh in *The Deluge*, his book on contemporary Vietnamese literature. "Only three hundred years old, it is way overpopulated, its congestion broken up only by sewer-like rivers and creeks. Hung over from decades of wars and revolutions, it's a cocktail of unpredictable sights, noises, and smells, and has a raw, exasperating energy. There is nothing refined about Saigon. It'll hug you tight, molesting you, and won't let go until you either strangle or marry it."

Dinh was a twelve-year-old refugee when he left Vietnam in 1975. He worked in Philadelphia as a house cleaner and a window washer before emerging as a translator, a poet, an essayist, and a guide to Vietnamese culture, both in Vietnam—where he lived from 1999 to 2001—and in the Vietnamese diaspora. "Scooters, cyclos, careening vans, overloaded trucks, pushcarts and beggars on dollies swarm in streets from five in the morning until two at night," Dinh says of Saigon. "Its architecture is a moldy French/Vietnamese hybrid left over from Colonial times, mixed with no-nonsense box-like buildings from the 60's and 70's, American style, and slick new skyscrapers downtown. Soviet statuary mars its rare parks. Sly, crass, incoherent and frankly infatuated with all things foreign, Saigon mimics everyone and proclaims itself an original."

In terms of entrepreneurial verve and insouciance, southern Vietnam is more dynamic than the north. But if this difference is good for business, it does nothing for art and culture, which is even more ferociously suppressed in the south. Literature written before 1975, writers with vaguely Republican sentiments, Cochinchina's intelligentsia before the communists arrived on the

Linh Dinh, Philadelphia, 2015.

scene—this legacy has been wiped clean out of mind by Vietnam's historical amnesia.

Vietnam insists on a kind of Robespierrean purity in its historical studies. The clock begins with the communists. Certain emperors are considered proto-communists. Other emperors are dismissed as reactionaries. (Nguyen Huy Thiep got into trouble when his stories confused the brutality of the proto-communists with the brutality of the reactionaries.) The scorecard is dictated by the culture police. Historical research begins with ideology. Facts are employed merely to confirm this ideology. Facts that contradict the party line are dismissed, and publication of these facts is a treasonable offense.

Because history is the most politicized and dangerous subject in Vietnam, only one graduating high school student had the temerity to present himself as a candidate in history at this year's exams in Nghe An province, the birthplace of Ho Chi Minh. When he entered the exam room, Pham Xuan Hai found himself facing forty-eight examiners and eighteen guards and monitors. He passed his exam, but instead of going on to study history, he says he is dropping out to join the army.

A TV journalist who asked me not to use his real name, for fear of reprisals, described how he had to read books by French authors when he wanted to learn about Vietnam's recent history. Vietnam is not a culture of readers. While the country spends $3 billion a year on beer, the average Vietnamese reads 0.8 books per year. "I think this is the end result of obliterating history, censoring the news, faking up stories with bribes," says my journalist friend. "There are 24,300 Ph.D.s in Vietnam, a higher number than in Japan, but the country does no original research and has among the lowest levels of intellectual productivity. After *Fifty Shades of Grey* was published, what was already a flood of trashy novels—what we call 'Chinese rubbish novels'—became a torrent. These romantic novels are mostly about love between a perfect man and a clumsy girl or between two perfect men. (Young girls in Vietnam go crazy for gay couples.) In the past, these novels avoided explicitly erotic scenes. Oriental culture dictated discretion. But thanks to the American influence, we are now having our *Fifty Shades* moment, with trashy erotic novels becoming our primary cultural product."

Saigon is building a new university, the Fulbright University of Vietnam, which will be the country's first private institution of higher education. Affiliated with Harvard University's Kennedy School, it will open in 2017. The school is supposed to have airtight guarantees of academic freedom, although this might be hard to accomplish, given that its first $20 million in funding is coming from the Vietnamese government.

Very few people know this fact because the origin of the money has been obscured. In 2000, the Vietnamese government, desperate for normalized relations, agreed to "repay" the United States

$5 million a year for debts incurred by the Republic of Vietnam—a country that, by then, had not existed for twenty-five years. To make the deal less embarrassing, it was structured as a scholarship-for-debt program run by something called the Vietnam Education Foundation. The act of Congress that established the foundation describes it as an "independent U.S. federal government agency." This "agency" is financing the university by taking Vietnamese money, sending it to the United States, and then sending it back to Vietnam. "The Vietnamese government has agreed to the creation of this new private university on three conditions," someone involved in the project told me confidentially. The university will not teach history, law, or journalism."

In 2016, the university became embroiled in a scandal after naming Bob Kerrey, a former U.S. senator who is also a confessed war criminal, as chairman of its board. An exhibition at Saigon's War Remnants Museum describes how Kerrey, as a young naval officer, led a swift-boat raid on an isolated village in the Mekong Delta. He rounded up civilians (the drainpipe in which some of them were hiding is on display at the museum) and ordered the killing of twenty-one villagers, including women and children.

As reported by the *New York Times* (which was also responsible for forcing Kerrey's confession in 2001), his appointment as board chairman generated fierce opposition in Vietnam. "Please tell me the name of any prestigious university in this world, where a killer in cold blood of women and children—he admitted it and he is not charged for it—could be the president," wrote Bao Anh Thai, a lawyer in Ho Chi Minh City, in a Facebook post. "It is not about the Vietnam War, it is not about reconciliation between the two countries, it is a common sense of education. Would you send your children to a university like that?

Sometime in the spring of 2017, making no public announcement, Kerrey resigned as chairman of FUV's board of trustees.

Envelopes Full of Money

Corruption is the scourge of Vietnam. It is also the scourge of journalism in Vietnam. Information is not only censored but also trafficked, with people paying for coverage and placement, or paying not to be covered. Every column inch, whether for a news story or an advertisement, is sold. A person's natural reflex while being interviewed by a journalist is to stuff money into an envelope and hand it over.

"Once I phoned up the government's department of statistics, looking for some numbers for a story," a journalist friend told me. "When I went to pick up the data, the department head gave me four envelopes. 'What's this for?' I asked. He looked at me like I was an alien creature. Why would I be refusing money for my bosses and me?

"Everywhere I go on assignment people try to put money in my hands. Coverage at press conferences is bought. This is why my colleagues love to go to them. When I first began working as a journalist, I tried to refuse the envelopes, but my cameraman and other crew members glowered at me. They wanted their cut."

Master of Ceremonies

Nguyen Cong Khe is a demonstrative man who makes his points by thrusting his finger in the face of anyone who might have the temerity to disagree. When he calls the Vietnamese government cowardly for arresting bloggers and journalists, he does a lot of finger pointing. He wants the government to turn the press loose to do the kind of reporting that today in Vietnam is done only online. Vietnam has many good journalists, Khe argues, so why waste their talent on government propaganda, which no one believes, or drive them into the rumor-based, partisan world of blogging?

Khe is a hearty, round-faced, ebullient fellow whose office is decorated with photos of himself shaking hands with world leaders. There is Khe with Donald Trump and Nelson Mandela and Bill

Clinton. There is Khe with Trinh Cong Son (the Bob Dylan of Vietnam), and there are lots of photos of Khe presiding over beauty pageants, where the smiling master of ceremonies is dwarfed by the bikini-clad contestants who tower over him.

Today Khe is dressed in a dark suit and a tie, enlivened by a pink shirt. He keeps two cell phones at the ready, a silver one in his left hand and a gold one in his right. He uses the former to summon a photographer to snap our photo. This is insurance against the unlikely possibility that I become famous enough to hang between Donald Trump and Miss Universe.

Khe's office is really two offices, with the wall between them knocked down. One space holds his desk, and the other area has been converted to a salon with facing couches. Behind. Khe's couch is a curio cabinet filled with his Hero of Labor medal, wooden carvings of Thai dancing girls, a smiling Buddha, two golden bulls, and other awards from his service to the Vietnamese Communist Party. On the wall to my right is another curio cabinet. Here, framed and positioned at eye level, in a place of honor, is a November 19, 2014, editorial that Khe published in the *New York Times*.

"The Vietnamese government must allow the media to operate freely," Khe wrote in his opening paragraph. "This is essential to the country's continued economic and political liberalization, and to the Communist Party's efforts to regain the support of the people, which it needs for the sake of its own survival."

It may not be apparent, but Khe is himself a victim of Vietnam's culture police. In his case, rather than being beaten and thrown in jail, he was kicked upstairs to the boardroom. In 2008, he was fired as founding editor of *Thanh Nien,* one of Vietnam's two leading newspapers, and sent to edit a glossy magazine filled with advertisements from real estate developers. Every few months, he manages to slip into his magazine a short article exposing political corruption—which is what got him fired in the first place—but this is barely a whisper compared to his days as a crusading newspaperman.

Khe spent a half-dozen years pacing in his oversized office

until he sensed that the time was right to call for press freedom in Vietnam. "Vietnam's media landscape has changed significantly during the past five years, and the Communist Party has lost much of its control over the industry, with disastrous consequences," he wrote in his editorial.

"There are now hundreds of official media outlets, all owned by the government, and all controlled by the Ministry of Information and Communications and its local counterparts. All senior editors are appointed, after careful vetting, by the government and the Communist Party. Vietnam also has some quasi-private outlets, which produce TV shows, host online news portals and publish local versions of foreign magazines, like *Esquire* and *Cosmopolitan*. But private operators are required to partner with a state entity, which means that they, too, must be mindful of censorship.

"As the government continues to expand news categories it considers to be sensitive—relations with China, land disputes, the medical conditions of top leaders—many media companies are providing increasingly sanitized news. Readers, particularly young ones, have deserted them in droves, looking for less propaganda. Both circulation and the advertising revenues of the two most popular official dailies, *Tuoi Tre* and *Thanh Nien*, have dropped by almost two thirds since 2008, according to highly placed sources at these newspapers. Other publications have turned tabloid, featuring sensational scandals in an attempt to stem the reader hemorrhage.

"Instead the Vietnamese public is turning to foreign news sources, which are easily accessible online. Facebook and social media have also blossomed: Some intellectuals and former party members have their own blogs on which they openly criticize the government, attracting tens of thousands of visitors every day. Although the government has imposed internet firewalls, workarounds are well known and readily available. Vietnam has one of the highest rates of internet penetration among countries with comparable per capita incomes.

"But the emergence of alternative sources of information is a problem in its own right, because these are not uniformly reliable. The public, including the intelligentsia, has grown so distrustful of state media and the state itself that it is too quick to accept accounts criticizing the government as true, even when they are not well substantiated."

One hears in Khe's editorial the voice of the old newspaperman with ink in his veins. He doesn't trust news that comes from anywhere but a newsroom, and he regrets that Vietnam's once ubiquitous papers have become threadbare shadows of their former selves. He goes on to give examples of the country's unreliable media.

"A slew of books has been published in recent years claiming to reveal state secrets on virtually every major national issue: from the origins of the Communist Party to the epic battle against the French at Dien Bien Phu, from China's real designs on Vietnam to Ho Chi Minh's private life. The recent 'Den Cu,' by Tran Dinh, questions Uncle Ho's nationalist credentials. It also claims he was directly involved in the forced land redistribution program of 1953–56, which killed more than 170,000 people, and may have attended the show trial of some wealthy landowners.

"The party and the government tend not to refute such allegations. Instead, they insist on maintaining outdated forms of control and micromanaging trivial issues, like the depth of the decolletage on singers' dresses. This reflects their lack of confidence, and it undermines the party's credibility, including on vital national interests, like combating corruption and curbing China's regional ambitions."

Khe's editorial goes on to argue that Vietnam's press censorship hinders the country's fight against corruption. With the press muzzled, no one is blowing the whistle on theft at state-owned enterprises. "When senior officials and corporate chieftains are arrested for graft, the public presumes it is the result of factional score settling," he wrote.

People who get their news from blogs are susceptible to rumor-mongering, paranoia, and disinformation, the editorial argues. "The lack of media transparency has also been a problem in Vietnam's tussle with our centuries old enemy, China." The piece mentions the anti-Chinese riots that swept over Vietnam in the summer of 2014. China had moved an oil-drilling rig into Vietnam's offshore waters, which provoked the "extreme nationalism of anti-Chinese demonstrations and virulent online petitions." Many of these petitions cite something called the Chengdu meeting. At this secret gathering in Chengdu, China, in 1990, aimed at the ending of the Cambodian war, the Communist Party of Vietnam is believed to have sold itself to the Communist Party of China—swapping offshore oil, bauxite, and other natural resources for massive bribes.

"Alternative sources of information are not the antidote to state control of the mainstream media," wrote Khe. "They are welcome,

Nguyen Cong Khe, Ho Chi Minh City, 2014.

but they cannot be relied upon alone. Especially in Vietnam's existential fight against corruption and China, the traditional Vietnamese media must be allowed to freely disseminate timely and impartial information. Vietnam has many experienced journalists who have been cowed by censorship for too long and want nothing more but to do their jobs properly."

Good Party Man

"Freedom of the press is good for the country, and it is good for the regime," Khe's editorial concludes. A cynic would describe his call for press freedom as a last-ditch effort to get his old newspaper back into the game. The Facebookers and bloggers are eating him for lunch. A discredited press will not claw its way back to profitability. It will be lucky to survive on government subsidies and bribery, until the day arrives when *everyone* in Vietnam is getting the news online from former journalists turned bloggers or from bloggers who have never been journalists in the first place.

"Freedom of speech is the most basic and important right for human beings," Khe tells me. "A free press is even more important in developing countries. It helps people to raise their voices. In other parts of Asia, the Philippines, Singapore, leaders have chosen to use the press rather than block it."

I ask him to give me details. "There has been a dramatic decline in press circulation," he says. "Ten years ago, we used to sell 500,000 copies a day. Now we're down to 150,000 copies a day. There are eight hundred newspapers in Vietnam, including online papers. As the quantity increases, the quality declines."

"I started *Thanh Nien* in 1985 and worked as director for twenty-three years," he says. "We were freer to express opinions then. We played an important role in the development of the country. In 2008 the government started to attack the press. I was hoping to stop the huge amount of corruption that was blocking our development." Instead, he got fired. Other editors were sacked, and two journalists were sent to prison for "abusing democratic freedoms." They had discovered that the director of Vietnam's state-controlled road building company, PMU 18, had embezzled nearly $2 million to gamble on football matches and pay prostitutes.

"It was our idea to cover the PMU 18 scandal," Khe says. "We protected our sources. For the first time in the country's history, hundreds of newspaper directors were summoned to the Ministry of Police. Two reporters for *Thanh Nien* and *Tuoi Tre* were arrested. I wrote articles calling for their release. This is why I lost my job. The director of *Tuoi Tre* and I were fired. The order was given by the highest-ranking officials in the Politburo. The president of the country disagreed with the decision, but he was overruled."

"The Youth Union of the Vietnamese Communist Party controls the newspaper. There are no private newspapers in Vietnam, no private press," says Khe, who remains a good party man, even when calling for press freedom, which he sees as a strategic move that would actually strengthen the party.

"Blogs and Facebook can post rumors and false information. This is dangerous to the government," he tells me. "It is necessary to have a private press in Vietnam. It will happen someday. It is inevitable. We should apply laws rather than giving orders. I believe the country needs the rules of law, but the path from speech to action is very long."

Given its precipitous decline in circulation, how is the mouthpiece for communist youth staying in business? "We started a website in 2006, and today we are Vietnam's biggest online newspaper," Khe says. "We earn $15 million a year from the newspaper, and $2 million a year from the website. We earned $5 to 10 million dollars a year in profit at the height of the paper. Today we're lucky to earn a million dollars a year.

"With the current management of the press by the government, it is unavoidable that journalists will go to alternative media. More and more journalists are leaving the mainstream press. Hundreds of reporters have done this. Some of these bloggers are under surveillance. It is an arbitrary and chaotic system.

"I disagree with the arrest of bloggers. This is not a good move by the government. The government should be brave enough to use mainstream media to argue with the bloggers. The government is a stronger force. It is potentially more effective than the bloggers. The government should adapt and be brave enough to confront alternative media.

"The party, the state, and congress are all agreed on the fight against corruption, but they don't give us the means to do this. We need to restore the faith of the people in the government. Investigative journalism needs freedom of the press to survive. Bravery is the most important factor for a great reporter."

As my final question, I ask Khe about corruption, not of government officials but of journalists. His smile disappears. His finger stops wagging. "Press corruption and bribery, yes, they exist," he says. "This is a painful reality. *The* most painful reality in Vietnamese journalism—corruption of the press in Vietnam."

He and I sit in silence for a minute, pondering his confession, and then his silver and gold cell phones start ringing, both at the same time.

Netizen

One journalist who quit Vietnam's state-controlled press to become a blogger is Huynh Ngoc Chenh, a former editor at Khe's newspaper, *Thanh Nien*. "I consider myself arrested in a huge cage," Chenh says of his new job, which is riskier and far less lucrative than his old one. But he is not going back.

For my afternoon meeting with Chenh, I walk down Pasteur Street, one of Saigon's main boulevards, turn into an alley, and climb three flights of stairs to a café, where the stereo is playing Nina Simone's "Pastel Blues." The café is furnished with gray sofas with red cushions. I look around the room and then out the windows at the treetops blowing in the wind. The sky is darkening before an afternoon shower. Chenh enters from the balcony, where he was smoking a cigarette, introduces himself, and slouches into a chair at my table. With the seasoned look of a newspaperman, he scans the room. His glance projects a mixture of suspicion, disdain, and curiosity.

Chenh wears blue jeans and a purple tee shirt, with reading glasses draped at the neck. He sports a chin beard and a floppy silver watch, and he has the creased face of a man who smokes too much. In 2013, Reporters Without Borders named him "Netizen of the Year." This honor, co-sponsored by Google, goes to a journalist who has opted out of mainline publishing to do his reporting online. Chenh tells me that now, a year after receiving his award, things are not going so well.

"I'm discouraged," he says. "I'm posting fewer articles. The government is blocking blogs and throwing up firewalls. Sometimes they lower the speed of the internet, and sometimes they shut it down completely, claiming that a shark bit the cable or some other natural disaster took place."

"Lately I've switched to using Facebook," he tells me. "It's much easier. Facebook is a huge newspaper for the Vietnamese. It's where we post sensitive information and get our news. It's 50 percent reliable. The rest is gossip and rumor."

Chenh has 17,000 followers and another 5,000 friends, for a total circulation of 22,000 daily readers. "Celebrities have a lot more, in the millions, but I rank in the top two or three among political commentators," he says.

When I ask him what he did as editor at *Thanh Nien*, he tells me that a big part of his workday was enforcing political dogma. "It was my job to scan and check articles. Now I write commentary. Of course, I prefer this kind of writing. Before, I represented the government and the newspaper. I was the censor. That was what they paid me for."

"Every newspaper in Vietnam is under the control of the government," Chenh says. "They exercise strict control over the content. I wasn't a communist, which is why I couldn't become the newspaper's director. I was just the editor. The editorial board is in charge of ideology. I worked for the board.

"Every week, on Wednesday, the director of the paper went to a meeting with the Ideology and Propaganda Committee. There was another staff meeting on Friday where we got our instructions. We were told which political subjects were sensitive. We could write about sports and culture, but the sensitive stories we had to avoid.

"For example, incidents at sea involving the Chinese, where they shot at Vietnamese fishing boats—we had to avoid these subjects. Currently, we have to avoid talking about street protests and farmers getting displaced from their land.

"Because of this kind of censorship I decided to leave *Thanh Nien* and write about these subjects. The press in Vietnam is completely different from what it is in the West. Here, only the state can run newspapers."

I ask Chenh where he gets his news. "I get information from friends," he tells me. "I find pieces of news buried in state papers. Demonstrators send me photos. Fishermen call me on the phone. Facebook is another source. I work at home. I'm divorced, so my wife can't complain about my taking up too much space or working all the time."

"How often do you get into trouble with the police?" I ask.

"In the past year I have been summoned to police interrogations six times," he says. "Many of my friends have been arrested. I'm an experienced journalist. I have evidence for my news. I make sure that what I write is legal. The last time I was summoned, I spent eight hours in the police station convincing them that I had done nothing illegal.

"Sometimes I have to compromise. I have to stop writing about certain topics, like fellow blogger Ba Sam, who is currently in jail.

Altogether, I know ten bloggers who have been arrested, and now the police have detained Nguyen Quang Lap, the writer, who they say has posted illegal articles."

"We are always prepared to be arrested anytime," Chenh says. "There are a hundred bloggers on the government list of people dangerous to the state, but there are *millions* of Facebook accounts. The government can't control all of us."

Born in 1952 in Danang, Chenh graduated from the university as a chemistry major and moved back to his native city to become a teacher. "After the war, in 1975, I realized the government was facing a lot of problems. I wrote some critical articles, some of which were published. In 1992, I dropped chemistry and switched to journalism. That's when I moved to Saigon and started working for *Thanh Nien*.

"Mr. Khe was my boss. He was fired because of the PMU 18 scandal. They removed him from directing the paper and made him president of the Thanh Nien Corporation. This is not a real position of power. *Thanh Nien* had joined the anticorruption movement, but we got caught in a factional fight."

I ask Chenh how he makes a living as a freelance journalist.

"I have a pension, and I make some money from my blog, although sometimes the government blocks the cable, stops the internet entirely, and not just a few sites," he says.

"I thought this was more common in China," I reply.

"The Chinese have created a walled garden, but that hasn't worked here in Vietnam," Chenh says. "The Chinese foresaw the popularity of the internet, but the Vietnamese were too slow and too late. The Vietnamese leadership was not aware of what was happening. They underestimated Facebook. They didn't know it was dangerous. Blogging flourished, becoming too strong for the government to block. The government tried to develop alternatives, but these projects failed completely.

"Facebook is also a place for business in Vietnam. It's used for advertising and for reaching customers. Everyone in the provinces uses Facebook, and all the government ministers have accounts."

Introduced in 2009, Facebook in Vietnam has another feature worth noting. It maintains a parallel universe of fake websites devoted to government officials. Every site is updated daily with biographical and other information, but nobody knows who is doing the updating or if they even live in Vietnam. Orbiting around the government like political doppelgängers, these ghost sites offer nothing direct by way of satire or commentary, but they are unnerving because of their obscure origins.

"Vietnam has a seat on the U.N. Human Rights Council," says Chenh. "Vietnam joins every international organization, but in reality none of these accords is applied in Vietnam. There's a difference between theory and reality. Our government is a dictatorship. They claim to be a democracy, which they have to say to engage in these organizations. We are a dictatorship pretending to be a democracy."

"They deny us our basic rights, freedom of speech, assembly, travel," he tells me. "But I'm just a journalist. I'm not a member of the democracy movement, although I want to stand by the people's side."

For Chenh to receive his Netizen award, he had to slip out of the country surreptitiously. The prize was announced only after he had crossed the border. He was harassed and detained on his return. His passport was seized, and he was blocked from leaving Vietnam when he later tried to travel to the United States.

"I consider myself arrested in a huge cage," he says. "Vietnam is full of people like me. On special occasions, the police follow me. On other occasions, I am blocked from leaving my house by security guards."

He tells me that reporting on corruption is still a prime subject, although hard to do in Vietnam, even without censorship and police surveillance. "There is no public registry for companies. In most of the corruption cases the press can't reveal anything. Evidence only comes from outside the country, when foreign

Shiva the Destroyer

investors are caught bribing Vietnamese officials. This information is revealed in the foreign press, but the press in Vietnam plays almost no role in the fight against corruption."

"I myself never received any envelopes full of money," he says. "My colleagues received huge amounts of money. Members of the editorial board get the largest bribes. The security forces, tax collectors, and the press—these are the most corrupt jobs in Vietnam. You receive small salaries and lead rich lives.

"The press is controlled by censors, corrupted by bribery, and completely unreliable. You have censorship pushing down from the top and bribery pushing up from the bottom to produce a press that's utterly corrupt.

"Most of the people I hired when I worked at *Thanh Nien* had not gone to journalism school. This school is called the Journalism and Propaganda University, and just from the name alone, you can tell the students are no good. We couldn't hire them. They were unqualified, and whenever we were forced to hire one of them, for political reasons, we had to begin all over, retraining them.

"Professors at the university have fake degrees and no real knowledge. Half the graduates can't find jobs. The other half only get hired because they pull strings. These are the ones we have to retrain. The important staff come from other fields. They were trained as lawyers, engineers, writers, and teachers.

"The press in Vietnam has seen a huge decline in circulation. There are seven hundred newspapers in Vietnam, but only ten or fewer are profitable. Circulation is declining day by day. Others survive only because they are supported by the government or the party.

"The strong papers, *Thanh Nien* and *Tuoi Tre*, used to sell 200,000 copies a day. Now they're down to a daily circulation of 120,000 to 150,000 per day."

I notice that Chenh's circulation figures are lower than those given by his former boss, but press circulation is tied to advertising revenue, which makes it a famously sensitive topic of conversation.

Huynh Ngoc Chen, Ho Chi Minh City, 2014.

"What are the three biggest subjects that the press isn't covering?" I ask.

"The sovereignty of Vietnam, mainly involving Chinese-Vietnamese relations," he says. "Democracy in Vietnam and human rights. There is also bauxite mining in the highlands. I opposed the project, but we lost that battle."

At the end of our conversation I ask Chenh if there is anything that he thinks is too sensitive for me to mention. "I have a small suggestion," he says. "You should go easy when talking about press corruption."

Leaving the Party

Pham Chi Dung leads the charge for press freedom in Vietnam, a position he assumed reluctantly because he was once a party official.

On July 4, 2014, a date chosen because it is Independence Day in the United States, Dung founded Vietnam's Independent Journalists Association, which now counts eighty-one brave souls as members.

We meet in the courtyard of his neighbor's house, which in the morning doubles as a café serving coffee and drinks. Along with a crying baby and a yapping dog, the space is filled with neatly dressed people on their way to work. The décor is half chic, half bricolage. Electrical wires sprout from junction boxes, while elsewhere flowerpots adorn the white and gray brick walls.

Dung is wearing creased green slacks and a green shirt rolled up at the sleeves. He is lean, with spindle-thin arms and the erect bearing of a former military man. He has a narrow face with a mustache, bowl-cut hair, and bangs on his forehead, which make him look younger than someone who is about to turn fifty. We sit at a table wedged between a statue of Buddha and a parked Honda Dream.

Nursing a glass of iced coffee, Dung lights a "Fine" cigarette and tells me that the alley leading into the cafe is usually blocked by plainclothes police. "Members of the Journalists Association have been beaten, and I am often prevented from meeting with foreigners," he says.

A few weeks ago, as he was dropping off his son at kindergarten, he was rushed by twenty policemen. "They handcuffed my hands behind my back, like a common criminal, and took me to the police station to be interrogated. This is the second time I have been arrested on the street, and I am summoned weekly to the police station. They demand that I disband the Independent Journalists Association and stop writing for the BBC."

"Vietnam's official journalists association is run by the government," he says. "Journalists are state employees. Their job is to valorize the party and spread state propaganda. They receive weekly orders on the stories they are allowed to run and how to cover them. Journalists who disobey will be fired or sent to prison. All publications are state-owned, and no independent media are allowed. In this system, there is no room for something called an 'independent' journalists association. Such a thing could only be an association of criminals, traitors, and would-be wreckers of social stability."

In fact, China has proposed a U.N. resolution aimed at banning groups such as Dung's. It, like Vietnam, wants to curb "the dissemination of information that incites terrorism, secessionism, or extremism or that undermines other countries' political, economic and social stability."

"I remain silent in the face of questioning," Dung says. "This can last from morning to evening. 'I will not say a word to you,' I tell them. 'I do not have to answer your questions. I have done nothing wrong. I write only the truth.'"

I ask Dung what he and his fellow journalists are trying to accomplish. "We are opposed to corruption and social inequality," he says. "We want a multiparty state, human rights, and civil society."

Dung was born in 1966 in Hanoi, where his father worked as a secretary to Vo Van Kiet, who emerged later as Vietnam's prime minister. In 1975, at the end of the war, his family moved south to Saigon, where Dung attended Le Quy Don—"the most expensive school for the rich." After graduating, he enrolled in the Institute of Military Technology, Vietnam's version of West Point.

"I was mainly taught in Russian," he says. "It's different today, when our educational system has given way to what the French call 'savage capitalism,' but back then our schooling was rigorous. I was strongest in chemistry and math. I loved reading books but was terrible in literature. I never imagined I would become a journalist. We have two phases in contemporary Vietnamese literature. From 1975 to 1990, we were dominated by the Russians. After 1990, western literature began coming into Vietnam, and Vietnamese writers began adopting western styles." Dung mentions Bao Ninh, Pham Thi Hoai, and Duong Thu Huong. "This is when my interest in literature began," he says.

After five years at the Institute of Military Technology, where many of his professors came from the Soviet Union, Dung graduated in 1989 as a second lieutenant specializing in logistics and military supply. "Altogether, I spent eight years in the military, including my five years at the institute," he says. As a souvenir from that time, Dung is missing part of the middle finger on his left hand.

"In 1992 I decided to leave the military and change to civilian life," he says. "I went to work for the People's Committee in Ho Chi Minh City, and then in 1994 I began working as assistant to Truong Tan Sang, who is currently the president of Vietnam."

"Would he help you if you got into trouble?" I ask.

"No, he would do nothing to defend me," Dung replies with a wry smile. "He would denounce me."

"For fifteen years, from 1997 to 2012, I worked as a national security analyst for the Communist Party. I also worked a freelance journalist for a variety of newspapers." Dung shows me the press card he was issued by the Cultural Information Department. I ask what benefits the card grants him. "You can avoid the traffic police," he says. "That's the only benefit."

"By 2011, I felt that corruption in Vietnam had reached unacceptable levels," he tells me. "I wrote articles about it, but no one would publish them. That's when I began writing for the Voice of America, Radio France, and the BBC. I wrote about Nguyen Tan Dung, the prime minister, and corruption.

"A year later the Ho Chi Minh City police arrested me. I was held in jail for five months. The party still considered me a 'comrade.' They tried to persuade me. I was released at the end of 2012. This is when my point of view changed dramatically. I realized the one-party system was no longer suitable for Vietnam.

"I decided to follow the democracy movement. I wrote more articles, and then, in 2014, I founded the Independent Journalists Association. To the government, I became a dissident. They no longer consider me a comrade."

In 2013 Dung resigned from the Communist Party of Vietnam. "I published a letter on the internet explaining what I was doing. The government demanded that the letter be withdrawn. The letter is still on the internet."

"The party today is nothing more than a protection racket for corrupt interests," he says. "It is no longer defending the people's interests."

Like Fish under the Blade

In China, someone like Dung would be incarcerated as an enemy of the state. "As Vietnam integrates into the bigger world, it can't act like the Chinese government," he says. "It can't block the internet. It can't suppress links, slow down access, and throw up firewalls. This has too big an effect on the economy. It cuts too deeply into profits. Vietnamese officials have shares in internet service providers. Google is blocked in China, but in Vietnam it is easy to access. Here we have power battles among officials, different factions exploiting media for their own ends."

Dung explains that Vietnam has two competing powers, the party and the state. Depending on who is in the ascendancy, a journalist can attach himself to one or another and be protected. "Generally, the party wants to block the internet, while the state wants to expand it, so long as it serves their interests."

Why did Vietnam fail to do what China did—build a parallel internet, replicating western services, under state control?

"Chinese officials think more strategically, more long-term," Dung says. "In 1989 Vietnam opened its doors to foreign investment. It had no plans on how to manage this investment. The focus was local. Each province or region had its own plan. Ten years later Vietnamese officials began to think nationally, but by then the internet had already been developed. This was another example of communist ignorance. They underestimated the power of the internet.

"In 2005, the internet began a rapid expansion in Vietnam, and it began serving democratic interests. Only then did officials get alarmed, but it was too late. They couldn't do anything without negatively affecting foreign investment. From 2005 to 2015, the government could only partially block the internet. China had their strategy. They had a domestic network in place from the beginning, but if Vietnam blocked Google and Facebook, the internet would collapse. Foreign investors would sue Vietnam in international court."

"The Vietnamese people are smart," Dung concludes. "The government is not."

Dung explains how Vietnam borrowed Chinese software and tried to emulate its model. In 2008 Vietnam launched a version of Baidu, China's Facebook. Everyone knew that the software was loaded with backdoors, tracking mechanisms, and code specialized in identity theft and censorship. "It failed two years later," says Dung. "It was boycotted by Vietnamese users."

I ask him about emails from dissidents, even those under house arrest, who seem to have free access to the internet. "This is the luck of the Vietnamese democrats, compared to our colleagues in China," he says. "Thanks to the internet we have a democracy movement in Vietnam. It's the most effective means for organizing. Telephones are not safe. Emails and Skype are safer."

I mention that none of the dissidents with whom I have been corresponding encrypt their messages. "I worked for six months with friends trying to encrypt my emails, but the police hacked them," Dung says. "We try to meet personally to exchange information. If they look at our emails, there is not much to discover."

"We are much better off than our colleagues in China," he tells me. "The current situation in China is like it was in Vietnam in 2005. They are arresting people, and the situation is getting worse under the current prime minister. In China, power focuses on one person, while in Vietnam, we have multiple power centers, or at least two, the party and the state. We have different interest groups. We have been decentralized throughout our history, even a thousand years ago, and that history is repeating itself in Vietnam."

Dung publishes two blogs, one called chandungquyenluc, or "Portrait of Power," which focuses on power struggles among party officials, and another, launched at the beginning of 2014, which focuses on political corruption. Needless to say, his former comrades are not pleased by his portraits.

"I am not allowed to travel outside the city," he says. "I can't go more than twenty kilometers from my house, and I'm always followed by four or five people."

"Are you prepared to go to prison?" I ask.

Dung nods. "Every one of us is prepared to go to prison," he says. "We are like fish under the blade, always ready to be arrested.

"Do you see any signs of progress?"

"Up until 2012, if you were arrested, you would get ten to fifteen years in prison. Now, thanks to international pressure on human rights, you get two to three years. Of course, it's a waste to sit in prison, but we don't have a choice.

"I have two sons, ages three and nine. My children have witnessed me harassed and stopped on the street and threatened by the police. My organization is the most influential civil organization in Vietnam. My name is on the top of the government black list."

Dung confirms what I have been told about corruption in Vietnam, which reaches to the top of the government and includes family members and clans. He tells me there is no corporate registry in Vietnam, no transparency regarding financial transactions or ownership. Information regarding these matters is secret, and revealing it is a crime. Hence, there is no paper trail, no documentation, no proof of malfeasance.

"We know the prime minister and his family are involved in various property dealings, where the government has forced peasants off their land. This is a big problem in Vietnam, dispossessed landowners—*dan oan*—who now number in the millions. But we have no proof of this. They bury the evidence. All we can do is describe the situation based on our observations. We write anti-corruption articles and are criticized. 'You write too sharply. Your influence is too great.'"

"Having evidence in my articles would make my situation worse," Dung says. 'The government would track down the sources of my evidence. In Vietnam we have no sense of western investigative reporting. Instead, we employ the French method of commenting on the news. Sometimes evidence leaks onto social media, but press freedom doesn't exist here."

"I went to a seminar in the Philippines on investigative reporting," he tells me. "The journalists from Vietnam had to admit that our press is so weak that we have no evidence. After my arrest, all my sources disappeared. We have no rules, no statutes, granting journalists access to information.

Pham Chi Dung, Ho Chi Minh City, 2014.

"We can't ask to see the corporate structure that shows how the prime minister's daughter owns a big housing project and lots of villas and estates outside Hanoi. The business records are hidden. This is why we want to build the laws of civil society in Vietnam.

"Censorship is dangerous in Vietnam, but self-censorship of the press is also very dangerous. Each journalist in Vietnam has his own self-censorship machine. I know that if I write another article about the prime minister, I will no longer be allowed to meet foreigners. I will be arrested. I can only criticize his policies, not his corruption."

All morning, people have been buzzing up the alley on their motorbikes and parking in front of the café. The crowd thins later in the morning, and then at noon a metal grill is rolled across the entrance and padlocked shut. The premises are closed, except to Dung, who is allowed to linger as long as he wants. The gate is unlocked for us when my translator and I slip into the alley and start walking toward the street where we can hail a taxi. I look back to see that Dung has untucked a pen from his shirt pocket and begun jotting notes for one of his daily dispatches.

CHAPTER VIII
Boiled—Steamed—Raw

On a warm evening in Saigon, the poet Ly Doi and I walk up a narrow flight of stairs to the roof of my hotel. We sit down on green plastic chairs and open a couple of beers. Staring at the boats on the Saigon River as the sun goes down, we discuss poetry and how writing it in Vietnam is dangerous enough to get you arrested. Doi is one of the four founders of Mo Mieng, the Open Mouth movement, which has been shocking Vietnam's bourgeoisie with surrealist, hip-hop, street-smart poetry since its founding in 2001.

Doi is an amiable man with a broad face, a mustache, and a mischievous grin. This evening he is wearing tan slacks, sandals, and an open-necked polo shirt. "They can arrest you for reading my poems in Vietnam," he says. The Open Mouth poets took their name from the Bible, he explains. "In the beginning was the word. God opened his mouth and spoke the world into existence. Words are the origin of the earth."

Doi supports himself as a freelance journalist for the newspaper *Culture and Sport*. "Every three months the security forces come to the paper to check on my work," he tells me. They limit the subjects he can write about. Nothing political. No cultural pronouncements. "We are summoned a lot by the police," he says of himself and his fellow Mo Mieng poets. "They try to get us fired from our jobs. The police told my landlady I was a dangerous character. I had to move four times. Sometimes I have 'accidents' on the road, with people running into me or knocking me down."

Doi's poetry is banned throughout Vietnam, and even his pen name is banned from appearing in print. (He publishes his journalism under his real name.) "It's hard for the government to arrest me," he says. "I'm just writing poetry. It would seem unreasonable to the public. They wouldn't understand that poetry is serious enough to get you arrested."

"The normal audience in Vietnam doesn't like our poetry," he tells me. "Poetry is supposed to be beautiful and rhythmic. People don't like poetry that's political. We use bad words, which is unacceptable in Vietnamese culture. Our poetry doesn't rhyme. We talk about bad things instead of beauty. This poetic tradition is borrowed from the West. It's really new in Vietnam."

The Open Mouth poets have read lots of Bukowski, Ferlinghetti, Ginsberg; French romantics such as Nerval; French symbolists such as Rimbaud and Verlaine; and French surrealists such as Breton, Aragon, and Eluard. It is a lucky break for Vietnamese literature that many of the surrealists, including the three just mentioned, were communists, even if only briefly. This allows their work to slip past the censors and circulate in Vietnam, where surrealism has been a major influence, particularly among the writers whom the culture police consider to be subversive.

"They practice literary vandalism," says the poet Linh Dinh of his Open Mouth colleagues. In *The Deluge*, his 2013 anthology of Vietnamese poetry, he writes, "Yes, sometimes they suck and say stupid things—who doesn't—but when they're on their game, they can also be brilliantly mad. Some applaud them as a turning point in Vietnamese poetry. Others sneer that they're all attitude and no substance. The Goethe Institut in Hanoi was intrigued enough to invite them to read in June 2005, only to have to cancel the event at the last minute under pressure from the Vietnamese authorities." Ly

Doi and his fellow poet Bui Chat were jailed for two days for passing out flyers at another canceled reading. As reported by the BBC, the Vietnamese government is on record as saying, "The poetry group Mo Mieng is not serious, with works that are downright obscene."

Here, translated into English by Kelly Morse and Nga L. H. Nguyen, is one of Ly Doi's more accessible works, "The Beggar of Hanoi":

> When I lived in Hanoi, by the door of the territorial headquarters where I worked was a beggar I'd toss some coins to before getting into my car with its tinted windows and imperial guard. One day, feeling that it was strange never to hear some "thank you," I looked carefully at the beggar. It was in this way, as I looked, that I realized the thing I'd mistakenly believed all this time to be a beggar was only a wooden pedestal, painted with care, upon which sat a bust carved in my likeness—the look crafty, the complexion ruddy and natural, the brain with termites eating holes through the rot.

Here is another example of Ly Doi's work, a section from Morse and Nguyen's translation of the poem "Boiled—Steamed—Raw," which satirizes Vietnamese culinary traditions:

> Life in Vietnam is best eaten boiled.
> They haven't found anything yet that the Vietnamese can't boil . . .
>
> Repeat after me:
>   Life in Vietnam is best eaten boiled.
>
> From boiled Honda motorbikes, property deeds, degrees, courtier titles
> From boiled food hygiene and safety, insurance
> From boiled intelligence, esthetics, culture, humanity
> From boiled human rights, liberty, ideology, spirituality
>
> They've yet to find a word that Vietnam can't boil

Repeat after me:
   Life in Vietnam is best eaten boiled.

From boiling to being boiled
All anyone thinks about is boiling
All households compete for Best Boilers
All professions boil with emulation . . .
The only reason why I myself am boiled: so as not to be boiled.

"Boiled—Steamed—Raw" was awarded the 2015 Gabo Prize for literature in translation and is described in the citation as a "biting trio of diatribes against many forms of repression and violence in present-day Vietnam."

In her introduction to Ly Doi's work, Morse wrote:

Vietnamese Publishing Law lists the following subjects as taboo. If a writer chooses to publish a piece that crosses these vague restrictions, there's a good chance he or she can expect a visit from the police, along with some combination of fines, job loss, surveillance, physical intimidation, or jail time. Since it is loaded language, I suggest substituting writing for wherever propaganda appears:

1. Propaganda against the Socialist Republic of Vietnam; destruction of the unity of all citizens.

2. Propaganda about or incitement towards war and aggression, causing rancor between the citizens and those of other countries; incitement towards violence; spread of reactionary ideology, depraved life styles, cruel acts, social evils and superstition, or destruction of good morals and customs.

3. Disclosure of secrets of the Party, State, military, defense, economics or external relations; disclosure of secrets from the private lives of individuals, and of other secrets as stipulated by law.

4. Distortion of historical facts; opposing the achievements of the revolution; offending citizens, great persons and heroes; slandering or harming the reputation of bodies and organizations or offending the honor and dignity of individuals.

"Ly Doi regularly breaks all these rules," Morse writes, "which is why his work is censored in Vietnam, and why for years he has been under surveillance and the victim of harassment by the Cultural Police. It is also why his poems are so interesting in contrast to most state-sanctioned work. Writing these poems has cost Ly Doi jobs, a steady place to live, and freedom of movement. And yet, he still keeps writing."

For the Open Mouth poets, "nothing is too base because everything has been debased," writes the American poet and essayist Hai-Dang Phan in his introduction to *The Deluge*. Phan says their nihilism is a reaction against three "targets": "the coercive aura of ancient Confucian teachings," "the absurd levels of corruption permeating Vietnamese society," and "the crass commercialism overtaking Vietnam." The country's hip-hop poets have created a tonic broth out of surrealism, street language, and cultural critique. Their verse mocks Vietnam's cultural czars and their own helplessness in the face of this deadening authority, which everyone around them seems to accept as ordinary and inevitable.

Garbage

Ly Doi was born in 1978 in Quang Nam province, the mountainous central part of Vietnam. His grandfather had gone north to fight for the communists. His father had gone south to fight for the republicans. After the war, his family was forced to spend a couple of hours every night receiving instruction in Marxist-Leninism. When he finished high school, Ly Doi moved to Saigon to study linguistics at the University of Social Sciences and Humanities. He graduated in 2001, which is also when he and three classmates founded the Open Mouth movement and began publishing their poetry in webzines and samizdats. That was also the year they emerged as Vietnam's foremost publishers of underground literature, an enterprise that for obvious reasons needs to remain obscure.

As night settles around us, we are joined on our Saigon rooftop by another Open Mouth poet, Bui Chat. Chat is a stocky man with a round, smiling face, a mustache, and a chin beard. He is an intellectual but looks like a midlevel weightlifter. Now thirty-five years old, he was born in Bien Hoa, outside Saigon, in an area settled by Catholic refugees, who, like his family, fled in 1954 from the communists in the north. His pen name is based on the words for two spices: one with a buttery taste, the other more acrid.

Chat presents me with a copy of his collection, *One-Rhyme Poems*, published in 2009. The book has a nicely glued perfect binding. The edges are a bit foxed, but otherwise the volume looks pretty good for a handmade book that is now six years old. Leafing through the pages, I stop to read a poem titled "Who?"

> I meet the communists
> Our brothers
> Who make us lose our memories
> Lose our own voices
> Lose things of value
> We possess but one thing
> Fear

I ask Chat to tell me about the two other Open Mouth poets, Khuc Duy and Nguyen Quan. Chat says that they have stopped writing to become monks, one Buddhist and one Catholic. To be certain that I have heard him correctly, I ask again about their becoming monks. Doi and Chat break into laughter.

"Depending on a slight variation in tone," Chat explains, "'to become a monk' can also mean 'to go to prison.'"

"I would like to become a monk myself," he says, by which he means he would like to go on a monastic retreat. But as the father of a six-month-old son, he is not likely to become a monk any time soon.

"I haven't done anything since university," Chat tells me. "I live with Mr. Ly Doi, who is 'the breadwinner' in the family." Chat spent three years in law school and graduated a year ago, but he never passed the English exam required to get his diploma.

Only after another round of questioning do I tease out of Chat the fact that he runs something called Giay Vun (Scrap Paper) Publishing, the largest samizdat publisher in Vietnam. Scrap Paper, which operates with photocopy machines and glue pots, was started in 2001 to distribute what the collective at the time called garbage poetry: poetry that was intentionally ungrammatical, ugly, shocking, and otherwise subversive in the eyes of the cultural commissars, who have been trying to put the publisher out of business ever since.

"We took our name from the fact that our publishing company had nothing on which to print books other than scrap paper," says Chat. Today he has print runs of 2,000 copies and a distribution network that stretches the length of Vietnam. The police are on to him, but he outsmarts them by scattering his stock around the city and making illegal books available first in the countryside and only later in Hanoi and Saigon, where they are more likely to be seized. "We are strategic about our publishing," he says. "It's hard for the police to withdraw a book after this kind of wide release."

Good Weather

Because it is illegal in Vietnam to sell banned books, Chat doesn't actually get paid for his work. He barters books, trades them, and otherwise keeps his publishing company running as a charitable enterprise. This explains why Doi is the breadwinner in the family.

"Scrap Paper is the first private publishing house in Vietnam. It has caused the most trouble," Chat says. "We have invested a lot of time in this." Vietnam is signatory to every international convention that allows for independent publishing companies, but these conventions—like others regarding human rights—are simply ignored.

"We used to store our books at home, but this became too dangerous," he says. "When the government started attacking publishing houses, we began working like guerrillas."

In 2011, Scrap Paper received the Freedom to Publish Award from the International Publishers Association. Announcement of the award was delayed until Chat had left Vietnam and flown to Argentina for the ceremony. On his return to Vietnam, he was arrested. Police seized his books and other materials, his computer, and passport. They even took his award.

"In Vietnam you can publish books, but you can't sell them," he says. He shows me Scrap Paper's latest publication, a nicely produced copy of Arthur Koestler's *Darkness at Noon*. Scrap Paper has started translating Koestler, Orwell, and other anticommunist writers from the 1950s. Vietnam is one of the few places in the world where this literature has lost none of its relevance.

"This book is very helpful to the Vietnamese," Chat says. "We translated *Animal Farm* and essays by Orwell and Václav Havel. During the past ten years, we have published fifty books. We use volunteer translators and a samizdat system of distribution. We time our releases to when the 'the weather is good,'" he explains, referring to momentary lulls in government censorship. "We do the opposite before 'sensitive' days, like September 2, which celebrates Independence Day in 1945, or Unification Day, which celebrates the end of the war in 1975, or right before the Communist Party General Assembly."

"Sometimes there are unexpected events and you accidentally publish a book that becomes sensitive, like a book with maps of the 'South China Sea,'" Chat says. "You have to check the political weather all the time, and sometimes the photocopy shops get scared. You can't really tell what's going to get you in trouble or when you'll get arrested."

"Do you practice self-censorship?" I ask.

"More or less, yes," he answers. "Our education system has brainwashed us. It takes more than a decade to get over this brainwashing. These people are really good at propaganda. This is the strength of the communists."

Recalling that he has lost two members of his poetry collective to monastic life, I ask Chat if more people are joining the Open Mouth movement. "The number of people like us? There are not very many," he says, "but we believe it is increasing day by day. Social media helps us. Vietnam's integration into international groups helps us.

"Recently twenty writers decided to quit the Writers Association. More and more writers in Vietnam are trying to change their point of view and expose themselves to the outside. We do our work. We don't indulge the government."

Sitting in the dark on our rooftop, watching the red-green lights of boats steaming up and down the river, we spend the rest of the evening talking about publishing in Vietnam. Chat tells me that the print run and sales figures for my recently published book are fake and that this is always the case with Vietnam's government-controlled publishers. "They say your book had a print run of 2,000 copies, but it really had a print run of 6,000 copies. Two thousand copies were reported, and the others were warehoused in case the book was seized, or they were sold to get the money to bribe the government for a publishing license." This helps to explain why I never knew when my book was actually published and never received any sales statements.

"They have to use the unreported copies to bribe officials," Chat says. "Most of the cost of book publishing goes to the government agency that issues the publishing license.

"Even a best-selling author like Thomas Friedman has an official print run of a thousand copies, and books with 'sensitive' content can be withdrawn at any time. Books are reprinted without telling authors, or they are sold in the black market, with no money going to the authors. The up side is that books get distributed.

Bui Chat and Ly Doi, Ho Chi Minh City, 2014.

They can be scanned and 'printed.' Sometimes the publishing files are 'leaked' from the printing company. Files can be stolen and taken to other publishers, or sometimes the entire book is retyped, which gives you better quality than scanning."

"The best time for selling books on the black market is when a book gets banned," he says. "That's when copies flood out onto the streets."

Huy Duc is the current model for book publishing in Vietnam. A former soldier and journalist, Duc wrote a two-volume history of the Vietnam War called *The Winning Side*. The book reveals, for example, how Vietnam's refugee flows were actually a money-making operation organized by communist officials. Duc published his book outside Vietnam. It is distributed by Amazon, but one finds many pirated copies for sale on the streets of Hanoi and Saigon. "A lot of parties joined hands to publish his book," Chat says. "The book is considered dangerous in Vietnam."

Night settles around us, and the streets seven stories below fall silent, except for the passing of an occasional motorbike, but we continue to talk late into the evening about how to escape the censors and publish samizdat books in Vietnam. "Please don't go into the details," Chat says. "The government is curious about how our books get distributed. We have to use a lot of different methods to get our books into the market. It would be helpful if you didn't make this too clear."

Pirates and Poetry

Nguyen Quoc Chanh has arrived early at the Morning Café and is already there by the time I climb the stairs and walk in. He is unusually tall for a Vietnamese, broad-shouldered and handsome, with a gray chin beard and a fine-featured face. He looks every inch the distinguished poet, and his partner, Thu-Huong Nguyen-Vo, who is wearing a calf-length black dress, has her own lanky charm. They make a striking couple, but Huong, a professor of Asian languages and cultures at the University of California in Los Angeles, can visit only during summer breaks and holidays, and their lives are unsettled, in large part because Chanh, who is Vietnam's leading poet, is no longer writing poetry.

He has decided that it's not worth the hassle, the interrogations, the nighttime visits from the police, the book bannings, and the blacklisting by reviewers. Nor is it worth being forced to publish overseas, which is a treasonable offense. "To be human is to be humiliated, to be Vietnamese is to be super humiliated," he writes in his poem "Disconnected Thoughts," which was published in one of his four volumes of poetry—two of them censored and pulped by the police, two others circulated only by internet and samizdat. Chanh's other banned book is a translation of T. S. Eliot's "The Waste Land."

Chanh was born in 1958 in Ca Mau, at the southern tip of Vietnam. His father, a northern Vietnamese who had joined the Viet Minh in 1943, had come south to fight the French. Billeted in the house of a landowner, he fell in love with his host's daughter and married her. "He and my mother had five children," Chanh says. "We were neglected by my father, who spent nine years in the Viet Minh and placed political commitment over family. I don't admire this decision. The path of the patriot is a wretched one."

Chanh's father was captured by the French in 1948 and sentenced to death. When his sentence was commuted to life in prison, he was shipped to the infamous tiger cages on the island of Poulo Condore. Instead of dying here, as many of his fellow prisoners did, Chanh's father managed to escape. While out on a woodcutting detail, he had fashioned a raft out of sap and cloth. After engineering a jail break, he set sail on this raft with a mixed crew of convicts and political prisoners. The leader of the convicts was Vo Tong, a strapping murderer who had named himself after a famous Chinese bandit known for killing tigers with his bare hands.

The escapees floated for a month in the South China Sea, surviving on urine, rainwater, and the blood of their less fortunate colleagues. While the crew was shipwrecked on a deserted island, Chanh's father heard that the convicts were planning to kill the political prisoners. He marched into Vo Tong's camp and challenged him to settle the matter. Chanh's father won the fight but later lost the war. After being rescued by fishermen and returned to shore, Chanh's father was arrested by the Viet Minh. He had been hoping to return to his military unit, but by then his commander, Nguyen Binh, had fallen out of favor with the communists.

"My father became leaderless after his general was killed," Chanh says.

Rather than valorizing his warrior father, Chanh takes a different lesson from his tale. "I thought patriotism extracted too big a price after I saw what had happened to my grandfather and my father. I was very wary of patriotism."

In 1969 Chanh's family moved to Long Khanh, a village northeast of Saigon, and Chanh, at age eleven, began school for the first time. "I saw my brothers and sisters being beaten in school. So I was afraid to go. I am afraid of all institutions, schools, hospitals, police stations. I prove Foucault's hypothesis that public institutions are sites of state control.

"I went to a Protestant school. I made forty mistakes in one page of dictation. I am still afraid of words. I am terrible at spelling, and I stutter. They kept jumping me from one grade to the next, because I was so old, and I had to be in school to stay out of the army.

"At the end of the war in 1975 I was in tenth grade. I stopped going to school for a year. That was when everyone was being moved out of the cities into New Economic Zones. We already lived in an NEZ. My family had cut down a plot in the forest to grow bananas, sugarcane, and tobacco, but I was sent back into the woods to clear more trees. I was working alongside city kids who had been moved into the jungles.

"My family was forced to 'donate' their land to the revolution. They had already lost all their land in the south, during the early phase of the revolution, and now they lost it again. I became a proletarian, unintentionally."

In 1979, Chanh was drafted into the army. "I could not avoid the fate of my father and grandfather," he says. "My unit was sent to fight in Cambodia. I got malaria and jaundice and was kept back. Many of my fellow soldiers were injured. They lost their legs to landmines or were wounded. They had nothing but tree leaves and roots for medicine. Only the officers got antibiotics. I saw the soldiers singing patriotic songs and thought this was scary. I had a nervous breakdown ['stomach ulcer' was the official diagnosis] and was discharged for health reasons."

Chanh enrolled in Saigon's University of Social Sciences and Humanities, this time excelling in his studies in literature. He graduated with high marks and was offered a lectureship at the university but was blocked from taking the post because his household registry, which listed an NEZ in the provinces as his residence, did not allow him to live in Saigon.

In 1990 he published his first book of poetry, *Night of the Rising Sun*. "The book was denounced as decadent, pessimistic, negative, and reactionary," he says. It was recalled and pulped. After being targeted in a denunciation campaign that called for his arrest, Chanh returned to Dong Nai province and went to work in a lumber mill owned by his brother. "I joined a band of illegal loggers to make more money," he tells me. "Madame Nhu—sister-in-law of the deposed South Vietnamese president—had cleared a vast area of jungle north of Saigon and planted it with teak wood. We went into this area at night and cut down her trees. This was done in the spirit of Marx and Robin Hood. We made five hundred dollars for every load. We did this for six months, until one of the team got shot. Then I bought some land. This is when I became what the French call a *rentier*, a petit bourgeois landowner."

In 1993, after marrying a former university classmate, a woman with a household registry in Saigon, Chanh moved back to the city. Four years later he published another collection of poems, *Inanimate Weather*. "This was written in a more roundabout way," he says. In other words, his political comments were more guarded and allusive.

Tre Publishing, the former cultural wing of the National Liberation Front, was his press, but his editors could do nothing to protect him from another denunciation campaign. The government blocked reviews of his work and any mention of his name. "I decided from this point on that I would publish only through online, unofficial channels and self-published samizdats," Chanh says. "I was the first poet in Vietnam to do this." Later, Scrap Paper Publishing and the Open Mouth poets would follow his lead.

Surreal

In 2001 Chanh published another poetry collection, *Of Metaphorical Identity*. "I just published my own stuff. I was the first to innovate, writing poetry on political and social issues and using street language," he says. "I didn't turn this into a movement. The younger poets gave it a wider following. I don't operate as part of any school or group. My relationship to society is problematic.

"My primary source is my social environment. My poetry has a lot of surrealist elements. Surrealism is appropriate for this social environment, which is full of contradictions. The environment gave rise to the surrealist language. The environment came first, not my borrowing from the West."

Chanh's poetry is also rich in scatological language, torrents of profanity that come from yet more "contradictions in the social environment." In this case, he is responding to being "bombarded by communist slogans and capitalist signs and symbols." The slogans are "commercial advertising," meant to imbue the populace "with visions of 'greatness' and 'plenitude.' Both of these contradict the everyday reality we live with. Political leaders and workers both use profanity. I'm trying to unite the two."

The denunciation campaigns and police harassment have continued unabated for the past twenty-five years. Every poem Chanh published meant a summons to the police station. "Security people would print out my poems. I had to sign every line they found problematic. They were using each line that I signed to build a case. They regularly visit in the middle of the night, knock on the door, and ask to check our household registration."

"Just last night, at midnight, we got a knock on the door. We were lying in bed reading your *New Yorker* article on Pham Xuan An. But by this point it's all political theater," he says.

"The latest crackdown began in 2008, after the summer Olympics in Beijing," Chanh tells me. "There was an earlier crackdown in 2006, right before Vietnam was allowed to join the World Trade Organization." That membership strengthened the political legitimacy of the communist government and allowed it to move with increasing ferocity against labor organizers and demonstrators, many of whom were arrested, right after Vietnam joined the trade group in 2007.

"By 2008, Vietnamese movements for self-expression had been reduced to nationalistic protests against the Chinese and what they were doing in the Spratly Islands and elsewhere in the Eastern Sea," Chanh says. "But there was a crackdown against these anti-Chinese demonstrations. The police started to round up dissident artists."

Remembering the fate of his father, he wanted nothing to do with patriotic demonstrations against the Chinese. "I was allergic to nationalism," he says. "So they put me in the third tier of threats to the state. Nationalism was the main reason to mobilize. Then came independent labor movements."

"Today, the pro-democracy movement in Vietnam has acquired anti-Chinese colors. The environmental movement is anti-Chinese. Protests over the Spratly and Paracel islands are anti-Chinese. Personally, I don't want to get imprisoned for being anti-Chinese. I wrote a poem about the communists in Vietnam and in China," says Chanh, who sees the two as indistinguishable. "It's a really obscene poem."

"I'm like a bullfighter," he tells me. "I alternate between being bored and scared. There's a significant amount of fear. I write at night. The sounds in the night always sound like the police knocking at the door. I live under a totalitarian government, ruled by fear. Poetry is an act of defiance against this fear. I cannot change the government. I can only fight my own fear. Fighting your fear is necessary for the act of writing. If you fear the government and you write with that fear, the government will allow you to publish. Only the fearless are prevented from publishing. Our first knowledge in Vietnam is the knowledge of fear."

Chanh admits that the police surveillance and interrogations, the blacklisting and nighttime knocks on the door have unnerved him. "I have decided to stop writing," he says. "It's a high-wire act. How do you fight your own fear and stay safe? In the last three years, I started working on becoming a sculptor."

After a residency at a sculpture studio in Bien Hoa, Chanh has begun making pottery in the style of that southern town, which lies on the outskirts of Saigon. "They have a particular tradition of pottery," he says. "It borrows from the Chinese, who migrated here in the seventeenth century. The Chinese tradition is mixed with the French to produce interesting glazes and new motifs. It's a very eclectic school."

"Now we have a house full of sculpture," says his partner, Huong. "He hasn't sold anything." Why? "No galleries can get a license to show his work, which is considered as dangerous as his poems."

"What are my choices?" says Chanh. "I could write for the market, or I could write anti-Chinese poems. These are the only two kinds of writing allowed in Vietnam today. Now even the Open Mouth poets are anti-Chinese. There has been a narrowing of our cultural views. The government is as repressive as it was in the 1990s, but the dissident writing is focused around nationalism rather than against totalitarianism. The state and the dissidents now share common ground. Everyone else has dissolved into factional fighting, with the bloggers caught between the faction of the prime minister, the faction of the president, and the faction of general secretary—all vying for power.

"The bloggers are fodder in the war. You can expose the corruption of one faction or another, but not all at once. This is like Kremlinology from the old days. It's like watching people fight under a rug. The prime minister controls the real money. He is pro-western and wants to be rich. The president is supported by intellectuals who oppose corruption, but he swings in the wind. The party secretary is nicknamed 'the Idiot,' but we know party members who are also very rich.

"I have extracted my lesson from history. The communists fought the capitalists for a hundred years, and then they turned into red capitalists. Whatever you fight against you become. This is why I don't want to fight the communists."

Marching Monks

I eat breakfast on the rooftop terrace of my hotel, looking out on the cargo boats that scuttle up and down the Saigon River. It was from perches like this that wartime reporters watched the surrounding countryside lit up with tracer rounds. Now, on the other side of the river, black-clad soldiers have been replaced by construction cranes that hover like praying mantises over the tops of Saigon's new tower blocks.

The terrace is outfitted with plastic tables, bamboo plants growing in pots, and a statue of Buddha presiding over a small fountain that flows into a concrete lotus leaf. A trellis shades me from the sun overhead, as the temperature creeps into the nineties and storm clouds gather on the horizon. It would be pleasant to linger here, but I have arranged to meet Chanh at his apartment, which doubles as his sculpture studio.

A taxi deposits me in front of a dilapidated building in District 1. I twist through a dark corridor and climb several flights of stairs before coming to Chanh's door. He and Huong welcome me into a stifling two-room apartment, where I wedge myself toward a seat at the kitchen table. Surrounding me are cardboard boxes piled to the ceiling, a motorcycle, overflowing bookshelves, and dozens of massive clay sculptures that look like human feet cut off below the knee. Actually, they *are* feet. Chanh explains that this series of spatulate-toed, earth-glazed sculptures was inspired by the monks who led Burma's 2007 Saffron Revolution. The room is chockablock with other sculptures—owls flying at night and mythical creatures, half-male, half-female—and even the table where I am seated is covered with smaller figures that I have to shove aside before I can set down a cup of tea.

Chanh is considered a dangerous artist, so art galleries, which need government licenses to show new work, will not exhibit his sculptures. He keeps making them, but even this room full of marching monks and mythical creatures is about to be taken away from him. He and his partner are being forced out. Although Chanh owns the apartment, which he bought with money earned during his logging days, eminent domain gives developers the right to evict him. They can make a lot of money from seizing a building like this, which is in a choice location, and so can the government officials who approve the deal. Chanh tells me that he is thinking of moving to Vung Tau, the coastal resort favored by the French when they ruled Vietnam. "Nobody knows me there," he says, "and I might be able to lead a quieter life, without any visits from the police."

Today, in his stifling apartment, Chanh is wearing a blue silk shirt and orange shorts, and a small fan next to the kitchen sink is blowing air in our direction. "You asked me yesterday about censorship and why I stopped writing. Huong," he says, gesturing toward his partner, who today is wearing a black top and white shorts, "told me I should give more revealing answers."

"I have been writing against the government from the 1990s to the mid-2000s," he tells me. "This is when the police reaction intensified. They called in my friends. I feared imprisonment. Government is a dogmatic truth. If you counteract dogma, then your writing becomes dogmatic. To counteract power, I was being transformed by that power.

"I was beating my head against the wall. It was creatively counterproductive. The police intimidation made me stop publishing online. The intimidation worked.

"At the same time, government censorship had failed. The government could no longer cross out lines and alter my work. So they switched to suppressing my work in its entirety.

"In the government tool bag they have direct censorship, permission to publish, and a larger set of repressive tools. In the 2000s, they switched to using these other tools, because of the rise of the internet.

"I had already reached the limits of poetry. Beyond that, I would have to become a soldier against the government. But the power was too lopsided. I would have to cease being a poet and become a militant.

"The government would isolate me and sanction me. They would take punitive measures, harass my family. My friends could no longer risk being my friends. The government would get you fired from your job and finally imprison you. The government power is too great.

"I feel defeated, but I also gained a life. My life was no longer reduced to reactions against the government and their repression.

"Am I a dissident? That's a word from the Soviet system. We are people fighting against an authoritarian system. We are critics of the government, opponents, offering resistance to communist authoritarianism.

"We are fighting party rule, which includes people who receive privileges from the government. Even if they criticize the government, they are sidestepping thorny issues and making the government look better. It also includes critics outside state privilege. They have to rely for protection on the cultural attachés at various western embassies. This is an insecure position to be in, having to rely on western powers.

"To be a critic of the government you have to go against global capital, the remnants of communism, and the organization of power in Vietnam. This resembles a mafia of organized crime.

"We have to resist these three sources of power in Vietnam, but our resistance is ineffective and pathetic. We sign petitions with two hundred signatures on them. People try to organize independent labor unions. One of them tries to shame the police by bringing her child to protests. This is both pitiful and ineffective. Then we have the support from western attachés and organizations. But what does this do for us? It turns us into tattletales who are always running to the western powers, asking them to save us. Again, this is both humiliating and ineffective. It gives the western powers too much power, which they don't always use well."

Nguyen Quoc Chanh, Ho Chi Minh City, 2014.

The Deluge

In his introduction to *The Deluge,* Hai-Dang Phan evaluates the work of Vietnam's contemporary poets. The best of them, he says, is Chanh, whom he praises for his "uncanny ability to invent a poetic language in Vietnamese that can still be heard in the cacophony of official language."

The Berlin Wall came down in 1989, and the Soviet Union disappeared soon thereafter. At the periphery of this collapsing world, Vietnam's communist rulers shook with fear, before realizing, after a couple of years of *doi moi* openness, that they could get back to cultural terrorism with impunity. Vietnam is a land, writes Phan, "where independent presses and journals are nonexistent, public poetry readings are broken up, Vietnamese literature written overseas [is] unacknowledged or derided, and where you can write whatever you want so long as you avoid politics."

Many of Chanh's poems were published in Berlin, on Pham Thi Hoai's *talawas* website. She and Chanh share an ironic appreciation of Vietnam's contemporary absurdities. As Hoai said in a 2004 talk at the University of California, Los Angeles, "Privatization in the field of culture and communication has not advanced as radically as the privatization of toilet paper, dishwashing detergent, liquid soap, shampoo, bath soap, toothpaste and tampons. Obviously this is not because the national demand for clean laundry, bathing, shampooing, and douching is more urgent, although the unbelievable density of advertisements for such products may make one think this way."

What blocks Vietnam from developing or even displaying its culture is the dead zone enforced by the country's censors. "The post-Renovation period is indeed one of strange empty spaces, of absent authority, of a train without an engine or an engineer," says Hoai. "The old prestige of ideology, of systems of thought and of certain spiritual values, have been abandoned, but the empty spaces have been sealed shut, leaving no opportunity for new sources of prestige or value to take their place."

Chanh and the Open Mouth poets evoke these empty spaces and loss of authority, the hypocrisy and perversion of Vietnam's one-party kleptocracy. Chanh writes in his poem "Contemporary Prick" about what he calls "the obscene counterfeiting of the intellect, arts, politics, and morals."

In another poem, "Post, Post, but not Post," he writes:

> Next to a Cambodian: I'm gloriously yellow.
> Next to a Westerner: I flatten myself in panic.
> Next to a Chinese: I timidly squint.
>
> Previous life: my core was monkey.
> This life: my community is ghostly.
> Next life: my country is a commune.

As Phan concludes in his introduction to *The Deluge* (whose title is borrowed from one of Chanh's verses: "he became lost and found himself in the deluge"), "Almost everywhere you go in Vietnam today, bright billboards and colorful street signs celebrate unprecedented growth and development, commemorate national unity and liberation, promote necessary policies to help curb societal problems, and cast Vietnam as the Asian tourist destination of the future. Not celebratory but critical, many of the poets in this anthology sully the disinfected portrayals of post-Renovation Vietnam. Their poems overflow with disgust, disillusionment, angst, and alienation, tottering dangerously on the edge of violence. In other words, they form distress signals of a collective unconscious in a moment of cultural crisis.

"One of the strongest distress signals has been sent by Saigon poet Nguyen Quoc Chanh. . . . Ever since his emergence during the Renovation years, Chanh has been fearless in his criticism of the government and unapologetic in his experimentation with poetic form. In effect, he has found himself and his work slandered and shut out of mainstream literary magazines and state-run publishing houses."

In the final victory for Vietnam's censors, Chanh will no longer be bearing witness from the deluge. The country's best poet will no longer be writing poetry.

All Things on Earth

In 2000 and 2004, the Vietnam Literature Project published two interviews online with Chanh. The first is by his fellow poet Linh Dinh, who lived in Saigon for two and a half years, between 1999 and 2001. During this time, Dinh, Chanh, and other poets began meeting weekly for a night of drinking rice wine, eating dog meat, and discussing "all things on earth." Chanh valued these meetings with his American friend, who also became one of his major translators and publishers. "What's wonderful was the fact that these small talks absorbed me into postmodernism without my knowing," Chanh says.

"I was born in Bac Lieu in 1958, into a family of opposing customs, with a Southern mother who chose action over words and a Northern father, nearly the opposite, who chose words over action," Chanh tells Dinh in their published interview. "I didn't fit in with Southerners because I had a little Northern blood, and I also didn't match with Northerners because I had a bit of the Southern temperament. I was the distorted product of that confused relationship. It influenced greatly my way of thinking and my attitude."

Chanh goes on to describe being drafted to fight in Cambodia. "During those two years, I came to recognize the nearly instinctive martial spirit latent in the majority of the Vietnamese people and it filled me with more terror than imagined gun battles against Pol Pot. But it's also lucky, because of the stomach ulcer, I was released from the ranks early."

Chanh talks about his wide reading of books by Albert Camus, Friedrich Nietzsche, and Henry Miller, works that he describes as "a mirror into the primal need to remove the sentimental waste of tradition from life and from literature. Those books formulated my individual consciousness, and caused me to resist the half-civilized environment of the collective power." He also acknowledges the influence of surrealism, which "immediately entered me like a toxic windstorm, and the surrealist method of verse indifferently turned into breath, flesh and blood, and grew into the most important part of my artistic consciousness."

The Open Mouth poet Ly Doi, who clearly admires his older colleague, conducted the other Vietnam Literature Project interview. "Creating is a way to link myself with life," Chanh says . "I don't know what the situation in foreign countries is like, but here, in this dark and miserable corner of the world, to live means being resigned to sinking [into] the shame. And writing poems is to rake up everything to make the shame stink."

Chanh keeps raking up the subject of censorship. "You can't do anything about it," he says, "because to them, the word *toc* (hair on your head) is OK but *long* (hair on other parts of your body) begins to be problematic; *mat* (eye) is extremely ethical, but *cac* (penis) surely corrupt; *can cu* (hard working) sounds patriotic while *dan ngu cu den* (people at the bottom rung) certainly reactionary. You can even be seen as the biggest reactionary when you fail to capitalize *bac Ho* (uncle Ho). State publishers are a black market that professionally sells printing permits to private printers, but it always sells them carefully because it is afraid of getting involved with some depraved or reactionary books. Its selling is well oriented. It is the socialist orientation."

Doi asks Chanh about distributing his works underground via samizdats. "Private persons can have rights to have dog meat, and even traffic in women and children, but they have no right to publish their works," Chanh replies. "Publishing is monopolized by the government. And a monopoly never supports innovations."

"Vietnamese poetry of today is not different from that under the Ly and Tran dynasties," he says. "It always makes the new by adopting the old from foreign countries. So Vietnamese poets can feel free to buy, steal, or rob the world poetic heritage. All trends, from futurism, dadaism, surrealism to new formalism and post-modernism, are necessary, because the Vietnamese poetry is like the Vietnamese economy in that it will be in the doldrums if there is no foreign investment."

Doi manages to get interesting answers from Chanh, even when posing questions that in the West would elicit canned responses. "What is freedom?" he asks, directing Chanh to talk about freedom "in its ordinary sense" and as "freedom in the arts."

"Freedom is the most beautiful concept among spiritual ones," Chanh answers. "This concept needs to be nurtured specially, and if it survives and grows up, other rubbish concepts will have no place in our mind. In my opinion, such concepts as 'The Socialist Republic of Vietnam,' 'The Liberation of the South Vietnam,' 'The Ideological

Front,' 'The Central Culture' . . . must be eliminated before the concepts of 'democracy,' 'development' . . . can be realized."

Vietnam, he says, is a crossroads culture, a borrower, a mimic of other people's ideas. This is reflected everywhere in the hammers and sickles and other communist insignia that festoon Vietnam's Marxist-Leninist state.

"What traditions does your poetry belong to, Oriental or Occidental?" Doi asks.

"My poetry may belong to the tradition of garbage, because Vietnam is a trashcan for both the East and the West," Chanh answers. "After some thousand years of struggle and coexistence with Chinese, French, Japanese, American and Russian imperialists, Vietnam developed a strangely tragic culture that is both virtuous and wanton, something like Thuy Kieu's life in *The Tale of Kieu*. Why are the Vietnamese people madly in love with the *Tale of Kieu*? I think the Vietnamese people, in their unconscious, feel similarities between the tragic fate of Kieu and Vietnamese history. It is a cultural complex, a defense. And it's this complex that unceasingly turns Vietnam into a trashcan for both the East and the West. Disputes between the old and the new, and traditions and innovations, are nothing but conflicts between two pieces of rubbish from the East and the West. In such an environment full of nonsensical conflicts my solution is to use and discard as quickly as possible all pieces of rubbish from both the East and the West."

Dupe

In his introduction to *The Deluge,* Hai-Dang Phan describes how Vietnam's southern writers, like the region's soldiers, suffered from being on the losing side in the war. The year 1975 "evokes not just the fall of the country but also the fall of a literature," he says. "Vietnamese literary history would be eventually dismantled, systematically re-written or outright erased; books would be banned, confiscated and burned; writers silenced, censored, and imprisoned."

At war's end, it became illegal to sell books and magazines published under the old regime, and all of Saigon's bookstores were shuttered. Their stock ended up in the city's flea markets, where connoisseurs such as Chanh picked up the world's great literature at cut-rate prices. Today, in its official literary history, Vietnam has erased every southern writer working between 1954 and 1975. Nguyen Quoc Chanh, the "unacknowledged visionary of new Vietnamese poetry," is merely the latest name subtracted from Vietnam's airbrushed history.

When Linh Dinh left Saigon in 1975, he was an eleven-year-old boat person. When he returned to live in the city in 1999, he was as a thirty-six-year-old poet whose work was infused with jazz and the American vernacular. Dinh claims to have been a major influence on Vietnamese poetry. He was certainly a cultural bridge, bringing an insouciant swing to Chanh, Ly Doi, and the other poets he met during his two and a half years in Saigon. In a recent email to me, Dinh wrote, "The Open Mouth poets were inspired by Chanh, and by me. Chanh and I did a reading at a Saigon restaurant/bar called Lotus in 2000. Then I started to publish these bawdy, cocky and politically aggressive Vietnamese poems. The cockiest and bawdiest Vietnamese poet, however, is Nguyen Quoc Chanh, and he's more politically aggressive than the Open Mouth guys. Though all of them are brave enough, Chanh is the bravest, and recklessly so."

"To kill artists, there is no better way than to herd them into the Writers' Union of Vietnam," writes Chanh in his poem *Dupe* (2004), before adding, "To understand the meaning of the word *dupe,* there is no better way than to become a citizen of the Socialist Republic of Vietnam."

The People Are Omniprescient

Early in 2017 I send Chanh New Year's greetings and ask if he can give me the latest news on censorship. A few days later he writes back to say, "I did a little digging and this is what came up with." Chan reports that the most recent book censored in Vietnam (which also happens to have been published by Nha Nam) is a biography of Pétrus Ky by the noted scholar Nguyen Dinh Dau.

Truong Vinh "Pétrus" Ky is a famous Catholic scholar and the author of more than a hundred published works that helped to popularize *quoc ngu*, the romanized script used in Vietnam today. Ky is a towering figure in Vietnamese literary history. He died in 1898, and today there are still schools named after him. To ban a book about Pétrus Ky is comparable to banning a book on John F. Kennedy, Jr., because he was insufficiently patriotic.

"After one month, the book was recalled without any mention in the state-sponsored press," writes Chanh. "People only learned of this incident on the internet, and the Vietnamese-language BBC later picked it up in an interview with the author. There was little to report because there's no trace of any order or stated reason for the recall, or even published critiques of the book.

"In his interview, Mr. Dau revealed that there was an 'order by mouth,' but we don't know from whose mouth to whose ears, and from whose ears to whose hands, before the book disappeared."

Chanh reached out to an informed source for news of why a book on Pétrus Ky would be censored. "Because the Vietnamese government says it is of the people, by the people, for the people, whatever it wants to hide from the people we can find out by asking the people. I grabbed one of the people, whose name is MS, a writer and translator."

"'Hey, you of the people,' he asked, 'do you know why this book was pulped?'"

Chanh was informed that the original complaint came "from MQL," a pro-government scholar and the editor of a nationalistic periodical, "who asked NVD, advisor to the party secretary of Ho Chi Minh City, to recall the book."

Chanh went to a second source to verify this story. "I got on top of another member of the people, a journalist named NV," who confirmed the account. "'The ideology cadres don't read books,' NV said. 'Only gate-keeping scholars would know enough about them to report up the chain.'"

"This makes absolute sense," Chanh writes. "The people are truly omniprescient!"

"The Party's secret weapon has always been to get prisoners to rat out fellow inmates, to use diligent peasants against lazy peasants, bike drivers against three-wheeled cyclo operators, writers against performers, ideological party members against banking party members, etcetera. Leaders are never guilty. It's all on you the people.

"And then there's the deal with disgruntled scholars. Chinese-trained versus Russian-trained, French-trained versus American-trained. Scholars of this region versus that region, except for the wretched places that support no scholars at all.

"Anything reported to the party becomes a problem. Descartes would say, 'It is a problem, therefore it exists!'"

CHAPTER IX

Information

Sigmund Freud defined censorship as resistance to unwelcome information. Such resistance produces "apparently meaningless deliria," or delusional structures of thought, that are "the work of censorship which no longer takes the trouble to conceal its operation." According to Freud, "instead of collaborating in producing a new version [of reality] that shall be unobjectionable," censorship "ruthlessly deletes whatever it disapproves of, so that what remains becomes quite disconnected." In the words of the Freud scholar Mary Jacobus, censorship produces a "psychotic text" containing "disconnected traces of impossible meanings."

The censor's black pen creates a distorted, funhouse view of the world. People disappear. Historical events are revised. Facts, quotations, data—all dissolve into a jumble of impossible meanings. This process of erasure is a defense mechanism. Powerful interests want to control our narrative. They want to tell a story without naming names, quoting actual people, describing real events, or analyzing the causes of these events. Reality dissolves into ideological blather, and the best we can hope to get from a censored story are the shadows revealing where meaning used to lie.

Anthropology tells us that no culture exists without taboos. Censoring of unwelcome information occurs in all societies, but the nature of what is censored and the means by which it is censored differ in crucial ways. Censorship by means of ideological conformity, which pushes dissenting views to the margins and then ignores them, functions differently from censorship regimes that suppress dissent and imprison or exile their critics. The liberal democracies of the West practice what might be called soft censorship (with occasional diversions into political assassination, imprisonment, or exile), while the former Soviet Union and China have developed centralized "watching agencies" for enforcing their censorship regimes. The divergence between soft and hard censorship explains some of the tension between the United States and Vietnam in their handling of "unwelcome information," including political dissent, human rights, and other contested issues.

Crystal Ball

After twenty-five years of traveling to Vietnam and watching the country emerge from its postwar devastation, I can only speculate about Vietnam's future. In one scenario, the Communist Party maintains its hold on political power and the state-operated enterprises that feed corruption. The party suppresses dissent through censorship and by imprisoning its critics. At the same time, as a sop to the restive public, it allows commerce to flourish at street level.

Vietnam now has a chain of McDonald's restaurants run by an overseas Vietnamese. He is a Harvard-trained venture capitalist who returned to his native country and married the prime minister's daughter. One-third of Vietnam's population is on Facebook, where political discourse overruns communist strictures. As Vietnam opens to the outside world, which includes its refugee communities scattered from Orange County to Berlin, will it start acting less like Nguyen Huy Thiep's "caged animal—ignorant and arrogant"?

Revolutions surprise people. Vietnam could flip suddenly from one kind of future into another. In the meantime, though, its greatest fiction writer is no longer writing fiction. Its best poet has given up poetry. The country's other artists have been forced into silence or exile. While crowing about its people's success as red capitalists, Vietnam has reduced its culture to rubble. Its literature and art exist in a kind of cultural ground zero, where propaganda replaces philosophy and history is the most dangerous subject one can study.

Vietnam is the test case for whether a country can have commerce without culture. The country has state-approved, ideologically correct, frozen forms of culture, but the culture that illuminates the world in fresh ways has been suppressed. The gambit is to see if this nation of brainwashed sloganeers can find its way into the future. Or will it be caught off guard by scenarios it never imagined? Welcome to Vietnam's brave new world—an experiment in real time to see if the suppression of memory, history, language, and art can result in any enduring facsimile of human happiness.

The Dead

There is no starker representation of what Vietnam does with its past than what it does with its dead. Certain bodies are valorized with grand crypts in ornate cemeteries. Others lie scattered under heaps of mud, where their caskets have rotted away and mourners are forbidden from tending their graves.

On my last day in Saigon, I rent a long-haul taxi and head northeast out of the city toward Bien Hoa and the coast. As we cross Saigon's canals and snake through traffic, I stare out the window at weedy lots filled with backhoes, cranes, bulldozers, fork lifts, semi-trailers, sky lifts, and cargo containers piled ten deep, all of them loaded with the tee shirts, tennis shoes, and other stuff that Vietnam ships around the world. The air is a toxic stew of dust and diesel. Thrusting up behind me are the city's new skyscrapers, while to my left rise the concrete piers for Saigon's new metro, which will eventually deliver workers to the Red Bull bottling factory, electronics assembly plants, and the other companies that dot this industrial landscape.

Passing a row of sweatshops in prefab sheds, we turn off the main road into countryside that mixes banana trees and bungalows with truck lots. We stop now and then to ask for directions and turn around a few times before coming to the gate of an unmarked cemetery. Here a policeman flags us to a halt, and other officials summon us into the gatehouse. I tell the superintendent that I have come to visit an old friend who is buried here. I make up a name, Nguyen Thanh Viet, the Vietnamese equivalent of Joe Smith. I know from photos that this cemetery for republican soldiers killed during the war is constructed in rings around a central memorial. I tell the superintendent that my friend is buried near the memorial.

The superintendent pulls out a ledger filled with names and plot numbers. He leafs through it, finding hundreds of Nguyens, but not Thanh Viet. He asks me to leave my telephone number and promises to call if he finds the man. I suggest instead that I be allowed to search for him. He has me fill out various forms in duplicate and leave my passport, and then the policeman leads us into the cemetery on his motorbike.

We drive past rows of untended graves that are being broken apart by trees and vines. Everything around us is dissolving into a riot of upended stones and vegetation. Other graves are nothing more than mounded heaps of red earth. The caskets that once contained these remains have rotted away. The Vietnamese care for their dead. They remember death days, not birth days. But here, with no one allowed to tend them, the graves are turning to mulch. In this forest blocked from memory, we are the sole visitors among thousands of graves.

Near the center of the cemetery, I stop the taxi and get out to walk. I peer at the names on the gray markers, many of them so weatherworn that they are no longer legible. I stare over the rows of men who died for a country that no longer exists. Around me are ring upon ring of what look like horizontal ant hills and tumbledown tombstones. The air smells of mud and mulch and the thick sweetness of vines happily propagating in the summer sunshine.

Back at the guardhouse, I tell the superintendent that I have failed to find my friend. He promises to call me when Viet's grave is located. I leave a small donation to thank him for his troubles.

Heading back toward Saigon, we turn onto an auxiliary road and stop at another cemetery. This flower-filled, meticulously groomed site is reserved for the heroes of the People's Armed Forces. Pham Xuan An is buried here. He wanted to be cremated and have his ashes scattered in the Dong Nai River. Instead, he was given a state funeral and interred with military honors in a massive granite tomb covered with votive urns and a stella eight feet tall.

An, a journalist and a spy, rests in a cemetery full of warriors and politicians because his spying was important enough to get him elevated to the rank of general. He never wore a uniform until the war was over, when he had to don one for state occasions. He had a puckish sense of humor about his fellow communists. They spoke a jargon-filled language that he pretended not to understand. Even here in this somber setting I can sense that An is having more fun than his neighbors. While everyone else lies under black granite, he is entombed in pink.

Enameled on his headstone is a ridiculous picture. The original, from which this one was copied, shows An, unaccustomed to the formality, wearing his military cap askew. His tie is crooked, and his shirt collar swims around his neck. But in this bigwig cemetery An's uniform has been switched from field green to white.

His cap has been straightened and his tie tightened around his neck.

Three porcelain statues sit next to An's tomb. They depict his favorite animals, from which he claimed to have learned important lessons. One statue shows the loyal German shepherd that guarded him at night while he wrote his reports in invisible ink. Another shows the rooster that represents the cockfighting he loved. (An was a sporting man who knew how to evaluate the odds. He bet on the winning side.) The third is a fish. "Fish teach you to keep your mouth shut," he told me in one of our last conversations. "Unfortunately, all my fish have died."

I am carrying a bundle of incense that I bought at the cemetery gate. Here at An's grave I try to light the entire bunch, which goes up in a whoosh of flame. I wave my torch of incense back and forth, struggling to extinguish it. Enveloped in a cloud of smoke, with the flames leaping toward my hand, I am forced to dump the incense into an urn full of water. I salvage a few sticks to burn at the foot of An's grave. The rest of the soggy mass has to be thrown away. This is when I discover that behind An's tomb lies a weedy lot filled with piles of wilting flowers and broken pottery. This garbage heap will eventually be covered with monuments, but for the moment it looks as forlorn as the republican cemetery down the road. Everywhere I look, even behind the grand stellae, Vietnam's red soil is reaching up to offer its cold embrace.

CREDITS

Unless otherwise noted, all photographs are by Thomas A. Bass.

P. [TK]. *The Dream of the Artist* (portrait of the writer Nguyen Huy Thiep) by Nguyen Dinh Dang, 1990. Oil on canvas, 97 x 130 cm. Used by permission of the artist.

P. [TK]. Pham Xuan An, *Time* correspondent, whispering in the ear of Robert Shaplen, *New Yorker* correspondent. On the left, Cao Giao, *Newsweek* correspondent. On the right, Nguyen Hung Vuong, *Newsweek* correspondent, and Nguyen Dinh Tu, *Chinh Luan* newspaper. Continental Hotel, Saigon, April 17, 1971. Photograph by Richard Avedon. © The Richard Avedon Foundation.

P. [TK]. Pham Xuan An, Ho Chi Minh City, 2005. Photograph by James Nachtwey.

P. [TK]. Pham Thi Hoai, Berlin, 2016. Photograph by Huy Don Ho Pham.

P. [TK]. Linh Dinh, Philadelphia, 2015. Photograph by Linh Dinh.

ACKNOWLEDGMENTS

I am indebted to the people named in this story. They braved prison, house arrest, exile, and other sanctions to speak to me about what Graham Greene called "the territory of lies." Others have chosen to remain unnamed, and I am grateful to them as well.

When she suggested that I write about being censored in Vietnam, the novelist-in-exile Pham Thi Hoai launched this project. It would not exist without her. And I might not have finished without more encouragement from Mary Mackay, who for many years has loaned me her critical eye.

They probably regret seeing their names in print, but I am also indebted to my Vietnamese censors, at least the ones who stepped forward to talk to me. During the five years spent slicing and dicing my manuscript, they honored the deal that kept me informed about what they were doing I salute the patience and decency of Nguyen Nhat An, Vu Hoang Giang, Nguyen Viet Long, Nguyen Thi Thu Yen, Nguyen The Vinh, and Duong Trung Quoc.

I owe a special note of thanks to Pham Hong Son. He had already spent five years in prison for translating an essay on democracy and another seven years under house arrest when he translated my essay on censorship. He is a brave man, and I am honored to count him as a friend.

I am grateful to the authors, journalists, and poets who welcomed me into their homes or sat for interviews in Paris, Berlin, Hanoi, Ho Chi Minh City, Philadelphia, and wherever else I could find them. They include Bui Chat, Bui Tin, Duong Thu Huong, Huynh Ngoc Chenh, Linh Dinh, Ly Doi, Nguyen Cong Khe, Nguyen Huy Thiep, Nguyen Quoc Chanh, Pham Chi Dung, Pham Doan Trang, Pham Hong Son, and Pham Thi Hoai.

Other people who helped me with this project, either by smiling on it benignly from a distance, or by sharing their knowledge of Vietnamese culture, or by sinking their editing teeth into the manuscript, include Geoffrey Cain, Calvin Godfrey, Christopher Goscha, Daniel Ellsberg, Christopher Hampton, Le Ly Hayslip, Gerry Herman, Thomas Herman, Alex Kodat, Sarah Logan, Nina McPherson, James Nach, Thuy Nach, Nguyen Ngoc Bich, Thu-Huong Nguyen-Vo, Stirling Silliphant, Tiana Alexandra-Silliphant, Nicholas Simon, and Peter Zinoman. I thank the Vietnamese research assistants and a friend who accompanied me on this assignment, even if they now wish to remove their fingerprints from the scene.

Roberta Krueger and Maude, Tristan, and Julian Bass-Krueger also accompanied me, both figuratively and literally when we celebrated my sons' twenty-first birthdays in Hanoi. Research on this book was supported by grants from the State University of New York at Albany, and the manuscript benefited from the advice of editors at the *American Scholar, pro&contra, Index on Censorship,* the *Washington Post,* and *Foreign Policy* as well as from two anonymous readers at the University of Massachusetts Press. Matt Becker, Mary Dougherty, Carol Betsch, Mary Bellino, Jack Harrison, Sally Nichols, Karen Fisk, Dawn Potter, and other colleagues at the press ushered the book into print. More help came from Lyndsey Blessing, Michael Carlisle, and Stephen Gillen.

My thanks to the Richard Avedon Foundation for permission to reprint Richard Avedon's photograph of Pham Xuan An; to James Nachtwey for permission to reprint his own remarkable photo of An, which illustrated an article in the *New Yorker;* and to Nguyen Dinh Dang, who painted the portrait of Nguyen Huy Thiep reproduced on page six and has his own tales to tell about censorship in Vietnam. Let me salute again the bravery of those people whose stories are told in this book. Their struggle is just, and I hope they prevail.

INDEX

50 Cent Party, 115
   See also du luan vien (public opinion agitators)

A87 (government department, formerly "A25"), 10–11, 105
Alexandra-Silliphant, Tiana, 16
Alibaba, 114
   See also China, internet and
America. *See* United States
American War. *See* Second Indochina War; Vietnam War
Anh Ba Sam ("Brother Gossip"), 156
   imprisonment of, 112, 116
   "Sidewalk News Agency" and, 112, 116
Anh-Minh Do, 109
Animal Farm, 176
   See also Scrap Paper (Giay Vun) Publishing
Army of the Republic of Vietnam (ARVN), 56–58, 60
Assange, Julian, 91

Baidu, 114
   See also China, internet and
Bao Ninh, 54–55
   on censorship, 60, 63–64
   censorship of, 51
   Central Highlands and, 52, 56, 72
   China, criticism of, 60–62
   denunciation campaign against, 51
   on Duong Thu Huong, 58–59
   family background of, 50
   military experience of, 50
   Nghe An province and, 56–57, 60
   on Pham Xuan An, 62–63
   on propaganda, 62
   self-censorship and, 60, 63, 73–74
   The Sorrow of War and, 51–53, 56
   unpublished novels and, 52, 55–58
   U.S. soldiers, meetings with, 53–54
Battle of the Sects, 26
   See also Binh Xuyen river pirates
bauxite mining, 36, 151, 160
   protests and, 116–117
   See also China, Chengdu meeting and
Bay Vien, 25, 33
   See also Binh Xuyen river pirates; colonialism, French
BBC, 36, 86, 171, 196
   Pham Chi Dung and, 161, 163

"The Beggar of Hanoi," 171
　See also Ly Doi
Berlin, 76–77, 81
Berlin Wall, 21, 48, 76, 189
　See also doi moi (Renovation)
Berman, Larry, 12, 22
　See also Perfect Spy
Beyond Illusions, 67
　See also Duong Thu Huong
Bien Hoa, 174, 185
Binh Xuyen river pirates, 25–27
　Battle of the Sects and, 26
　French colonial administration and, 25–26
　opium trade and, 25
blogs, 36, 149, 152–157
　arrest of bloggers, 90, 104–105, 108–109, 112, 157
　censorship of, 112–113, 155
　chandungquyenluc ("Portrait of Power"), 166
　"Confession" of Pham Doan Trang, 111
　criticism of, 151–154
　Huynh Ngoc Chenh and, 154–157
　legality of, 39–40, 112
　political factions and, 185
　"Sidewalk News Agency," 112, 116
　See also Anh Ba Sam ("Brother Gossip"); internet; news media, independent; Nguyen Quang Lap; Pham Chi Dung
Boat People, 33, 106
　See also exile, *viet kieu*
"Boiled–Steamed–Raw," 171–172
　See also Ly Doi
bribery
　as banned word, 33, 71, 159–160
　book publishing and, 177
　French government and, 71
　Gold Campaign and, 31
　government officials and, 38, 159, 177
　in journalism, 145, 147, 152, 154, 159

　police and, 90, 159, 163
　See also corruption
"Brother Gossip." See Anh Ba Sam
Brown, David, 37
Bui Chat, 174–178, 179 (photo)
　arrest of, 171, 176
　on publishing, 175–178
　Open Mouth poets and, 174, 177
　Scrap Paper (Giay Vun) Publishing and, 175–176
　"Who?", 174
Bui Tin
　as censored topic, 31, 43
　as colonel in the North Vietnamese Army, 31, 48
　on democracy, 48, 106
　in exile, 48
　as journalist, 48

Cain, Geoffrey, 38
Cambodia, war with Vietnam, 33, 151, 181, 192
censorship
　academics and, 196
　arguments for, 5–6, 96
　book banning, 10, 23, 44, 51, 67, 79–80, 122, 179, 182, 194–196
　book publishing and, 9–13, 28–31, 43–45, 80, 91, 172, 177, 193
　Chinese, 20, 83–84, 89–90, 114, 157, 162, 164–165
　Chinese, criticism of, 30, 43–44, 48
　controlled leaks and, 38
　control mechanisms for, 9–10, 35–36, 38, 90–91, 94, 187
　criticism of, 20, 63–64, 151–152, 192–193
　cultural effects of, 96, 132–133, 145, 190
　denial of, by Vietnamese, 29–30, 68, 102
　economic consequences of, 20–21, 152–153, 159
　editors and, 9–11, 100–101
　education and, 144–146, 173

exceptions to, 38
Freud, Sigmund, views on, 198
of history, 27, 102, 144–145
history of, in Vietnam, 89
internal exile and, 84, 132, 154, 158
journalism and, 90–91, 111, 148–161, 167, 169
Knausgaard, Karl, views on, 94
Kundera, Milan, views on, 14
land reform campaigns and, 150
laws on, 29–30, 38–39, 112, 136, 172
life under, 83, 96, 197
opposition to, 85, 96, 148, 152
organizations directing, 9–11, 105, 112, 115, 153
psychological effects of, 111, 119
rules of, 80–91, 94–96, 192–193
self-censorship, 29, 45, 83, 111, 124, 126, 168, 176–177
social control and, 94, 197
state-owned media and, 35–36, 38, 40, 187
theory of, 38
in Tunisia, 91
U.S.-Vietnamese relations and, 82–83, 116
Vietnamese training in China, 83–84
See also blogs; Communist Party of Vietnam; education; history; internet; news media, official; police; propaganda; publishing
Central Department for Propaganda and Education, 105
meetings with news media and, 107
Nguyen Phu Trong and, 105
Central Highlands, 111
Bao Ninh and, 52, 56, 72
bauxite mining in, 116
ethnic minorities and, 93
Second Indochina War and, 52
Central Propaganda Commission, 35–36
Cham, 32, 93, 122, 142
See also ethnic minorities; My Son (Cham temple complex)
chandungquyenluc ("Portrait of Power"), 166
See also Pham Chi Dung
China
50 Cent Party and, 115
bauxite mining in Vietnam and, 36, 116–117, 151, 160
censored criticism of, 30–31, 33–34, 37, 44, 149
censorship in, 20–21, 83–84, 89–90, 114, 157, 162, 164–165
Chengdu meeting and, 48, 151–152
criticism of, 43, 48, 60–62, 82, 101, 150
Cultural Revolution, 78
Document Number Nine and, 89–90
famines and, 20
Gold Campaign and, 32
Great Leap Forward, 20–21
internet and, 101, 109, 114–115, 157, 164–165
language and, 32, 42, 101
Pham Xuan An and, 31, 102
press freedom and, 40
protests, anti-Chinese, 40, 61, 151, 184, 188
South China Sea conflict and, 33, 60–61, 108, 156, 176
Thanh Do agreement and, 48
Vietnam, comparisons with, 90, 109, 114, 164–165
Vietnamese censorship, as model for, 83–84, 107, 114
Vietnamese sovereignty and, 48, 135–136, 151–152, 160
Vietnamese training in, 83–84
war with Vietnam, 34, 67
See also South China Sea conflict; *The Tale of Kieu*
China Beach, 141–142
cockfighting, 33
Cold War, 76, 82–83

colonialism, 70
    American, 26, 93
    French, 25–27, 56–57, 65, 92–93, 123, 180
    Vietnamese, 32, 93
    See also Vietnam, history of
communism
    Bui Chat poem on, 178
    in China, 90
    comparison with democracy, 69
    countries practicing, 133
    criticism of, 69–70, 133
    history and, 144, 174
    land ownership and, 33, 65–67, 99, 123, 150, 166, 181, 187
    language and, 32, 101, 202
    Pham Xuan An on, 32–33
    as "red capitalism," 185
    reeducation and, 17, 30, 42, 101
    See also land reform campaigns; reeducation
Communist Party of Vietnam, 2, 29, 44, 113, 176
    attitudes toward, 119, 135
    benefits of joining, 44
    Central Propaganda Commission, 35–36
    China and, 90, 151
    control of media by, 35–36, 38, 40, 90, 107, 148–151, 153
    criticism of, 135, 148–151, 163–164
    distinctions between party and state, 99, 165
    Duong Thu Huong and, 64–71
    history of, 138
    intelligence of members, 49, 78
    officials, 106, 115
    Pham Hong Son and, 133, 135–136
    propaganda and, 31–32, 115
    See also propaganda
Communist Party Propaganda Department, 36, 115
computers. *See* internet
Confucianism, 96–97, 173

corruption
    book publishing and, 177
    censored criticism of, 152–153, 157, 163, 167
    chandungquyenluc ("Portrait of Power") and, 166–168
    criticism of, 37–38, 82, 150, 152, 158, 164
    government and, 150, 153, 166–167, 185
    in journalism, 147, 159–160
    journalism and, 147, 154, 159, 166–168
    journalists encouraged to cover, 37–39, 83–84, 185
    Vietnam as emulating China, 84
    See also bribery; news media, official; PMU 18 affair
The Crystal Messenger, 79
    See also Pham Thi Hoai
Cu Huy Ha Vu, 36, 116
Cultural Information Department, 163
Culture and Sport (newspaper), 169
cyber trolls, 113–116
    See also du luan vien (public opinion agitators); Facebook; internet

dan oan (dispossessed landowners), 166–167
    See also communism, land ownership and
Darkness at Noon, 176
Daydreaming During a Traffic Jam, 55–56
The Deluge, 183, 194
    culture of Vietnam and, 191
    Nguyen Quoc Chanh and, 189–190
    Open Mouth poets and, 170, 173
    Saigon, description of, 143
    See also Linh Dinh
democracy, 106, 121, 158, 160
    movement, 111–113, 119, 163, 165
    necessity of, argument for, 193

INDEX

Pham Hong Son and, 133, 135–136, 139
See also freedom of speech; protest movements
Den Cu, 150
denunciation campaigns
  against Anh Ba Sam, 122
  against Bao Ninh, 51, 55, 132
  against Duong Thu Huong, 71
  against Nguyen Huy Thiep, 122, 124
  against Nguyen Quoc Chanh, 182–183
  against Pham Doan Trang, 117–119
  See also disinformation, police
Descartes, René, 197
Dewey, A. Peter, 33
Dinh Dang Dinh, 116
disinformation, 115, 151
  du luan vien (public opinion agitators) and, 92, 109, 113–115, 118
  "fake websites," 115, 118
  See also denunciation campaigns; Facebook; propaganda
dissidents
  arrest and imprisonment of, 105–107
  challenges faced by, 183
  criticism of anti-Chinese sentiment, 151, 185
  democracy movement and, 111–113, 165, 193
  encryption and, 165
  illegal class on journalism, 119–121
  protests and, 61, 116–117, 120
  statistics on, 105–106, 112
  See also blogs; news media, independent; police; protest movements
"Di Thui" ("Stinking Whore"), 86
Document Number Nine, 89–90
doi moi (Renovation), 21, 69, 79, 124, 189
  Bui Tin and, 48
  Nguyen Huy Thiep and, 126

Do Thi Minh Hanh, 116
Do Tuan Kiet, 42
du luan vien (public opinion agitators), 92, 109, 113–115, 118
  See also Facebook; internet
Duong Thu Huong, 58–74
  banned work of, 67
  Bao Ninh and, 58–59, 72–73, 78
  charges against, 39
  Communist Party and, 64, 66–67
  criticism of American war, 70
  criticism of French, 71–72
  as "darling of the Communist Party," 64
  family history of, 65
  imprisonment of, 64, 137
  land reform campaigns and, 65, 67, 69
  as musician, 66
  The Sanctuary of Despair and, 70–71
  as screenwriter, 66
  translators, falling out with, 72
  war experience of, 66–67
  work published online by, 68
  The Zenith and, 68
  See also McPherson, Nina; Phan Huy Duong
Duong Trung Quoc, 41, 45, 49
  on Pham Xuan An, post-war career of, 46, 48
  See also publishing

eBay. See Alibaba
editors
  arrest and, 11
  as censors, 9–10, 27, 44–45, 99–102
  as "midwives," 100–102
  See also Nguyen Thi Thu Yen; Nguyen Viet Long; publishing
education
  as brainwashing, 4, 177
  Chinese, 60
  communist reeducation, 17, 30, 41, 101, 173

education (*continued*)
    Confucianism and, 96–97
    criticism of journalism programs, 159
    foreign languages and, 66, 78, 111
    Fulbright University of Vietnam, 145–146
    history study, as dangerous, 144–145
    Vietnamese training in China, 83
    See also reeducation
Ellsberg, Daniel, 22
erotica, 145
ethnic minorities
    autonomy of, 32, 93, 142
    as banned topic, 33, 37
    Cham, 32, 93, 122, 142
    democracy movement and, 113
    Hmong, 125
    Khmer, 93
    Montagnards, 32, 56, 93
    nam tien (march to the south) and, 32
exile
    authors and, 64, 69, 74, 77, 85, 106, 132, 200
    internal, 60, 84, 132
    U.S.-Vietnam relations and, 116
    viet kieu, 57
    See also censorship, self-censorship

Facebook, 117, 149, 157
    compliance with police, 114–115
    criticism of, 153
    failed attempts to block, 114–115
    failed emulation of, 165
    government accounts and, 115, 118, 158
    hacking and, 115
    introduction into Vietnam of, 114
    legality of, 109
    as news source, 111, 155–156
    See also China, internet and; *du luan vien* (public opinion agitators); internet

Fate of Love. *See The Sorrow of War*
"Fired Gold," 129
First Indochina War, 65, 180
    Dien Bien Phu (battle of) and, 150
    See also Binh Xuyen river pirates; colonialism, French
For a Green Hanoi, 120
    See also journalism, illegal instruction in
France
    Binh Xuyen and, 25–27
    colonialism and, 25–27, 93, 180
    opium trade and, 25
    release of Duong Thu Huong and, 71
    as teaching Vietnamese, 33
    war with Vietnam, 180
freedom of speech
    arguments for, 20, 152, 193
    Confucianism and, 97
    democracy movement and, 113, 121
    history of, in Vietnam, 89, 140
    Knausgaard, Karl on, 94
    laws on, 39
From Hollywood to Hanoi, 16
Fulbright University of Vietnam, 145–146

garbage poetry, 175
    See also Open Mouth poets (Mo Mieng)
"The General Retires," 121–122, 129
Giay Vun Publishing. *See* Scrap Paper Publishing
Goethe Institut, 170
Google, 114, 155
Goscha, Christopher, 92
Greene, Graham, 15, 207
Guantánamo Bay prison, 82

Hai-Dang Phan, 194
    on Nguyen Quoc Chanh, 189–191
    on Open Mouth poets, 173, 191
Hanoi, 53, 110, 119–120, 128
    Cinémathèque, 7
    Hoan Kiem Lake, 127

Harvard University. *See* Fulbright University of Vietnam
Hayton, Bill, 37–38
The Hills of Eucalyptus, 68
  See also Duong Thu Huong
history
  banned topics in, 10, 32–33, 68
  Chinese, 20–21
  dangers of, 102, 144–145
  of press freedom, 89
  totalizing approach toward, 27, 144
  See also Vietnam, history of
Hmong, 125
  See also ethnic minorities
Hoang Minh Chinh
  democracy movement and, 135
Ho Chi Minh
  aliases of, 8–9, 90, 193
  Bao Ninh and, 56–57, 60
  birth place of, 56, 60
  books on, 68, 150
  Gold Campaign and, 32
  land reform campaigns and, 67–68, 78, 150
  mistress, assassination of, 68
Ho Chi Minh City. *See* Saigon
Hoi An, 141
  See also My Son (Cham temple complex)
Hong An, 36
Hong Duc, 11–12, 41
  as "powerful" publisher, 43
  See also Ministry of Information and Communication; publishing
Ho Quang Loi, 125
human rights, Vietnamese, 1, 98
  China, comparisons with, 40, 90, 165
  criticism of, 154
  Human Rights Council and, 108, 158
  international relations and, 85, 108, 116, 135, 166, 175–176
  journalists and, 108
  Nguyen Phu Trong and, 105–107

  reports on, 106–108
  statistics on, 40, 105–107, 112, 166
  See also Ministry of Public Security; police
Huxley, Aldous, 3, 133
Huy Duc, 178
Huynh Ngoc Chenh, 154–160, 160 (photo)
  arrests, 155
  on corruption, 158–160
  as editor at *Thanh Nien*, 155–157, 159
  Facebook and, 155–157
  as "Netizen of the Year," 155, 158
  sources for, 156
  See also journalism; news media, independent

Ideology and Propaganda Committee, 156
Inanimate Weather, 182
  See also Nguyen Quoc Chanh
Independent Journalists Association, 161, 163
  See also Pham Chi Dung
Index on Censorship, 20, 89, 103, 208
India, 20
information
  absence of, consequences, 21, 105
  alternative sources of, 150–154
  electronic, 39, 109
  journalism and, 99, 147, 156, 166–168
  resistance to, 198
  state control of, 40, 115
  as trafficked, 147
  See also journalism; news media, independent; news media, official
intelligence
  journalism and, 16–17, 21
  military, 15–17, 22, 26, 34, 46
  spies and, 16, 19, 48–49, 63
internet, 107–119, 149–158
  censorship and, 107–109, 149, 187
  cyberspace, 86

internet (*continued*)
    as difficult to control, 109, 114–115, 157, 164–165, 187
    du luan vien (public opinion agitators) and, 92, 109, 113–115, 118
    economy and, 164
    encryption, 165
    firewalls, 81, 149, 155, 164
    government hacking and, 46, 81, 112, 115, 165
    government manipulation of, 113, 115, 155, 157
    hardened computers, 46
    laws on, 39–40, 89
    policies on, 109
    as replacing news media, 149–154
    as replacing print, 63
    Vietnam as emulating China, 165
    See also blogs; Facebook; news media, independent; Pham Thi Hoai; publishing, online
Irrawaddy Magazine, 35

jargon. *See* reeducation; Vietnamese language
journalism
    arrests and imprisonment for, 107–108, 113, 116, 153, 161, 163
    as "betrayal," 94–95
    bribes and, 145, 147, 152, 154, 159–160
    "free press" and, 89
    illegal instruction in, 119–121
    independent, 108–113, 116–117, 154–168
    lack of sourcing, 90–91, 166–168
    political factions and, 150, 164, 185
    practices, 90–91
    press freedom ranking, 40
    quoting sources in, 88, 90, 94, 97
    training, by state, 159
    unofficial sources, 156
    use of pseudonyms, 90–91, 97
    writers as "informal police force," 38
    See also blogs; Huynh Ngoc Chenh; internet; news media, independent; news media, official; Pham Chi Dung
Journalism and Propaganda University, 159

Karlin, Wayne, 54
Kennedy, John F., 33
Kerrey, Robert ("Bob"), 146
Khmer, 32, 93
Khuc Duy, 174
Knausgaard, Karl, 94
Korea, 69

land reform campaigns
    death toll, 150
    Duong Thu Huong and, 65–67, 69
    Duong Thu Huong, family history and, 65–66
    as elimination of intellectuals, 78
    Ho Chi Minh, involvement in, 150
    Ho Chi Minh, pen name and, 99
    Nguyen Quoc Chanh, family history and, 181
    Paradise of the Blind and, 67
language. *See* translation; Vietnamese language
Lansdale, Edward
    Binh Xuyen campaign and, 26
    as training Pham Xuan An, 15, 26, 32
Lao Dong (Labor) Publishing Company, 31–35
laws
    on censorship, 39, 112
    on Communist Party control, 38
    on espionage, 136
    on internet, 39–40
    on publishing, 29–30, 39, 43, 172
    on "state secrets," 39
    See also censorship, control mechanisms for; censorship, rules of; publishing, rules of
Le Hoang, 107
Leninism. *See* Marxist-Leninism

Le Thi Cam, 65–66
Linh Dinh, 68–69, 144 (photo)
    background of, 143
    The Deluge and, 143
    influence on Vietnamese poetry, 195
    with Nguyen Quoc Chanh, 191–192
    See also The Deluge
Logan, Sarah, 109
Ly Doi, 86, 169–173, 175, 179 (photo)
    arrest of, 171
    "The Beggar of Hanoi," 171
    "Boiled–Steamed–Raw," 171–172
    family history of, 173
    Open Mouth poets and, 169–170, 173

Malcolm, Janet, 94
Maoism. *See* Document Number Nine; land reform campaigns; Marxist-Leninism
Mao Tse Tung, 10, 21
Marxist-Leninism, 5, 38, 42, 76, 80, 173, 194
McPherson, Nina, 67, 70–71
    See also Duong Thu Huong
media. *See* blogs; internet; journalism; news media, independent; news media, official; publishing
Ministry of Information and Communication, 105
    guidance meetings and, 36
    Hong Duc (publisher) and, 11, 43
    laws on blogging and, 39
    media and, 37, 149
    See also Central Department for Propaganda and Education
Ministry of Public Security, 36
    General Tran Dai Quan and, 112
    guidance meetings and, 36
    People's Public Security Publishing House and, 22
    as police, 112
    publishing and, 19, 42
    See also police

Mitterrand, Danielle, 71
Mo Mieng. *See* Open Mouth poets
Montagnards, 32, 56, 93
    See also ethnic minorities
Morse, Kelly, 171–173
My Son (Cham temple complex), 142–143

nam tien (march to the south), 32
    See also colonialism, Vietnamese; ethnic minorities
"Netizen of the Year" (award), 155, 158
    See also Huynh Ngoc Chenh
New Economic Zones, 181
news media, independent, 108–113, 116–117, 154–168
    arrests and imprisonment and, 108–109, 111, 113, 116, 161
    blackmail and, 117–119
    Facebook and, 155–156
    government hacking and, 81, 112–113
    Huynh Ngoc Chenh and, 154–160
    Independent Journalists Association (Vietnam), 161, 163
    laws and, 39–40
    Pham Chi Dung and, 160–168
    Pham Doan Trang and, 111–120
    sources and, 155–156, 167
    surveillance and, 158, 161, 165
    See also blogs; Facebook; internet
news media, official, 147–157
    arguments for independence of, 147–154
    arrests and, 153
    banned topics and, 156, 160
    bribes and, 147, 159–160
    as censors, 155
    Chinese, 90
    circulation and earnings of, 152–153, 159
    government control of, 89–90, 107–108, 147–156, 161
    ideology and, 156
    Journalism and Propaganda University and, 159

news media, official (*continued*)
    lack of sourcing, 90–91, 166–168
    meetings with government, 35–36, 107, 157
    online newspapers, 111, 153
    press freedom ranking and, 40
    purge of writers, 132
    relations with China, 151–152
    replacement by internet, 149–154
    reporting on corruption, 38, 153, 157–159
    as useful for factions in government, 37, 150, 164, 185
    See also China, Chengdu meeting and; internet; journalism; Nguyen Cong Khe
Ngo Dinh Diem, 24
Nguyen Ai Quoc National Political Academy, 42, 46, 101
    See also reeducation
Nguyen Chi Vinh, 17
Nguyen Cong Khe, 148–154
    on corruption, of government, 150, 152, 154
    on corruption, of press, 154
    criticism of online media by, 150
    firing of, 107
    PMU 18 affair and, 107, 153
    press freedom, arguments for, 148–154
    on print media, decline of, 149, 152–153
    See also news media, official; *Thanh Nien*
Nguyen Dinh Dau, 196
Nguyen Du, 129
    See also The Tale of Kieu
Nguyen Du Writers School, 51, 73
Nguyen Huu Cau, 116
Nguyen Huu Vinh. *See* Anh Ba Sam ("Brother Gossip")
Nguyen Huy Thiep, 4, 127 (photo), 144
    aristocratic background of, 123–124
    art by, 128
    Buddhism and, 122, 124–125
    on censorship, necessity of, 4–6
    Chinese literature and, 125
    denunciation campaign against, 122
    family history of, 121, 123
    "The General Retires" and, 122
    Hmong and, 125–126
    self-censorship and, 124, 126
Nguyen Ngoc, 129–133
    Bao Ninh and, 129, 139
Nguyen Nhat Anh, 7–14, 15 (photo)
Nguyen Phu Trong
    America, visit to, 105
    human rights and, 105–107
    See also Communist Party of Vietnam; human rights, Vietnamese; news media, official, meetings with government
Nguyen Quan, 174
Nguyen Quang Lap
    arrest of, 108–109, 157, 166,
    blogging and, 108
    protests and, 109
Nguyen Quoc Chanh
    anti-Chinese sentiment, criticism of, 184–185
    banned work of, 182
    family history of, 179–181, 192
    Night of the Rising Sun and, 182
    Open Mouth poets and, 182, 185, 195
    police harassment of, 179, 183, 188
    pottery of, 185–186
    samizdats and, 182, 193
    street language and, 183
    surrealism and, 183, 192–193
    on Vietnamese culture, 190, 194
Nguyen Tan Dung, 109
Nguyen The Vinh, 41, 45–46
    as censor, 12, 45
    Hong Duc (publisher) and, 11–12
    Perfect Spy and, 12
    The Spy Who Loved Us and, 11–13
Nguyen Thi Thu Yen, 8, 14
    publishing negotiations with, 31, 34–35
    See also publishing, editing and

Nguyen Van Phu, 98
Nguyen Vien, 86–87
Nguyen Viet Long, 29, 41
  background of, 9, 43
  as editor and censor, 23–28, 44, 101
  interview with, 42–44
  response to article on, 100–102
  See also Nha Nam (publishing company); publishing, editing and
Nha Nam (publishing company), 7–11, 13–14, 30
  book banning and, 10–11, 23
  contract with, 22–23, 34–35
  criticism of author, 103
  as independent publisher, 23, 29, 43
  See also Nguyen Thi Thu Yen; Nguyen Viet Long; publishing; The Spy Who Loved Us
Nhan Dan (Communist Party newspaper), 48
  denunciation of Nguyen Huy Thiep, 122
nhan van giai pham affair, 10
Night of the Rising Sun, 182
North Vietnamese Army, 32, 43, 152
  Bao Ninh and, 50–56, 62
  Bui Tin and, 48, 106
  Duong Thu Huong and, 65–66
  Pham Xuan An and, 15–19, 21–22, 33–34
  post-war activities of, 106
  psychiatric camps, 70
  Tet Offensive and, 33
  Vo Nguyen Giap and, 31, 65
  See also Army of the Republic of Vietnam (ARVN); Second Indochina War; Vietnam, Republic of (South)
Novel Without a Name, 58–59, 64, 68, 72
  See also Duong Thu Huong

O'Brien, Tim, 54
Of Metaphorical Identity, 132
One-Rhyme Poems, 174
  See also Bui Chat
Open Mouth poets (Mo Mieng), 169–175, 177, 190
  Bui Chat, 174–175
  criticism of, 171
  founding of, 173
  imprisonment and, 174
  influences of, 170, 182, 195
  Khuc Duy, 174
  language, use of, 170
  Ly Doi, 169–174
  meaning of name, 169
  Nguyen Quan, 174
  Nguyen Quoc Chanh and, 182, 185, 195
  Pham Thi Huong on, 85–86
  poems of, 171–172, 174
  surrealism and, 170
  See also garbage poetry; samizdats
opium trade, 25
  See also Binh Xuyen river pirates; colonialism, French
Orwell, George, 176
  See also Scrap Paper (Giay Vun) Publishing

Paradise of the Blind, 67
  See also Duong Thu Huong
The Penguin History of Modern Vietnam, 92
People's Public Security Publishing House, 22, 42
  See also Ministry of Public Security; police
perestroika, 124
  See also doi moi (Renovation)
Perfect Spy, 14–15
  attempted cancellation of release, 19–20
  censorship of, 14–15
  Nguyen The Vinh and, 12
  omissions from, 17–18, 22
  See also Berman, Larry
Pham Chi Dung, 160–168, 167 (photo)
  blogs of, 166

Pham Chi Dung (*continued*)
  Communist Party and, 163–164
  corruption and, 163, 166, 168
  Independent Journalists Association and, 161–163
  internet and, 164–166
  investigative reporting and, 166–167
  military background of, 163
Pham Doan Trang, 35–36, 111–120
  arrests, 113, 117
  blackmail of, 117–118
  blocked website of, 113
  democracy movement and, 111, 113
  family history of, 111
  on internet, effect of, 114–115
  journalism, illegal instruction in, 119–120
  as journalist, 111
  psychological trauma of, 118–119
  surveillance of, 119
  Vietnamese censorship, summary of, 37
Pham Hong Son, 92, 133–140, 137 (photo)
  arrest and imprisonment of, 133, 136–137
  democracy and, 133, 135–136, 139–140
  family history of, 138
  Nancy Pelosi and, 135
  police surveillance of, 134, 136, 140
  translation and, 92, 133, 136, 139
Pham Quynh, 78
Pham Thi Hoai, 74–86, 87 (photo), 91, 131–132, 162
  censorship of, 79–80
  on commerce in Vietnam, 189–190
  cooking and, 76–77, 81–82
  The Crystal Messenger and, 79–80
  defense of author, 98–99
  doi moi (Renovation) and, 79
  family history of, 78
  government hacking and, 81
  at Humboldt University, 74, 79
  land reform campaigns and, 78
  meeting her censors, 99
  Pham Quynh and, 78
  pro&contra and, 81
  publishing works online, 80
  on self-censorship, 83
  talawas and, 74, 81
  as "untrustworthy," 79
  on Vietnamese relations with west, 82–83, 85
Pham Xuan An, 1–2, 28, 41, 47 (photo), 49, 54
  American brain, 32
  CIA and, 15
  communism and, 18, 32–33
  criticism of Chinese, 101
  criticism of post-war policies, 19
  distrust of, by government, 48, 54
  Edward Lansdale and, 15, 32
  as Hero of the People's Armed Forces, 22
  intelligence training of, 15–16, 32
  as journalist, 16–17, 21
  language and, 9, 42, 101
  "official" heroic image of, 12, 17–19, 45–46, 63
  police surveillance of, 22, 54
  post-war career of, 15–19, 46, 48
  reeducation camp and, 18, 42, 101
  retirement of, 15–17
  sense of humor, 17, 22, 32, 101
  as southerner, 9, 22, 42, 48
  state funeral of, 17, 34, 202–203
  tomb of, 202–203
  Tran Kim Tuyen and, 16
  U.S., love of, 32, 100–101
  on Vietnam, disunified nature of, 93
  See also The Spy Who Loved Us; Vietnamese language
Phan Huy Duong, 69, 71
PMU 18 affair, 153, 157
  See also Thanh Nien
poetry
  as arrestable offense, 170

banned works, 10, 170, 182
"The Beggar of Hanoi," 171
"Boiled–Steamed–Raw," 171–172
"garbage," 174, 195
language and, 86, 173, 182–183, 189
Nguyen Quoc Chanh and, 178–197
Open Mouth poets and, 169–175
The Tale of Kieu, 51, 86, 129, 194
Tran Dan and, 10
See also Linh Dinh
police, 39–40, 105–108, 111–114
  agencies, 105, 112, 153
  arrests, 113, 117, 156–157, 161, 169–171, 176
  beatings, 105–107, 111, 113, 115, 119, 135, 161
  blackmail, 117
  China, comparisons with, 40, 90, 165
  corruption and, 90, 155, 163
  criticism of, 154
  denunciation, 170
  as enforcers in "gangster state," 106–107
  Facebook and, 114–115
  hacking, 112, 115, 165
  house arrest, 92, 108, 133–134, 165, 207
  imprisonment, 39–40, 64, 71, 92, 105–109, 112, 133, 135–137, 140, 153, 163, 166, 174
  international relations and, 108, 116, 135, 166, 183
  interrogation, 117–118, 124, 156, 161, 183–184
  Nguyen Phu Trong and, 105–107
  Pham Doan Trang and, 113–120
  phone tapping, 115
  plainclothes, 106, 113, 116, 134, 161
  psychological effects of abuse, 118–119, 184
  raids, 10, 122, 124
  statistics on, 40, 105–107, 112, 157, 166
  surveillance, 22, 40, 48, 54, 119, 133–134, 140, 158, 184
  torture 33, 107, 113, 118
  traffic accidents, 106, 113, 170
  undercover informants, 136
  See also human rights, Vietnamese; Ministry of Public Security; U.N. Human Rights Council
Politburo, 19, 48, 153
political prisoners, 40, 112
  sentencing, 166
  statistics on, 40, 106, 112
  trade of, for economic gain, 108, 116
  See also police, imprisonment
"Post, Post, but not Post," 190
  See also Nguyen Quoc Chanh
Poulo Condore, 180
press. *See* blogs; journalism; news media, independent; news media, official; publishing; samizdats
prisoners of war (POWs), 56–57, 180
pro&contra, 74, 81, 92
  See also Pham Thi Hoai
propaganda, 19, 66–67, 70
  arguments against, 147, 149
  dangers of, 20–21
  du luan vien (public opinion agitators), 92, 109, 113–115, 118
  Duong Thu Huong and, 66–67
  education and, 4, 90, 159, 177
  government use of term, 30, 39, 172
  loudspeakers in streets and, 61–62
  organizations directing, 35–36, 105, 107, 156, 159
  press and, 90
  Vietnamese training in China, 83
  Western writers as "mouthpiece" for, 31–32, 34
  See also Central Department for Propaganda and Education; Central Propaganda Commission; Communist Party of Vietnam; Communist

Party propaganda (*continued*)
  Propaganda Department; education; Ideology and Propaganda Committee; Journalism and Propaganda University; Ministry of Information and Communication
protest movements
  anti-Chinese, 61, 151, 184, 188
  bauxite mining, 116–117
  democracy movement, 111–113, 163, 165
  discussion of, 156, 188
  For a Green Hanoi, 120
  ineffectiveness of, 188
  outside Vietnam, 109
  See also dissidents; Pham Chi Dung; Pham Doan Trang
publishing, 7–14, 21–25, 28–35, 43–45
  agencies overseeing, 10–11, 102
  black market and, 177–178, 194–195
  book banning, 10, 23, 44, 51, 67–68, 80, 122, 170, 179, 182, 195–197
  book banning as "silent," 44, 80, 122, 195–197
  book sales, as grounds for censorship, 79–80
  bribes and, 177
  decline of print media, 149, 153–154
  Duong Thu Hong and, 67–68
  editing and, 9–10, 23–28, 44–45, 99–102
  editors as "midwives," 99–102
  guidance meetings and, 35–36
  "hiding behind your finger" (foreign release), 91
  Huy Duc and, 178
  independent, 7–14, 22–23, 28–29, 43
  independent, permits, 10–11, 28–31, 34–35, 41–43, 193
  laws on, 29–30, 38–39, 43, 172, 194–195
  limited print runs, 55
  Ministry of Information and Communication and, 11, 43
  Nguyen Huy Thiep and, 126
  Nguyen Quoc Chanh and, 182–184
  online, 35, 68, 74–75, 80–81, 88–92, 178, 187, 189
  Perfect Spy and, 19–20
  pre-censorship and, 9–10, 31–34, 41
  print run records, 177
  rules for, 9–10, 28–29, 35–36, 43–45, 80, 91, 176
  samizdats and, 175–178, 182, 193
  seizure and, 10, 12, 23
  state-owned publishers, 11, 31, 34–35, 45–46, 193
  See also Hong Duc; Lao Dong (Labor) Publishing Company; news media, official; Nha Nam (publishing company); People's Public Security Publishing House; Scrap Paper (Giay Vun) Publishing

quoc-ngu, 196

reeducation, 173
  as censored topic, 30, 33
  Duong Thu Huong, film about, 70
  Pham Xuan An and, 18, 42, 101
  See also Vietnamese language, bureaucratic jargon and
refugees
  as banned word, 33
  Boat People, 33, 106
  See also exile, *viet kieu*
Reporters Without Borders
  internet and, 40
  "Netizen of the Year Award," 155
  on Nguyen Phu Trong, 105, 107
  press freedom rankings, 40
Rung Sat
  Binh Xuyen river pirates and, 25–27

naming of, 26–27, 100–101
  See also colonialism, French; Second Indochina War; Vietnamese language

Safer, Morley, 22
Saigon, 104–105, 200–201
  anti-Chinese protests and, 61
  Linh Dinh on, 143
samizdats, 2
  distribution methods, 175–176
  Nguyen Quoc Chanh and, 179, 182
  Open Mouth poets and, 86, 173
  Scrap Paper (Giay Vun) Publishing and, 175–176, 178
The Sanctuary of Despair, 70–71
  See also Duong Thu Huong
Sanctuary of the Heart, 68
  See also Duong Thu Huong
Scrap Paper (Giay Vun) Publishing, 175–178
  distribution methods of, 175–176
  "Freedom to Publish Award" and, 176
  garbage poetry and, 175
  George Orwell and, 178
sculpture
  Nguyen Huy Thiep and, 124
  Nguyen Quoc Chanh and, 184–186
Second Indochina War
  A. Peter Dewey and, 32
  Bao Ninh and, 50–54, 56–58
  Bui Tin and, 31
  censorship of, 32–33
  China Beach and, 141
  criticism of, 70
  Edward Lansdale and, 25, 26, 32
  My Son (Cham temple complex) and, 142–143
  Ngo Dinh Diem, Jean Baptiste and, 24
  Pham Xuan An and, 15–22, 26, 32–33
  PTSD and, 70, 141, 152

  Rung Sat and, 25–27
  as struggle between family members, 67
  Tet Offensive and, 17
  Thiep family history and, 124
  Tran Kim Tuyen and, 16
  Vietnamese unification and, 93
  Vo Nguyen Giap and, 31
  The Winning Side and, 178
  See also Army of the Republic of Vietnam (ARVN); Pham Xuan An; prisoners of war (POWs); Vietnam, Republic of (South)
Sen, Amartya, 20–21
Shadows and Wind, 96–97
Shiva (Hindu god), 142
  See also My Son (Cham temple complex)
"Sidewalk News Agency," 112, 115
  See also Anh Ba Sam ("Brother Gossip")
Simon, Nicholas, 63
Snowden, Edward, 91
The Sorrow of War, 131
  censorship of, 51
  criticism of, 84
  Duong Thu Huong and, 58–59, 72–73
  film adaptation of, 63
  narrative of, 52–53
  re-release in Vietnam, 56
  See also Bao Ninh
South China Sea conflict
  as banned topic, 33, 60–61, 103, 156, 176
  blogging and, 108
  description of, 60–61
  protests and, 61
  See also China, Chengdu meeting and; dissidents
South Korea, 69
  Koreans in Vietnam, 61
  See also South China Sea conflict
South Vietnam. See Army of the Republic of Vietnam (ARVN); Vietnam, differences between

South Vietnam (*continued*)
  north and south; Vietnam, Republic of (South)
The Spy Who Loved Us, 1–2, 11–35, 54, 59
  censorship of, by Lao Dong (Labor) Publishing Company, 11, 31–34
  censorship of, by Nguyen The Vinh, 11–12, 41, 45
  censorship of, by Nha Nam, 23–30
  contract for, 23, 34–35, 41
  Duong Trung Quoc and, 45–46
  footnotes and, 24–27, 100–102
  Hong Duc (publisher) and, 11–12, 41, 43
  Nguyen Thi Thu Yen and, 30–31, 35
  Nguyen Viet Long and, 23–30, 42–44
  Nha Nham and, 22, 29
  online publication of, 35, 81
  Perfect Spy and, 12, 14–15, 17, 19–20
  publishing license and, 28–29, 34–35, 41
  release of, in Vietnam, 41
  Rung Sat and, 25–27, 100
  story of, 15, 21–22
  translation and, 42
  See also Pham Xuan An
Stasi, 79
surrealism, 170, 183, 192
  See also Nguyen Quoc Chanh; Open Mouth poets (Mo Mieng)
surveillance, 48, 184
  Facebook as tool for, 114–115
  internet and, 40, 108, 115
  Pham Xuan An and, 22, 54
  police and, 54, 119, 133–134, 136, 140, 158
  undercover informants, 136
  See also police

Swamp of the Assassins. *See* Rung Sat

talawas, 74
  poetry of Nguyen Quoc Chanh and, 189
  publishing of censored news by, 81
  See also Pham Thi Hoai
The Tale of Kieu, 51
  "Stinking Whore" ("Di Thui") and, 86
  Vietnamese culture and, 129, 194
Templar, Robert, 96–97
Thanh Nien (newspaper), 147–159
  arrest of reporters and, 107–108
  circulation and earnings of, 152–153, 159
  declining circulation, 149
  employee qualifications of, 159
  Huynh Ngoc Chenh and, 154–156, 159
  Nguyen Cong Khe and, 147–149, 152
  PMU 18 affair and, 153, 157
  reporting on corruption by, 107–108, 148, 152–153, 157
  See also bribery, in journalism; news media, official
The Things They Carried, 9
Thu-Huong Nguyen-Vo, 178
Time magazine, 21
To Huu, 97
Tran Dai Quang, 112
Tran Dan, 10
Tran Dinh, 150
Tran Kim Tuyen, 16
translation, 62
  of author's article on censorship, 88–92, 134
  of Bao Ninh, 51, 56, 84
  distinctions between northern and southern Vietnamese and, 9, 26
  Duong Thu Huong and, 71–72
  of George Orwell, 176

Nguyen Quoc Chanh and, 179
Perfect Spy, 12, 19
Pham Hong Son and, 133–136, 139
Pham Thi Hoai and, 74, 80
Rung Sat and, 26–27, 100
Scrap Paper (Giay Vun) Publishing and, 176
of *The Spy Who Loved Us*, 8–9, 21–23, 26–27, 32–35, 62, 101
unofficial rules of, 91
Vietnamese language and, 9, 26, 32, 84, 101, 192
of "The Wasteland," 179
See also Vietnamese language
Tre Publishing, 182
Trump, Donald, 147
Truong Tan Sang
Pham Chi Dung and, 163
Truong Vinh "Pétrus" Ky, 196
Tuoi Tre (newspaper), 107
declining circulation, 149, 159
PMU 18 affair and, 153
See also news media, official
Twitter. See Weibo

U. N. Human Rights Council, 106, 108, 158
United States
asylum and, 116–117, 119
Bao Ninh and, 53–54
battle in Rung Sat and, 25–27
as censored topic, 33, 101
China and, 61–62
Fulbright University of Vietnam and, 145–146
human rights and, 82
journalism and, 98–99
Linh Dinh and, 195
Nguyen Huy Thiep and, 5
Nguyen Phu Trong and, 105–106
Pham Doan Trang and, 117–118
Pham Xuan An and, 18–19, 21, 26, 32, 100
support of Vietnam, 82–83, 135
trade with China, 62

trade with Vietnam, 57, 82, 145–146, 109
Vietnamese appreciation of, 57, 100
Vietnamese prisoners and, 108, 116, 135
Vietnamese study in, 73, 92
See also Second Indochina War; Vietnam, international relations and; Vietnam War

Van Cao, 10
Viet Minh, 78, 180
See also First Indochina War
Vietnam
bauxite mining and, 36, 116–117, 151, 160
comparisons with China, 90, 129, 164–165
Confucianism in, 96–97, 173
cultural emptiness of, 5, 104–105, 142, 190, 193–194, 200
differences between north and south, 22, 67, 143, 192
disunified nature of, 92–93, 165–166, 185
embrace of commerce and, 104–105, 143, 145, 162, 183, 190–191, 193, 199–200
as "empire state," 92–93
ethnic minorities and, 32–33, 125
international relations and, 71, 82–83, 85, 108, 116, 183
Marxist-Leninist doctrine and, 5, 38
political factions and, 164–165, 185, 195
South China Sea affair and, 33, 60–61, 108, 156, 176
trading dissidents with U.S., 71, 108
U.N. Human Rights Council and, 106–108, 158
See also censorship; Communist Party of Vietnam; human

Vietnam (*continued*)
    rights, Vietnamese; police; political prisoners; propaganda; *The Tale of Kieu*
Vietnam Education Foundation, 146
Vietnamese language
    bureaucratic jargon and, 32, 89, 101, 202
    conflict avoidance and, 89
    distinctions between north and south, 9, 26, 42, 101
    "language of the people," 69
    "language of the street," 86, 173, 182–183
    Pham Xuan An on, 101
    poetry and, 86, 173, 182–183, 189
    translation and, 31, 84
    See also education, foreign languages and; Open Mouth poets (Mo Mieng); Pham Xuan An, language and; translation
Vietnam, history of
    Binh Xuyen river pirates, 25–27
    Boat People, 33, 106
    Buddhism and, 122
    Central Highlands and, 52–56, 111
    Cham peoples and, 32, 93, 122, 142
    doi moi (Renovation), 21, 69, 79, 122, 124, 126, 189
    Duong Thu Huong and, 65–71
    Edward Lansdale and, 26, 32
    France and, 26, 65, 93, 123, 180
    free press and, 89
    The Gold Campaign, 32
    Ho Chi Minh, 68, 78
    John F. Kennedy, 33
    Khmer peoples and, 32, 93
    Kingdom of Champa, 142
    land reform campaigns, 65–67, 69, 78, 99, 150, 181
    map as drawn by France, 93
    Montagnards and, 32, 56, 93
    nam tien (march to the south), 32
    nhan van giai pham affair (cultural purge), 10
    New Economic Zones, 181
    opium trade and, 25
    Poulo Condore, 180
    reeducation, 17, 30, 33, 41, 42, 101, 173
    Rung Sat (Swamp of the Assassins), 25–27, 100
    Stasi and, 79
    Tet Offensive, 17, 26, 33
    unification, 92–93
    Viet Minh, 78, 179–180
    Viets, 93
    war with Cambodia, 33, 181
    war with China, 34, 67
    war with France, 65, 180
    war with United States, 17, 26, 31, 33, 67, 70
    See also colonialism; First Indochina War; Pham Xuan An; Second Indochina War
VietnamNet, 117
"Vietnam: Programmed Death of Freedom of Information" (report), 107–108
Vietnam, Republic of (South), 31–32
    Pham Xuan An and, 16
    See also Vietnam, differences between north and south
Vietnam War, 15–17, 21–22, 24–25, 33, 46, 61, 67, 106, 137, 146, 178
    See also Second Indochina War
VNExpress, 111
Vo Nguyen Giap, 31, 43, 48, 65
Vu Hoang Giang, 7–14, 15 (photo)

Weibo, 114
    See also China, internet and
Wikileaks, 19
The Winning Side, 178
World Trade Organization, 183
Writers Association, 4, 122, 128
    denunciation campaign against Bao Ninh, 132
    writers leaving, 177

The Zenith, 68
    See also Duong Thu Huong

ABOUT THE TYPE

The text font used for *Censorship in Vietnam* is Apollo. This typeface was designed by Adrian Frutiger in 1962 and produced by the Monotype Corporation for use on their phototypesetting machines. The clear, elegant Apollo works well for long texts and headlines. Frutiger created some of the most widely used fonts of the twentieth, and now twenty-first centuries. He spent most of his career working for Deberny & Peignot updating typefaces and preparing them for phototypesetting, as well as designing nearly thirty original typefaces.

Myriad, used as the display type for this volume, was released in 1992 as a collaboration between type designers Carol Twombly and Robert Slimbach for Adobe Corporation. Myriad is distinguished from other san serifs by the special ' y" descender and the slanted cut of the "e." The font was developed as a multiple master format enabling the font to be rendered dynamically, from light to extra bold weights. Myriad's well-drawn letter proportions, clean, open shapes, and extensive kerning pairs ensure a comfortable level of readability across all of its variants and in languages ranging from Vietnamese and Greek, to basic and extended Latin.

THOMAS BASS, whose work appears in the *New Yorker*, the *New York Times*, *Wired*, *Foreign Policy*, the *Atlantic*, *Smithsonian*, and other publications, is the author of six previous books, including *The Eudaemonic Pie, Camping with the Prince, Vietnamerica, Reinventing the Future, The Predictors,* and *The Spy Who Loved Us*. Cited by the Overseas Press Club for his reporting, he has written two previous books on Vietnam, which he has been visiting regularly since the early 1990s. Recipient of awards from the Ford Foundation and the New York Foundation for the Arts, he is professor of English and journalism at the State University of New York in Albany.

www.ingramcontent.com/pod-product-compliance
Lightning Source LLC
Chambersburg PA
CBHW032213230426
43672CB00011B/2542